PERSPECTIVES ON
19th and 20th Century
Protestant Theology

PAUL TILLICH

PERSPECTIVES ON

19th and 20th Century
Protestant Theology

Edited and with an Introduction by

CARL E. BRAATEN

HARPER & ROW, PUBLISHERS

New York, Evanston, and London

FIRST EDITION

LIBRARY OF CONGRESS CATALOG CARD NUMBER: 67–11507

B-R

Preface

This book, *Perspectives on 19th and 20th Century Protestant Theology*, contains tape-recorded lectures which Paul Tillich delivered at the Divinity School of the University of Chicago during the spring quarter of the 1962–63 academic school year. He lectured from an outline and longhand notes; therefore, we did not have any manuscript against which to check the spoken word. Errors in the finished edition may very well be due to an acoustical gap between what was spoken by Tillich and what was heard by the editor, and should therefore be charged to the editor. We hope the readers will agree that taking this risk is a small price to pay for getting into print Tillich's views on modern Protestant theology.

While at one time Professor Tillich raised serious questions about publishing this material as a *history* of Christian thought, in considering the advice of his professional colleagues shortly before his death he was most open to the possibility of publishing it as *perspectives*. As such they provide deeper insight into the leading developments of modern thought as well as into the way in which Tillich drew from them as sources for his own constructive thinking. Students both of the Protestant tradition and of Tillich's thought will find these lectures to be an invaluable help to understanding.

Finally, I wish to express a word of gratitude to those whose good will and work have made this volume possible; first of all, to Jerald C. Brauer, dean of the Divinity School of the University of Chicago, who authorized the lectures to be taped and supported this venture all the way; to Armin G. Weng, who as president of the Lutheran School of Theology at Chicago made the necessary funds available to transfer Tillich's voice to a typed manuscript; to Robert H. Fischer, who used his historian's eye to keep the volume free of historical inexactitudes and also helped to smooth out the English; finally, to Mrs. Hannah Tillich and Robert C. Kimball, who cleared the path for this book to be published posthumously.

Carl E. Braaten
Lutheran School of Theology at Chicago

Table of Contents

Paul Tillich and the

Classical Christian Tradition

by Carl E. Braaten

THE RADICALISM OF PAUL TILLICH

It has been said that the real Tillich is the radical Tillich but the radicalism which moved Paul Tillich was not the iconoclastic spirit of those who wish to create *de novo* an original brand of Christianity; rather, it was the radicalism which moved the great prophetic spirits of the religious tradition. Tillich's term for it was the "Protestant principle." This radical principle was to be used not against but for the sake of the "catholic substance" of the Christian tradition. One question which Tillich posed for his own theological effort was this: "How can the radicalism of prophetic criticism which is implied in the principles of genuine Protestantism be united with the classical tradition of dogma, sacred law, sacraments, hierarchy, cult, as preserved in the Catholic churches?"[1] Tillich also saw the danger in prophetic criticism. The prophet hopes to get to the heart of the matter with his knife of radical protest; the false prophet is known in the tradition as one who cuts out the heart itself. It was the true radicalism rooted in Biblical prophetism

[1] Tillich, "The Conquest of Intellectual Provincialism: Europe and America," *Theology of Culture* (New York: Oxford University Press, 1959), p. 169.

xiii

which drove Tillich to criticize our religious and cultural forms of tradition. Thus, like the Old Testament prophets, his criticism *of* the tradition was always *from* the tradition, from some deeper level in it, not from some arbitrary, neutral or alien standpoint outside the "theological circle."[2]

Most of Tillich's commentators and critics in America have had the impression that Tillich was a radical, perhaps even dangerous, innovator.[3] The chief reason for this impression was often cited by Tillich himself. Americans—and perhaps moderns in general—have little sense of history. They are not aware of the sources of tradition from which they come. Europeans possess a more vivid historical consciousness than Americans, and for this reason European theologians are much less inclined to stress the innovating features of Tillich's thought. Many of Tillich's favorite ideas and terms, which sounded utterly novel to American students, came originally from a long line of honored ancestors. His basic categories and concepts, the style and structure of his thinking, were not unprecedented in the Christian tradition—to those who knew their history of thought. Tillich's uniqueness, his creativity and originality, lay in his power of thought, the comprehensive scope of his vision, his depth of insight, the systematic consistency with which he developed the internal relations of the various elements of his philosophy and theology, and the daring he displayed in crossing borders into new fields. He could be so actively immersed in the currents of his time and exert such vital influence on the shape of things to come because his roots were deeply embedded in and nourished by the classical traditions of the Christian Church.

DIALOGUE WITH THE CLASSICAL TRADITION

Tillich was a son of the whole tradition of the church in a measure that can hardly be said of any other theologian since the Reformation.

2 To be in the "theological circle" is to have made an existential decision, to be in the situation of faith. Cf. Tillich, *Systematic Theology* (Chicago: The University of Chicago Press, 1951), Vol. II, pp. 6, 8, 9–11.

3 See Tillich's answer to a student's question, "Is Paul Tillich a dangerous man?" in *Ultimate Concern*, edited by D. Mackenzie Brown (New York: Harper & Row, 1965), pp. 188–93.

Although Tillich confessed he was a Lutheran "by birth, education, religious experience, and theological reflection,"[4] he did not rest comfortably within any traditional form of Lutheranism. He transcended so far as possible every limiting feature of his immediate heritage. The transconfessional style of his theology made it difficult for many of his Lutheran contemporaries to recognize him as a member of the same family.[5] He did not have to *try* to be ecumenical; for the substance of his thinking was drawn from the whole sweep of the classical tradition. His theology was a living dialogue with great men and ideas of the past, with the fathers of the ancient church, both Greek and Latin, with the schoolmen and mystics of the medieval period, with Renaissance humanists and Protestant reformers, with the theologians of liberalism and their neo-orthodox critics. His method of handling the tradition was eminently dialectical, in the spirit of the *Sic et Non* of Abelard.

Tillich's systematic theology was built up through the rhythm of raising and answering existential questions. Each of the five parts of the system contains two sections, one in which the human question is developed, the other in which the theological answer is given. He admitted that there could very well have been an intermediate section which places his theological answer more explicitly within the context of the tradition.[6] The dialogue with the tradition mediated through the Scriptures and the church, the sort of thing which appears in small print in Karl Barth's *Church Dogmatics,* thus receded pretty much into the background of the *Systematic Theology.* This sacrifice of explicit attention to the historical tradition had the result, I believe, in gaining for Tillich the reputation in some circles as a speculative theologian who arbitrarily projected ideas whether or not they squared with the central thrusts of the church's tradition. If that was the result, it is unfortunate. It conceals the catholicity of Tillich's mind and the extent

---

[4] Tillich, *The Interpretation of History* (New York: Charles Scribner's Sons, 1936), p. 54.

[5] Cf. my brief article, "Paul Tillich as a Lutheran Theologian," in *The Chicago Lutheran Theological Seminary Record* (August, 1962), Vol. 67, No. 3. See also the chapter by Jaroslav Pelikan, "Ein deutscher lutherischer Theologe in Amerika: Paul Tillich und die dogmatische Tradition," in *Gott ist am Werk,* the *Festschrift* for Hanns Lilje, edited by Heinz Brunotte and Erich Ruppel (Hamburg: Furche Verlag, 1959), pp. 27–36.

[6] *Systematic Theology,* I, p. 66.

to which his systematic ideas were won through an intense intellectual struggle with the sources of the tradition.

To reveal more of this living background of Tillich's systematic theology, it has seemed important to us to publish some of his lectures on the history of thought. Seldom did he publish in the field of historical theology. He had a fear of being judged by the strict canons of scientific historiography. On the occasion of the Tillich Memorial Service in Chicago, Mircea Eliade was not exaggerating when he stated: "But, of course, Paul Tillich would never have become a historian of religions nor, as a matter of fact, a *historian* of anything else. He was interested in the existential meaning of history—*Geschichte,* not *Historie.*"[7] Yet, very few minds were so laden with the consciousness of history, with memories of the classical tradition. Tillich's students were awed by his ability to trace from memory the history of an idea through its main stages of development, observing even subtle shifts in the nuances of meaning at the main turning points. In fact, a great part of Tillich's career in teaching theology was devoted to lectures and seminars in the history of thought. Students who were privileged to study under Tillich at Union, Harvard, or Chicago reminisce today about their most memorable courses, such as the basic sequence in The History of Christian Thought, or The History of Christian Mysticism, or The Pre-Socratics, or German Classical Idealism. Even students from backgrounds uncongenial to Tillich's views on the Christian faith could not fail to learn from him as an interpreter of the Christian tradition. Many were liberated from the strait jacket of a given denominational tradition to become more open to the fullness of the common Christian heritage.

The Interpretation of History

The key to an understanding of Tillich's handling of the tradition is his fundamental proposition that every interpretation is a creative union of the interpreter and the interpreted in a third beyond both of them.

[7] Eliade, "Paul Tillich and the History of Religions," in *The Future of Religions,* by Paul Tillich, edited by Jerald C. Brauer (New York: Harper & Row, 1966), p. 33.

The ideal of unbiased historical research to report only the "naked facts" without any admixture of subjective interpretation Tillich called "a questionable concept."[8] Without a union of the historian with the material he interprets there can be no real understanding of history. "The historian's task is to 'make alive' what has 'passed away.' "[9] The dimension of interpretation is made unavoidable because history itself is more than a series of facts. An historical event "is a syndrome (i.e., a running-together) of facts and interpretation."[10] Furthermore, the historian himself is unavoidably a member of a group which has a living tradition of memories and values. "Nobody writes history on a 'place above all places.' "[11] The element of empathic participation in history is basic to the act of interpreting history.

Tillich was too much influenced by both the existentialist and the Marxist understandings of history to imagine that one could grasp the meaning of history by surveying the past in cool detachment. In a crucial passage Tillich emphatically states: "Only full involvement in historical action can give the basis for an interpretation of history. Historical activity is the key to understanding history."[12] This dynamic view of history arose out of Tillich's own struggle with the historical actualities of his situation. In one of his autobiographies he acknowledged that many of his most important concepts, such as the Protestant principle, *kairos,* the demonic, the *Gestalt* of grace, and the trio of theonomy, heteronomy, autonomy, were worked out for the sake of a new interpretation of history. "History became the central problem of my theology and philosophy," he said, "because of the historical reality as I found it when I returned from the first World War."[13] With prophetic zeal he sounded forth the theme of *kairos,* that moment in time when the eternal breaks into history, issuing to his contemporaries a summons to a consciousness of history in the sense of the *kairos.* He

8 *Systematic Theology,* III, p. 301.
9 *Systematic Theology,* I, p. 104.
10 *Systematic Theology,* III, p. 302.
11 *Ibid.,* p. 301.
12 *Ibid.,* p. 349.
13 Tillich, *The Protestant Era,* translated by James Luther Adams (Chicago: The University of Chicago Press, 1948), xvii.

allied himself in these years with religious socialism, and was no doubt the main theoretician of this movement.

When Tillich turned toward the past he had little interest in it for its own sake. His involvement in the present and his sense of responsibility for the future drove him to search out meanings from the past. "Whoever would maintain the idea of pure observation must content himself with numbers and names, statistics and newspaper clippings. He might collect thousands of things which could be verified but he would not for that reason be able to understand what is actually happening in the present. One is enabled to speak of that which is most vital in the present, of that which makes the present a generative force, only insofar as one immerses oneself in the creative process which brings the future forth out of the past."[14] To act in the present, one must understand oneself and one's situation; to understand this, one has to recapitulate the process by which the present situation has evolved. In the "Introduction" of this volume Tillich states that the primary purpose of his lectures on Protestant theology is to show "how we have arrived at the present situation," or in other words, "to understand ourselves."[15] The fascination for the past on its own account is given as a second and subordinate purpose. We have tried to indicate the primacy of Tillich's existential interest in the historical tradition by characterizing these lectures as "perspectives." The term "history," which Tillich requested us not to use, would have suggested to many people a historiographical treatment less preponderantly interpretative.

TILLICH AND EARLY CATHOLICISM

The knowledge of Tillich's theology could serve as a prerequisite to an advanced course in patristic studies, or vice versa. There are many bridges in Tillich's theology to the traditions of the ancient church. One immediately thinks, of course, of the centrality of the trinitarian and christological doctrines in Tillich as well as in the leading church fathers. No doubt it was Tillich's love for Greek philosophy which pre-

[14] Tillich, *The Religious Situation,* translated by H. Richard Niebuhr (Cleveland: Meridian Books, 1956), p. 34.
[15] Cf. *infra,* p. 1.

pared him for a sympathetic understanding of the development of these dogmas. Quite unlike the great historians of dogma in the Ritschlian school, especially Adolf von Harnack, Tillich esteemed the classic dogmas of the Trinity and the Christ very highly as the appropriate reception of the Christian message in the categories of Hellenistic philosophy. Harnack's thesis that the "Hellenization of Christianity" was an intellectualistic distortion of the New Testament gospel resulted, Tillich claimed, from a misinterpretation of Greek thought. What Harnack did not understand was that "Greek thought is existentially concerned with the eternal, in which it seeks for eternal truth and eternal life."[16] On the other hand, Tillich did not believe that the conciliar formulations of the ancient church were binding on all future theology. The categories that were used then are not unquestionably valid for our time. His reconstructions of these dogmas in his *Systematic Theology* are serious efforts to get beneath the outer crust of the old formulas to clear the way for an understanding of the reality which originally they were meant to protect from heretical attacks. Critical essays and books have been and will continue to be written for a long time to come to assess to what extent Tillich succeeded in reinterpreting the old doctrines of the church.

The concept of the Logos in the early Greek fathers also found one of its stanchest allies in Tillich. Of all the leading contemporary theologians, Tillich was the only one who integrated the Logos doctrine into his own theological system. Without it he could not have been the apologetic theologian he was. When Tillich referred to himself as an apologetic theologian, he had in mind the example of the great second-century apologist, Justin Martyr, for whom the Logos doctrine was, as for Tillich, the universal principle of the divine self-manifestation. If the apologist is to answer the questions and accusations of the despisers of Christianity, he must discover some common ground. The common ground for both Justin and Tillich was the presence of the Logos beyond the boundaries of the church, making it possible for men in all religions and cultures to have a partial grasp of the truth, a love of beauty, and a moral sensitivity. Tillich could stand "on the

[16] *Systematic Theology*, III, p. 287.

boundary"[17] between theology and philosophy, church and society, religion and culture, because the Logos who became flesh was the same Logos who was universally at work in the structures of human existence. Tillich's apologetic writing demonstrates how he shared the conviction of the Apologists that Christians by no means have a monopoly on the truth, and that the truth, wherever it may be found, essentially belongs to us Christians. The Logos doctrine saved Tillich's theology from a false particularism that has hampered so much of the ecclesiastical tradition.

Tillich was never under any illusion that the first five centuries of the church provide any clear support for Protestantism against Roman Catholicism. What he stressed instead was *how early* the formative principles of Catholicism developed, especially in the defense against the onslaughts of Gnosticism. The closing of the canon, defining the apostolic tradition, the rule of faith, the formation of creeds, and also episcopal authority were developments which occurred very early, and cannot be written off as aberrations of the "Dark Ages." Of course, Tillich was never able to endorse the rise of early Catholicism as an unambiguously salutary occurrence. In the light of the "Protestant principle" he could point out that the church paid a dear price in its struggle against heresies. What he called the heteronomous structures of an authoritarian church, which later resulted in the church of the Inquisition, had their beginnings in the anti-Gnostic response of Orthodoxy. Also every definition entails exclusion. When the church was pressed by heresies to defend itself, it had to define itself. This self-definition, Tillich believes, inevitably has a narrowing result. "The whole history of Christian dogma is a continuing narrowing down, but at the same time a *defining*. And the definition is important, because without it many elements would have undercut the whole church, would have denied its existence. The dogma, therefore, the dogmatic development, is not something merely lamentable or evil. It was the necessary form by which the church kept its very identity. . . . The tragic element in all history is that if something like this must be

[17] Tillich's autobiographical sketch by this title, *On the Boundary* (New York: Charles Scribner's Sons, 1966). This edition is both a revision and a new translation of Part I of *The Interpretation of History*.

done, it immediately has the consequence of narrowing down and excluding very valuable elements."[18] The theologian today has the onerous task of breaking through the definitions to recover if possible those valuable elements which for *tragically necessary* reasons were temporarily excluded. With this sort of dialectical insight Tillich could affirm that the church was basically correct in each instance in which it rejected a major heresy, but wrong when its self-defining formulations became rigid, as in the case of post-Tridentine Roman Catholicism and Protestant Orthodoxy. There is no solution to this problem of self-reduction through self-definition except by the continual reformation of the church (*ecclesia semper reformanda*).

The two theologians of the ancient church who had the greatest influence on Tillich were Origen and Augustine. Clearly it was their common bond of Neo-Platonism which attracted Tillich to their way of thinking. When Tillich expounded the doctrines of Origen and Augustine, it was often difficult to distinguish Tillich's own doctrine from theirs.[19] This was not simply a case of Tillich reading his own ideas into Origen and Augustine; I think it was rather that he had read such ideas out of them, probably at first backtracking his way from Schelling, through Boehme, German mysticism, medieval Augustinianism, and early Christian Platonism. At any rate, whatever occasioned his interest in Origen and Augustine, he felt at home in them.

Origen's mysticism, his understanding of the symbolic significance of religious language, his doctrines of the Logos, the Trinity, creation, the transcendental fall, and his eschatology, especially its universalism, were all features which Tillich was able to adapt to his own systematic theology. I do not suggest that Tillich did this uncritically. In particular, it was evident that despite his kindred feeling for Augustine, Tillich rejected his conservative philosophy of history, namely that aspect of it which resulted in the ecclesiastical interpretation of the Kingdom of God as ruling on earth through the church's hierarchy and its sacramental mediations. This is a decisive deviation from Augustine. It meant that Tillich could ally himself more with the prophetic in-

18 Brown, ed., *Ultimate Concern*, pp. 64–65.

19 Tillich's lectures on the history of Christian thought have been recorded and edited by Peter H. John, and have circulated on a limited scale among Tillich's students. A new edition of these lectures will be published soon.

terpretation of history, receiving its impulses from Joachim of Floris, the radical Franciscans, and the left-wing Reformers. His own doctrine of the *kairos* could hardly be accommodated by the traditional, ecclesiastical interpretation of history, with its antichiliastic, nonutopian character. For Tillich and the prophetic line of interpretation the future may be pregnant with a decisively new meaning for which the past and the present are merely preparations. The conservative ecclesiastical tendency has always managed to quash too vivid expectations of the future; such expectations are the spawning bed of revolutionary attitudes toward the present situation and the church's place in it.

THEONOMY AND MYSTICISM IN THE MIDDLE AGES

Moving on to Tillich's interpretation of the Middle Ages, our first observation must be that he made important contributions toward overcoming the deep-seated rationalistic and Protestant prejudices against the so-called "Dark Ages." The one thousand years from Pope Gregory the Great to Doctor Martin Luther have often been pictured with contempt as a monolithic age of ignorance, priestly tyranny, and religious superstition. Directly against this stands the idealized image of the Middle Ages in Romanticism. Tillich was no romanticist, but he was influenced by its outlook on the Middle Ages. Christian romanticists look back to the Middle Ages as an ideal unity of religion and culture, as an organism in which the religious center irradiates through all forms of cultic, legal, moral, and aesthetic activities. Tillich could not share the hope of Romanticism to re-create a society according to the pattern of an idealized Middle Ages. On the other hand, Tillich drew the inspiration for his own concept of theonomy from this romanticist outlook on medieval society. "Protestantism cannot accept the medieval pattern either in Romantic or in Roman terms. It must look forward to a new theonomy. Yet, in order to do so, it must know what theonomy means, and this it can find in the Middle Ages."[20]

Tillich was able to give a sweeping overview of historical periods in terms of the principles of autonomy, heteronomy, and theonomy. "Theonomy can characterize a whole culture and give a key to the inter-

[20] *Systematic Theology*, I, p. 149.

pretation of history."[21] The ideal of a theonomous culture can never be fully realized on earth because of man's existential estrangement that runs through all history. But there may be partial realizations. Such a culture is one in which the inner potentialities of man are being fulfilled through the driving presence of the Spirit, giving power, meaning, and direction to the autonomous forms of life. Autonomy describes a situation which cuts itself off from the transcendent source and aim of life. Examples of more or less autonomous periods are those of skepticism in Greek philosophy, the Renaissance, the Enlightenment, and present-day secularism. Heteronomy represents the attempt to impose an alien law upon the autonomous structures of life, demanding unconditional obedience to finite authorities, splitting the conscience and the inner life. The struggle between the independence of autonomy and the coercions of heteronomy can only be overcome through a new theonomy. This is a situation in which religion and culture are not divorced, where instead, according to one of Tillich's most famous formulations, culture provides the form of religion, and religion the substance of culture.

Applying these principles to the Middle Ages, Tillich emphasized, not their homogeneous nature, but the great diversities and transitions within medieval culture. He contrasted the relative openness of the medieval church toward a variety of ways of thinking to the narrowness of the church of the counter-Reformation. The high point of the Middle Ages was attained in the thirteenth century in the great systems of the Scholastics. Particularly, the Augustinian line from Anselm of Canterbury to Bonaventura represented a theonomous style of theologizing. Here, beginning with faith, the mind was opened to perceive the reflections of the divine presence in all realms and facets of life. The end of the Middle Ages was characterized by nominalism and heteronomy. The world was split; the realms of religion and culture were separated. The double-truth theory was invented as a way of maintaining philosophy and theology side by side, in a state of mutual contradictoriness. A statement that is true in theology may be false in philosophy and one that is true in philosophy may be false in theology. Adherence to the creeds of the church can be maintained only on

[21] *Systematic Theology*, III, p. 250.

the basis of an absolute authority. This positivistic notion of authority came to clear expression in Duns Scotus and William of Ockham. The concept of authority became heteronomous and was applied more and more in a heteronomous way by the church.

What seems unique in Tillich's interpretation of the Middle Ages is the fact that he attributed the disintegration of theonomy and the emerging gap between scientific autonomy and ecclesiastical heteronomy to none other than Thomas Aquinas. In one of his most self-revealing essays, "The Two Types of the Philosophy of Religion,"[22] he traces the roots of the modern split between faith and knowledge back to the Thomistic denial of the Augustinian belief in the immediate presence of God in the act of knowing. For Thomas, God is first in the order of being but last in the order of knowledge. The knowledge of God is the end result of a line of reasoning, not the presupposition of all our knowing. Where reason leaves off, faith takes over. The act of faith, however, becomes the movement of the will to accept truth on authority. Tillich's verdict is clear: "This is the final outcome of the Thomistic *dis*solution of the Augustinian *solution.*"[23]

This essay on "The Two Types of the Philosophy of Religion" reveals how alive the philosophical debates of the Middle Ages were in Tillich's own thinking. He saw that fundamental issues were being decided with tremendous consequences for world history. When Tillich lectured on this period, he was no impartial observer of the debates; he was definitely a passionate participant. On most issues he took the side of the Augustinians against the Thomists, the Franciscans against the Dominicans, the realists against the nominalists, etc. The background to all these controversies was what Tillich called the eternal dialogue that continues in history between Plato and Aristotle. It is the dialogue between a philosophy of wisdom (*sapientia*) and a philosophy of science (*scientia*), or as Tillich put it, between the ontological and the cosmological approaches to God.

Tillich's alliance with the Middle Ages appears also in his high evaluation of its mysticism. For Tillich there is an ineliminable element of mysticism in every religion. A question he often posed to his students

22 *Theology of Culture*, pp. 10–29.
23 *Ibid.*, p. 19.

was whether "mysticism can be baptized by Christianity." His answer was "yes," provided we distinguish between the abstract type of mysticism of Hinduism and the concrete mysticism of Christianity. Concrete mysticism is Christ-mysticism. Such a mysticism may be taken up into Christianity as an historical religion. Without the mystical element in religion Tillich observed that it becomes reduced to intellectualism or moralism. True doctrines or good morals become the essence of a religion without the mystical dimension. In this he agreed basically with Schleiermacher and Rudolf Otto against Kant and Albrecht Ritschl. He never joined Karl Barth and Emil Brunner in their wholesale rejection of Christian mysticism. In this regard both Barth and Brunner were still clinging to the Ritschlian prejudice that Christianity and mysticism are irreconcilable opposites.

The eradication of all mystical elements in the Christian tradition would leave us but a torso. In Tillich's judgment this would require getting rid of half of the apostle Paul's theology, its Spirit-mysticism; the Christ-mysticism of men like Bernard of Clairvaux whom Luther prized so highly would have to go; indeed, much of the theology of the young Luther would have to be cut out, and along with it his understanding of faith. The Christian tradition would be a vast wasteland without its enrichment through mysticism. Of all the labels that have been applied to Tillich's theology, none of them come close to fitting unless they bring out the mystical ontology which undergirds his whole way of thinking. This is why it is not very revealing to label Tillich an existentialist as popularly done; it tends to obscure the underlying essentialism of his reflections on existence. Tillich's doctrine of existence is cradled within the framework of his mystical ontology. Only from this perspective should we understand many of Tillich's expressions which have created either offense or puzzlement, such as "God beyond the God of theism," "Being itself," "absolute faith," "ecstatic naturalism," "belief-ful realism," "symbolic knowledge," "essentialization," etc. These terms are echoes of the mystical side of Tillich and of the Christian tradition.

THE REDISCOVERY OF THE PROPHETIC TRADITION

The mystical side of Tillich's thought was always kept in tension with the prophetic aspect. Some of his sharpest judgments were made against mysticism as a way of self-elevation to the divine through ascetic exercises. In the name of the *sola gratia* principle of the Reformation he condemned mysticism as a method of self-salvation. The enigma many have sensed in Paul Tillich is due to this polygenous character of his thinking. Although his roots were planted deeply in the soil of neo-Platonic mysticism, German idealism, and nineteenth-century Protestant liberalism, nevertheless, Tillich placed this entire heritage under the criticism of the "Protestant principle." This principle he derived from the Pauline-Lutheran tradition. The estrangement between God and man is overcome solely on the basis of divine grace, without any merit or worthiness on man's part. The existential power and theological relevance of the Reformation doctrine of justification by grace alone through faith alone was mediated to Paul Tillich by his teacher Martin Kähler. Tillich, however, radicalized it to meet even the situation of the doubter. "Not only he who is in sin but also he who is in doubt is justified through faith. The situation of doubt, even of doubt about God, need not separate us from God."[24]

Tillich bemoaned the fact that modern man can scarcely understand the meaning of justification. For this reason he exchanged the legal imagery taken from the courtroom for new expressions borrowed from the psychoanalytic situation in which the therapist accepts the patient *as he is*. Justification by grace through faith is interpreted as our being accepted *in spite of* the fact we are unacceptable. The whole gospel is contained in the phrase "in spite of." In spite of our sin and guilt, in spite of our condemnation and unbelief, in spite of our doubts and our total unworthiness, the miracle of the good news is for just such people. "Justification is the paradox that man the sinner is justified, that man the unrighteous is righteous; that man the unholy is holy, namely, in the judgment of God, which is not based on any human achievements but only on the divine, self-surrendering grace. Where this

[24] *The Protestant Era,* xiv.

paradox of the divine-human relationship is understood and accepted, all ideologies are destroyed. Man does not have to deceive himself about himself, because he is accepted as he is, in the total perversion of his existence."[25]

An important part of Paul Tillich's mission to American Protestantism was to reinterpret in contemporary terms the message of the Reformation. He felt that American Protestantism had scarcely been touched by the prophetic message of Luther and Calvin. Lectures he delivered at The Washington Cathedral Library, Washington, D.C., in 1950, dealt with "The Recovery of the Prophetic Tradition in the Reformation" and are now published in Volume VII of the collected works of Paul Tillich in German.[26] The great doctrines of the Reformation, which have become mummified for many of its heirs, are in Tillich's treatment living symbols of the new relationship to God which provided the explosive power of Luther's reformatory work. The poignancy of Tillich's own prophetic criticism of American Protestantism's pseudo-orthodoxies, shallow liberalisms, and puritan moralisms was due to his grasp of Luther's message. His observation on Protestant preaching in America was that it too often tends to make the grace of God, that is, God's attitude toward man, depend on the individual's moral earnestness, religious devotion, or true beliefs. The formula "justification by faith" has been retained, to be sure, but then, as Tillich rightly pointed out, faith is transformed into a work which a man is exhorted to perform on his own conscious decision. To avoid this Pelagianizing implication Tillich suggested that it might help to say justification *through* faith instead of *by* faith. This would mean that faith does not *cause* but *mediates* God's grace. Tillich's little book, *Dynamics of Faith*,[27] was written in part to overcome dreadful distortions of the concept of faith. Faith is distorted when it is conceived anthropocentrically as either a knowing (intellectualism) or a doing (moralism) or a feeling

---

[25] *Ibid.*, p. 170.
[26] "Die Wiederentdeckung der prophetischen Tradition in der Reformation," *Der Protestantismus als Kritik und Gestaltung* (Stuttgart: Evangelisches Verlagswerk, 1962), Gesammelte Werke, VII, pp. 171–215. An English version of these lectures was published; the German edition, however, is by Tillich's request the authoritative one.
[27] New York: Harper & Row, 1957.

(emotionalism). Tillich's own definition of faith as a state of being grasped by an ultimate concern was an attempt to use an expression which suggests that faith involves both the depths and the totality of the self, and is therefore not merely the function of a particular faculty of the mind.

The extent of Luther's influence on Tillich's mind cannot be detailed here. Several connections may, however, be worth a brief mention. Luther said that what makes a theologian is his ability to distinguish rightly between law and gospel. This means that like the two natures of Christ, law and gospel must be differentiated without being separated (Nestorianism) or being confused (Monophysitism). Tillich rarely ever used the categories of law and gospel as an explicit theological formula. The structure of his thinking is, however, clearly patterned after this feature of Luther's theology. It makes its appearance in Tillich's system as the methodological principle of correlation. He does not develop a doctrine *about* law and gospel; instead all his thinking is structured in terms of it. His essays dealing with theology and culture, the plan of his *Systematic Theology,* and all his sermons show that before he would announce the Christian answer, the kerygma, he would carefully describe the human predicament. The description of the human predicament is man's existence *under the law;* the presentation of the Christian answer offers the new possibility of life *under the gospel.* The sequence is always law before gospel, that is, always the posing of the question before the attempt to answer. For Tillich this is the proper theological method, and at just this point he deviated from Karl Barth who placed the gospel before the law, who spoke of Christ before turning to the analysis of the actual human situation as man today experiences it. Tillich's plea for a fruitful correlation between philosophy and theology also rests upon this law/gospel basis. When he states that philosophy raises the question which theology must answer, he is saying in another way that the gospel is the divine response to the questionability of human existence under the law. Philosophy functions analogously to the law as theology does to the gospel.

Tillich believed that the "law of contrasts" in Luther's doctrine of God can help to counter the trend in Protestant theology to rationalize and moralize the picture of God. This law of contrasts is expressed in a series of terms that must be maintained in a relation of dialectical tension to each other: e.g., the hiddenness of God and the revealedness of God, the wrath of God and the love of God, the strange work of God (*opus alienum*) and the proper work of God (*opus proprium*), God's kingdom on the left hand and his kingdom on the right hand, etc. This style of thinking in terms of dialectical tension between contrasting concepts also characterized Tillich's theology. One can see shades of this in Tillich's analysis of the ontological polarities in the depth of the divine life and in his trinitarian principles. The difference, of course, between Tillich and Luther must also be acknowledged. Between them stood Jacob Boehme who through German classical idealism, especially Schelling, provided Tillich with a powerful model of dialectical thinking in mystical-ontological categories. Thus, for example, Luther's idea of the devil as the agent of God's wrath makes its appearance in the tradition of mystical theology, running from Boehme through Schelling to Tillich, as a negative principle, as the principle of nonbeing, gnawing at the foundations of reality. Also the mystical feeling for depth is brought out by the idea of the abyss in the divine life, the *Ungrund* in Boehme's language. Tillich saw that both Luther and Boehme's ideas of God had their common background in late medieval mysticism as expressed, for example, in the *Theologia Germanica*. He drew upon this tradition in protesting the reduction of the picture of God in late nineteenth-century Protestantism to the simple image of a loving father. Hence, for Tillich the symbol of the wrath of God was not merely an outdated notion of primitive mythology that can be excised from our picture of God. Tillich was always grateful to Rudolf Otto's book, *The Idea of the Holy,* for making him more deeply aware of the abysmal mystery of God, the *mysterium tremendum et fascinosum*. And on this point he was convinced that Otto was a better interpreter of Luther's theology than the leading Ritschlians had been.

FROM ORTHODOXY TO NEO-ORTHODOXY

The rest of the story of Tillich as an interpreter of the Christian tradition can be had by reading this book. Although its title promises to bring out Tillich's perspectives on theology in the nineteenth and twentieth centuries, he actually reaches back to the period of Protestant

Orthodoxy to begin his account of the development. He lays out the main principles of theology in the seventeenth and eighteenth centuries. The period of Protestant Scholasticism did not evoke in Tillich, as in many of his contemporaries, a feeling of revulsion. He ranked it as part of the "classical tradition," not as an aberration from which we have nothing to learn. Not the theologians of Orthodoxy but their modern imitators were the butt of Tillich's scorn. The original pietists, men like Spener and Zinzendorf, were likewise not to be disparaged, only their followers who tried to make a method out of their piety. In numerous places in Tillich's writings he shows how he would mediate between Orthodoxy and Pietism on the question whether theology could be done only by those who are regenerated.[28] His answer was that the Pietists were right in stressing that theology involves existential commitment, but wrong in making that commitment a matter of absolute certainty. This leads to subjectivism in theology against which the Orthodox theologians rightly protested.

One of Tillich's most provocative theses in this book states that mysticism is the mother of rationalism. Both have in common a subjectivist outlook; the "inner light," by a slight shift of emphasis, becomes the autonomous reason. This hypothesis can perhaps best be tested by examining to see to what extent the pietists and the rationalists allied themselves in the attack on Orthodoxy and to what extent rationalism prospered most where Pietism had gained the strongest foothold. The exact nature of the alliance would be an interesting subject for careful historical research.

The sections on Schleiermacher and Hegel are revealing of Tillich's indebtedness to them. It must be remembered that Tillich kept alive the memory of these figures at a time when it was generally popular in theology to debunk them. Schleiermacher was glibly dismissed as a mystic and Hegel as a speculative philosopher. Søren Kierkegaard's verdict on Hegel was accepted by many as the last word, and Emil Brunner's book on Schleiermacher charged the ills of modern Protestantism to his account.[29] Tillich used to recall how hostile the reaction was during the twenties and thirties to his seminars on these men. It

[28] *Systematic Theology*, I, p. 11.
[29] *Die Mystik und das Wort* (Tübingen: J. C. B. Mohr, 1924).

is to Tillich's credit that he maintained for himself and imparted to others a sense of balance toward the era of liberalism. Today there is a renewed interest in the thought of both Schleiermacher and Hegel, not only for historical reasons, but also for their constructive theological significance. The new affirmation of Hegel, that is, the early Hegel, in German theology is a movement with which he was not intimately acquainted, but with which, nonetheless, his own theology has certain strong affinities.[30]

Tillich's attitude toward liberalism was dialectical. When he first became known in America, he tended to be classified with the neo-orthodox movement. He shared its critique of the liberal doctrine of progress and sounded similar notes on man's radical estrangement. He attacked the illusory schemes of self-salvation and pointed to the grace of God, to the new being in Christ, and to the Kingdom of God beyond history as the source of man's hope for a real fulfillment. The brand of liberalism he most readily rejected was the reduction of Christianity to the religion of Jesus. Liberalism's attempt to apply the methods of higher criticism to recover the historical Jesus beneath the various apostolic portraitures of Jesus as the Christ provided no adequate basis for Christian faith. He pronounced the search for the historical Jesus a failure, and believed that Bultmann's skepticism toward the sources was largely justified. In his student days the ascendant form of liberalism was the Ritschlian school. Tillich could never share the basic outlook of the Ritschlian theologians, neither their antimetaphysical bias nor their rejection of mysticism, neither their "back to Kant" posture nor their ethicization of Christianity. The University of Marburg was the center of the Kant-Ritschl sphere of influence. Tillich came from the University of Halle, where the traditions of German classical idealism and the theology of revivalism or pietism were mediated to him by his professors of philosophy and theology, the most often acknowledged of whom was Martin Kähler. This difference between Halle and Marburg symbolizes, perhaps even accounts for, the opposition between Tillich and Bultmann, the Marburg professor of New Testament. Bultmann was trained under Wilhelm Herrmann, who tended to teach dogmatics in

[30] *Inter alia,* Jürgen Moltmann, Wolf-Dieter Marsch, also Wolfhart Pannenberg.

the form of ethics. Tillich criticized Bultmann's demythologizing of the New Testament because only its ethical symbolism remains in his existentialist interpretation. The cosmic symbolism drops out of sight; it is removed as so much primitive mythology. Tillich, the ontologist *par excellence,* was passionately interested in the cosmic symbols. Therefore, demythologizing for Tillich did not mean the removal of such symbols, but deliteralization and interpretation. Since ethics is the focus of Bultmann's interpretation, the basic appeal is for decision; his is a theology of decision. By marked contrast Tillich's interpretation is in terms of ontological categories; he spoke of participation in the reality becoming transparent through the symbols. The idea of participation suggests that even the dimension of the unconscious is involved in the religious act; the idea of decision confines the religious act to the level of consciousness. In this light we can understand why Tillich's thinking was thoroughly sacramental; the decisionism of existentialist theology, on the other hand, leaves no room for the sacramental aspects of religion.

The main body of this volume deals with the great prophetic voices of the nineteenth century. Many of these were on the fringes of the Christian tradition, some even among its most bitter opponents. Tillich's selective treatment of this period focuses on the critical thrust from the philosophical side. He leaves largely out of account the developments in historical criticism, the investigation of the origins of primitive Christianity; also he pays little attention to the reconstructions of church doctrine that were being advanced by professional theologians. The reason for this selectivity is Tillich's conviction that the impetus to historical research and doctrinal reformulation came from changes in philosophical outlook. One has only to think of the dependence of historical critics like David F. Strauss and Ferdinand C. Baur on Hegel's philosophy of history, or of the dependence of dogmatic theologians like Alexander Schweizer and J. C. K. von Hofmann on Schleiermacher's philosophy of religion. The greatness of Tillich's interpretation lies in his masterful ability to detect and trace out the repercussions of a philosophical concept upon the subsequent course of things.

The more immediate reason, however, for slanting the selection toward the *philosophical challenges* to Christian theology was Tillich's own mind-set and vocational self-understanding. He communicated best with persons of a philosophical orientation and he had an almost evangelistic zeal to recommend the Christian message to the intellectual doubters and scoffers of the faith. His account of the nineteenth-century critics of Christianity is simultaneously a revelation of Tillich's intellectual autobiography; it serves as a mirroring of Tillich's dialogue with the radical questions which modern culture places on the theological agenda. I think it provides documentary evidence of the assertion that Tillich was a *radical* theologian who searched into the depths of the *tradition* to find positive answers to the questions of modern man. One of his last statements confirms this estimate of his own theological intention: "I presuppose in my theological thinking the entire history of Christian thought up until now, and I consider the attitude of those people who are in doubt or estrangement or opposition to everything ecclesiastical and religious, including Christianity. And I have to speak to them. My work is with those who ask questions, and for them I am here."[31]

Tillich's career was begun when liberal theology was on the wane; he lived through the transitions of theology from the rise of "crisis" theology to its transformation by Barth into neo-orthodoxy, and from the decline of Barth's influence to the paramountcy of Bultmannianism after World War II. In half a century theology had gone a full cycle; Tillich observed the signs of the revival of liberalism. In his last Chicago address entitled "The Significance of the History of Religions for the Systematic Theologian," Tillich turned to the question of the future of theology. He saw that we were standing at a kind of crossroads. Theology could go with the secular group down a road strewn with the paradoxes of "a religion of non-religion" or of a "theology-without-God language,"[32] or it could take an opposite route toward a theology of the history of religions. Tillich's hope for the future of theology was the latter. He saw no promising future for theology if it clings to the exclusive attitudes of neo-orthodoxy or joins the "death of God" group. Theology would have to meet a new challenge: "Therefore, as theologians, we have to break through two barriers against a

[31] Brown, ed., *Ultimate Concern*, p. 191.
[32] *The Future of Religions*, p. 80.

free approach to the history of religions: the orthodox-exclusive one and the secular-rejective one."[33] A theology fully informed by the universal revelation of God in the history of religions and purified by the concrete event on which Christianity as a particular religion is based points to a way beyond these two barriers. A religion which combines both the universal and concrete aspects Tillich called "The Religion of the Concrete Spirit."[34]

Tillich's vision of the future of theology was formed in part through his association with Professor Mircea Eliade in their joint seminars on "History of Religions and Systematic Theology" in 1964. Eliade reports how Tillich opened his mind to the new stimulus from the side of the history of religions. For Tillich, Eliade states, this was an occasion for the "renewal of his own Systematic Theology."[35] He did not ask his theological students to look upon his system of theology as an achievement that could not be transcended. To the end Tillich displayed an amazing freedom to press beyond the limits of his own system and to point out new options for theology. Eliade's picture of Tillich in their seminars is the way Tillich himself would have had us remember him; it is the picture of "how Tillich was fighting his way to a new understanding of systematic theology."[36]

[33] *Ibid.*, p. 83.
[34] *Ibid.*, p. 87.
[35] "Paul Tillich and the History of Religions," *op. cit.*, p. 33.
[36] *Ibid.*, p. 35.

PERSPECTIVES ON
19th and 20th Century
Protestant Theology

Introduction: Problem and Method

O ur task is to cover in this series of lectures the tremendously large subject of Protestant theology in the nineteenth and twentieth centuries.[1] We can do this only because this course has a definite purpose and particular limits.

The primary purpose of this course is to understand our own problems by seeing their background in the past. I do not intend that you should learn merely a lot of facts which have no meaning for you. Instead I want to show you how we have arrived at the present situation. In view of this purpose it will be possible to draw from a great amount of material.

I hope you will discover that the past can be interesting even in itself, and not merely because it is *our* past, the past from which we come as religious people and theological thinkers. Perhaps the *erōs*, the word for love in Platonic Greek, will be aroused to interest you in some of the events in the past. This would be a beautiful by-product, but I do not know to what extent I will succeed in evoking that *erōs*.

In any case, there always exists this twofold purpose of a course in history, and especially of a course in the history of thought. The main purpose is to understand ourselves; yet there is the other purpose of

[1] Editor's Note: These lectures were delivered at the Divinity School of the University of Chicago during the spring quarter of 1963. They were offered under the course title "Protestant Theology in the Nineteenth and Twentieth Centuries." The class met eighteen times for sessions lasting an hour and a half. All material in the footnotes has been supplied by the present editor.

responding to a fascination for things which have happened in the past. This latter purpose might even be the more important for some of you now; as a rule, however, it is not the main reason for historical research.

This double purpose, especially the primary and basic one of trying to understand ourselves, leads us to emphasize the trends of thought more than the individual personalities who shaped them. We will see how these trends lead into our present situation. Of course, individual theologians will be discussed because they are the bearers of the development, but only those will be discussed more fully who happen to represent the great turning points in the course of events leading to us.

The orientation of this course makes it impossible to limit ourselves to a discussion of theologians. We must relate ourselves also to philosophers. In some cases they are more important than the theologians of their time because their philosophy of religion made decisive inroads into the history of Christian thought. In other cases the scientists will be more significant than the philosophers; also literature and even music—to allude to Karl Barth—will form an important part of the historical development.

I was very much interested and surprised when I read how Karl Barth dealt predominantly with the history of philosophy, and even music, in his beautiful book on the history of nineteenth-century theology.[2] And if Karl Barth does this, considering his attitude toward philosophy, then I certainly feel justified in doing the same thing. I recommend Barth's book as an illustration of the greatest convergence between his thinking and my own. Therefore, we will have to trespass the limits of the theological circle by dealing with philosophers, men of science and literature.

There is another kind of limit that we must trespass in order to understand the problems of the nineteenth century. We will have to go back into the eighteenth century, and occasionally even before that, because the principles of the modern mind were formulated in the centuries preceding the nineteenth. You can find these principles

<hr/>

[2] *Die protestantische Theologie im 19. Jahrhundert* (Zürich: Evangelischer Verlag, 1952). The English translation is entitled *Protestant Thought from Rousseau to Ritschl* (New York: Harper & Row, 1959). Unfortunately, only eleven chapters, less than one half, of the German edition are included in the English version.

implicit in all the great thinkers of the Renaissance, and certainly in the great scientific systems of the seventeenth century. But it was only during the eighteenth century that these principles became fully formulated as criticisms of theology. Every university and college worthy of their names are dependent on the thinkers of the eighteenth century and on their fundamental criticisms of the traditions of Orthodoxy and Pietism. And if you should come from Europe to America as I did thirty years ago, you would be astonished at how much more Americans are dependent on the eighteenth century than Europeans. The reason is very simple. America experienced every little of the romanticist reaction against the eighteenth century. Therefore, there is a very strong relationship here to the eighteenth century; thus I will be speaking very much to your situation when I go back to the principles out of which the criticism of orthodox and pietistic theology came.

We must also go beyond the nineteenth century into the twentieth because certain fundamental theological events have taken place in the last sixty years. I will now mention only a few of them in passing: the end of liberalism represented classically by Adolf von Harnack; the great all-embracing victory of the existentialist point of view; then the resurgence of what is called neo-orthodoxy in America and the theology of crisis in Europe. It is unfortunate that the latter is also called dialectical theology, because it is really more antidialectical than dialectical. Finally, there has been an appearance in recent years of what one could call neoliberalism. Now, these four movements have appeared in the twentieth century, and if we did not include them, this course would have no existential conclusion for our situation.

Now, I repeat, this is a large program for a single quarter, but it can be carried out if we select and interpret the material from a particular point of view, or better, from an overarching point of view. This means that we do not simply say that there was Mr. X and he said this, and a little later Mr. Y came along and he said that, and so with all the Xs and the Ys we reach the present time. That is a nonsensical way of dealing with history, even though it might be claimed to be the most "factual." Actually, it has nothing to do with real facts. Of course, there are factual elements in an interpretation of history, otherwise the interpretation becomes a misinterpretation of the course of history. History has an inner *telos*. *Telos* means "end," the "end" toward which something runs. Every period has an inner *telos*, and a given period must be interpreted historically in the light of its "end." Everything in this period receives its significance for us from its relation to the *telos*. In every moment innumerable things happen. In one hour like this more things are happening than all the books in the world could describe if we were to enter into the microcosmic elements in ourselves, in our brains and minds. Therefore, the interpretation of history must be selective; everything depends on the point of view from which we select and on the principle used in establishing what is important. For example, what is most important in church history? The answer is, of course, the Christian Church and its theological work. This also includes Western culture and the relationship of cultural activities to religion. In any case, a point of view in the interpretation of history must be found.

There is a point of view which I want to use, namely, the continuous series of attempts to unite the diverging elements of the modern mind. The most important of these attempts will seek to unite the orthodox and the humanist traditions. If the word "orthodox" seems too narrow for you, then we can speak of the "classical" tradition instead. All modern theology is an attempt to unite these two trends in the recent history of Christian thought. But, of course, this is only a very general formulation. The situation is infinitely richer, both culturally and religiously, than this can indicate. But if we look carefully, we will find that all the theologians, especially the great ones, will try to answer the question: What is the relation between the classical and the humanist traditions? One answer could be: There is no positive relation between them at all; the one simply stands beside the other. There could be the opposite answer: There is a complete unity between them, either in the one direction or in the other. But between these two opposite answers there can be many others, not as onesided as these two, which try to find a vital relationship, filled with many problems, tensions, and possible solutions.

First, I will develop the different elements in this divergent situation which had to be united. After having shown these elements, namely, Orthodoxy, Pietism, the Enlightenment and Romanticism, etc., I will discuss the greatest, the most embracing and effective, but in the last analysis unsuccessful attempts to bring about a union of all of them. I call these *the great synthesis*. *Synthesis* in Greek means "putting together," but in English this word has a negative connotation. Synthetic pearls are not genuine pearls. However, the theology of Schleiermacher and the philosophy of Hegel—these two great representatives of the synthesis in the early nineteenth century—are certainly not artificial pearls. They are very genuine and have had a tremendous impact on the whole history of thought to the present day. Hegel, for example, through the reactions of his pupils, has changed the surface of the earth in the twentieth century, perhaps more than any philosopher has ever done. We have only to think of the Communist Revolution.

These two thinkers, Schleiermacher and Hegel, are the points toward which all elements go and from which they then diverge, later bringing about the demand for new syntheses. We will see how these new syntheses have been attempted again and again, and finally what in my opinion has to be done today. So the whole story has a dramatic character. It is the drama of the rise of a humanism in the midst of Christianity which is critical of the Christian tradition, departs from it and produces a vast world of secular existence and thought. Then there is the rise of some of the greatest philosophers and theologians who try to unite these divergent elements again. Their syntheses in turn are destroyed and the divergent elements collide and try to conquer each other, and new attempts to reunite them have to be made. The Ritschlian school is an example of this, with Harnack as its leading representative. And in our century there is the Bultmann school, and so on.

Thus we really have a drama before us, a drama in which many tragedies are involved. All the disruptions of inner, personal, spiritual life of countless people are involved in the conflicts of this drama—conflicts which do not stop before the sacred doors of theological schools and seminaries. They are inescapable for all of us, whether we like it or not.

There is one thing in what I have said that you might tend to question, namely, the predominance of German theology in the nineteenth and early twentieth centuries. This is simply a fact which I cannot help. The reason for this is that other Protestant countries were not involved in this conflict to the same intense degree. If we look at Great Britain for a moment, we see that there was no great depth of genuine theological interest. The Anglican Church put its main emphasis on liturgical questions, and on questions of political structure and ethical consequences. This is its genius, its greatness, but it is not theology in the strict sense. In the Scandinavian countries there is only one man who made a great difference in the nineteenth century, and he is Søren Kierkegaard. He was not only a religious writer, as Martin Heidegger calls him, but in his religious writings the existentialist philosophy was present. Many modern existentialists have derived their philosophy from Kierkegaard's writings. Kierkegaard was what he was because he had to struggle to overcome his master, Hegel. Hegel's thought permeates his whole work, almost every sentence. And contemporary with Kierkegaard there was another theologian greatly influenced by Hegel, Bishop Hans Martensen of Denmark (1808–1884). He was a theologian of mediation,[3] to use a term dating from the middle of the nineteenth century.

In Holland during the nineteenth century there developed a split between the critical attitude on the one side (the liberal church took into itself all the critical elements of liberalism) and the orthodox Calvinist Church on the other side, which maintained the traditional theology with great tenacity. But during this period there were no new theological solutions in Holland.

In Switzerland the older traditions were preserved, but here there arose certain other influences which were later to shape modern theology. Three names must be mentioned. The greatest of them is Friedrich Nietzsche (1844–1900), whose attack on Christianity had an enormous influence on the whole later theological development. The second is Jacob Burckhardt (1818–1897), the historian, who wrote the beautiful books about the Renaissance and the art of Florence and Rome. And the third one is Franz Overbeck (1837–1905), who declared —something which Barth often mentions—that if Christianity has arrived at the point of nineteenth-century liberalism, then one must ask

---

[3] The expression "theology of mediation" is a technical term referring to various nineteenth-century efforts to correlate the Christian faith with the modern mind. For a discussion of this *Vermittlungstheologie*, see below, pp. 208–215.

the question: Are we still Christians? and he passionately denied that. He had a great influence on later thought. These are some of the vital new impulses that were experienced in Switzerland, and which played an important role in the theological revolution that occurred in the twentieth century (Barth and Brunner).

In France, which has only a small number of Protestants, the modernist movement was the most interesting, comprising those who represented what was called "symbolofideism." This means literally the "symbolism of faith." Alfred Loisy (1857–1940) is the best known of the modernists. These modernists had an interesting theory of religious symbolism. They were excommunicated by the Pope, but their influence has never ceased. Often I meet Catholic laymen, especially highly educated ones, who take it for granted that most of the dogmas have to be taken symbolically. But officially this is not permitted. The modernistic symbolofideists were condemned by the Pope.

Now the United States followed generally the continental development, first orthodoxy, then pietism, usually called revivalism here, and then liberalism. But there are two differences. The first is that in this country liberalism took the form of a church, namely, Unitarianism. This has never happened in Europe. There liberalism was a theological movement in the established churches, but it never established itself as a church. Perhaps this was a better solution because it seems that Unitarianism in this country suffers from its separation. It tends to be less flexible than liberal theology in Europe because it becomes bound to a church tradition.

The second important difference is the rise of the social gospel movement. There were also social ethical elements in the late nineteenth-century liberal theology represented by Harnack, but they were not essential. Only with the rise of religious socialism, a comparatively small movement after the first World War, did similar things occur in Germany. Before this they had already occurred in Switzerland and in England. But the transformation of all theology from the point of view of social ethics, thus creating a theology of the social gospel,[4] is something original in this country.

---

[4] Cf. Walter Rauschenbusch, *Theology of the Social Gospel* (New York: The Macmillan Company, 1918).

Now that gives us a broad overview of things. It is enough to show you that the central and most dramatic movements of theology took place in Germany. This also means that it happened on Lutheran soil. This is not strange, because there is no other Protestant church which places such a heavy emphasis on doctrine, on the pure doctrine as it was called in the Reformation period. What Luther called the Word of God over against the Roman Church was embodied in the Lutheran confessions and doctrines. And Lutheranism, at least in some sections, still preserves this tremendous emphasis on the doctrinal side of Christianity. Calvinism lays more stress on the disciplinary, ethical side, and Episcopalianism more on the liturgical side.

All this shows that the kind of history of Christian thought to which I will introduce you is, so to speak, the historical dimension of systematic theology. It is not church history and I am no church historian. And when you ask, Why should I learn all this? Why these studies of the history of Christian thought which only seek to establish dates that can soon be forgotten again?—then I must answer that this is not the way in which I intend to deal with the past.

CHAPTER I

Oscillating Emphases in Orthodoxy,

Pietism and Rationalism

A. The Period of Orthodoxy

First I want to say a few words about what followed the period of the Reformation, namely, the development of orthodoxy. Now the word "orthodoxy" has two meanings. There is both Eastern Orthodoxy and Protestant Orthodoxy. The Eastern Churches which call themselves Orthodox (e.g., Russian and Greek) do so not so much because of their doctrinal interests, but because of their interest in the tradition. The Eastern Orthodox Churches, of course, have fixed liturgical forms and they also have doctrinal statements, but they are very flexible in this respect. They have the good fortune of not having a Pope. Because they feel that they are in continual development, they can work in close relation with Protestantism in the World Council of Churches. The term "orthodoxy" in Greek simply means "right opinion," but in Eastern Orthodoxy it connotes the "classical tradition." The tradition is expressed in the councils, in the creeds, in the acknowledged Fathers, and in the whole liturgical development. This is Eastern Orthodoxy. It is clear that here orthodoxy means something quite different from what it means when we speak of Protestant Orthodoxy.

We must also be sure to distinguish between orthodoxy and fundamentalism. The orthodox period of Protestantism has very little to do
with what is called fundamentalism in America. Rather, it has special
reference to the scholastic period of Protestant history. There were great
scholastics in Protestantism, some of them equally as great as the
medieval scholastics. One of them is Johann Gerhard (1582–1637) who
in his monumental work[1] developed fully as many problems as the
tomes of the medieval scholastics in the thirteenth and fourteenth centuries. Such a thing has never been done in American fundamentalism.
Protestant Orthodoxy was constructive. It did not have anything like the
pietistic or revivalistic background of American fundamentalism. It was
objective as well as constructive, and attempted to present the pure and
comprehensive doctrine concerning God and man and the world. It was
not determined by a kind of lay biblicism as is the case in American
fundamentalism—a biblicism which rejects any theological penetration
into the biblical writings and makes itself dependent on traditional
interpretations of the Word of God.

You cannot find anything like that in classical orthodoxy. Therefore it
is a pity that very often orthodoxy and fundamentalism are confused.
One of the great achievements of classical orthodoxy in the late sixteenth and early seventeenth centuries was the fact that it remained in
continual discussion with all the centuries of Christian thought. Those
theologians were not untheological lay people ignorant of the meanings
of the concepts which they used in biblical interpretation. They knew
the past meanings of these concepts in the history of the church which
covered a period of over fifteen hundred years. These orthodox theologians knew the history of philosophy as well as the theology of the
Reformation. The fact that they were in the tradition of the Reformers
did not prevent them from knowing thoroughly scholastic theology,
from discussing and refuting it, or even accepting it when possible.

All this makes classical orthodoxy one of the great events in the
history of Christian thought. I feel that the superiority of the more
educated Catholic theologians in our century over the more educated
Protestant theologians is largely due to the fact that they know their

[1] The reference is to Gerhard's 9-volume work on dogmatics, *Loci theologici*
(1610-22). This is a classic expression of the "local" (or topical) method of
scholastic theology.

Latin as well as you know your English. They are able to formulate the classical doctrines of Christianity in continuity with the Latin language that in theology goes back at least to Tertullian in the second century. We have in the Latin language something that I sometimes call a philosophical and theological clearing house. Its sharpness of linguistic and logical distinctions overcomes much of the vagueness that is prevalent in Protestant thought. There is no modern language that has this kind of sharpness. Now I would not suggest that you should all speak Latin as well as our theological fathers used to do. They had to write an essay in Latin in order to pass an examination for admission into the university. They had to be able to use Latin freely, without a commentary. Although this ability has been lost—and it represents a great loss of sharpness in theological thinking—we should at least be able to read the Latin texts with a translation running on one side. I hope somebody will take this to heart and write such a book. We could have a compendium, as it was called in Germany in my time, of classical orthodoxy, Lutheran or Calvinist, or better both united in one compendium, where you have on one side the classical formulations in Latin—which you could recognize because there is so much of the Latin language in English—and on the other side the English translations, which are never as good as the Latin.

In this connection I often think of the saying of one of my former teachers, Martin Kähler, who lived in the period immediately following Goethe, and who knew his Goethe as well as the Bible by heart. He used to say that the orthodoxy of the sixteenth and seventeenth centuries is the abutment against which the bridge of all later Protestant theology leans. That is a very good symbol, because all later Protestant theology becomes a bit vague and is suspended in the air if it is not related to the classic formulation of Reformation theology in Protestant Orthodoxy. The vagueness of much theological thinking in modern Protestantism stems from this lack of knowledge of Protestant Orthodoxy.

Friedrich Schleiermacher, the father of modern Protestant theology, was theologically educated within the framework of Protestant Orthodoxy. If you read his dogmatics, *The Christian Faith*,[2] you will find that

---

[2] Edited by H. R. Mackintosh and J. S. Stewart (Edinburgh: T. & T. Clark, 1928).

he never develops any thought without making reference to classical orthodoxy, then to the pietist criticism of orthodoxy, and finally to the Enlightenment criticism of both, before he goes on to state his own solutions. This is an important procedure for all theological thought.

Orthodoxy is the most objective representation of Protestant theology. Of course, when I use the word "objective," I find that I must always carefully define what "objective" means as over against "subjective." Today the word "objective" means scientifically verified or empirically true. This is not the sense in which I mean it. One cannot simply transpose categories from science to the humanities. When we speak of Orthodoxy as "objective" we have in mind a representation of doctrine as such without particular reference to the individual who accepts or rejects it. The "subjective" element—the word "subjective" does not mean willful or arbitrary as it is usually used today—has reference to the believing subject, construing something in what we today call existential terms. Orthodoxy tried to be as objective as possible, but even this system was open to subjective elements. First of all, there was the subjective element which belongs to all Protestantism, namely, Luther's personal experience, or Zwingli's, or later on Calvin's. All three of them broke through the objectivism of the Roman Church. This break-through was an element in the orthodox system itself. This becomes very clear when we look at the two main principles of Orthodoxy. These have been called the "material principle" and the "formal principle."

The material principle of the Reformation is the doctrine of justification by faith, or rather by grace through faith. Excuse me for this slip of the tongue! Never say what I just said by mistake, but always say, justification *by* grace *through* faith. The justifying power is the divine grace; the channel through which men receive this grace is faith. Faith is by no means the cause, but only the channel. In the moment in which faith is understood as the cause of justification, it is a worse work of man than anything in Roman Catholicism. It results in destroying one's own honesty by compelling oneself to believe certain things. This is the consequence of the phrase, justification *by* faith. If faith is a human work which makes us acceptable to God, and if this human work is the basis or cause of salvation, then we can never be certain of our salvation in the sense in which Luther sought for certainty when he asked the question, "How do I find a merciful God?" Therefore, whenever you are dealing with Protestant theology, dismiss forever this distortion of faith —*sola fide* in Latin—which sees faith as a cause instead of as a channel. Luther made this clear repeatedly when he said that faith is always receiving and only receiving; it does not produce anything. Certainly it does not produce the good will of God.

Here the linguistic problem becomes the profoundest theological problem. The great distortions in Protestantism have come from this basic confusion—as if Luther ever said that an intellectual acceptance of doctrines can be the saving power for men. For Luther faith is the result of the divine Spirit, and the divine Spirit and grace are one and the same thing. God gives us grace by giving us the Spirit. It is the Spirit who makes it possible for us to accept the message that our sins are forgiven. It is absolutely contrary to the whole Reformation if somebody should say that before you can be forgiven you must first have belief in God, in Christ and his atonement, plus Luther's doctrines and Catechisms. That is anti-divine and anti-Reformation. The primary thing is to be open for the divine grace, and not the attempt to produce it. The worst form of trying to produce it—at least today—is to try to accept doctrines, to believe in something which somehow we believe is unbelievable, force it upon ourselves and repress honest doubt. That is the worst kind of distortion.

There is the other principle, the "formal principle," on which the system of Orthodoxy was built. This is the principle of Scripture which became fixed and rigid. Is it not possible to rest confidently on this? But we all know that ever since Origen there have been many interpretations of the Bible. Every period of history has a different understanding of what is decisive in the Bible. The Bible is an object of interpretation. If somebody does not believe that, just ask him, "Do you know what the Greek words meant at the time they were written so that you can identify them with the Word of God?" Then very likely he will say, "I don't even know Greek, but I have the King James Bible, and of course, that is the true Word of God. All of the modernistic Bibles should be burned." That is the typical point of view of somebody who simply does not know. It may be a repression of willingness to face the real situation. The Bible is the book which contains the reports of the events which have happened both in the Old and the New Testaments. It presents the history of revelation and its fulfillment in the Christ as the foundation of the Christian Church. This is the central event which the Bible proclaims.

But if we say that this protects us from being subjective, then we have never tried to translate even one verse of Scripture. The right translation of all the great passages of the New Testament is dependent on an understanding of their meaning, and this is a work for which rigorous scholarship is needed. At the same time, the religious tradition is at work in the understanding of Scripture when simple believers read it. Their reading does have saving power for them. This is the meaning of the Protestant formula *Scriptura suiipsius interpres,"* (Scripture interprets itself). It does this to every pious layman who reads the Bible; this does not mean, however, that he may make a theological dogma out of his ignorance of the situation, as fundamentalism does. So here we have the principle of subjectivity unavoidably entering in, although the Reformers tried to prevent it by putting the authority of the Bible in place of the authority of the church. This is most clear in Calvin. For Calvin the Bible does not say anything to anyone, either to theologians or to pious readers, without the divine Spirit. The divine Spirit is the creative power in which our own personal spirit is involved and transcended. The spirit is not a mechanism for dictating material as in some forms of the theory of inspiration.

There is another dangerous element in classical orthodoxy to which I must refer. This is the two-storied character of orthodoxy theology. The lower story is called "natural theology," which works with reason, and the upper story is called "revealed theology." The theologians always had difficulty determining what belonged to each. Naturally, doctrines like those dealing with the trinity and the incarnation were placed into revealed theology, but already the doctrines of creation and providence were doubtful. Where did they belong? Thus Johann Gerhard, of whom we spoke earlier, distinguished between pure and mixed doctrines (*doctrinae purae et mixtae*). The pure doctrines are those which can be deduced only from divine revelation; the mixed doctrines are those which can be dealt with partly in terms of reason and partly in terms of revelation.

Such a view is quite unsatisfactory and presupposes a concept of reason that itself is unsatisfactory. Thus it happened that a revolution occurred by the lower story fighting against the upper story. As often happens in society, the lower classes fight against the upper classes. But during the Enlightenment it was the lower story of the building of theology which revolted against the upper story. The lower claimed the right to become the whole building and denied the right to have any independent upper story at all. We call this "rationalism" in theology. There was something in the very structure of Orthodoxy which made it possible for this revolution of rationalism to take place.

B. The Reaction of Pietism against Orthodoxy

Before the revolution of natural theology against revealed theology took place, there was another type of criticism against the orthodox system which had recourse to a subjective element and recalled Luther's personal experience. In the power of the Spirit which speaks through the biblical message Luther had carried out a revolution against the objectivism of the Roman Church. In his earlier development Luther was very much influenced by mystical elements. He was profoundly influenced by the so-called *Theologia Germanica,* the classic of devotional literature from the period of German mysticism. It was Luther's experience of God which produced the explosiveness of his teaching that really transformed the surface of the earth. What was this experience? It was not the criticism of dogma. There had been much of that prior to Luther. Most of his positions had been theoretically formulated earlier by the so-called prereformers. But it was the explosion of a personal relation to God. Was that based on human achievements of an intellectual or moral kind, or was it based on openness for what God gives and in particular *forgives?* The latter was the decisive thing. Thus already in the period of the Reformation there were elements that we must call mystical, and which became pronounced again in the anti-orthodox movement of Pietism. This happened first in Germany in the seventeenth century (Spener and Francke), then in British Methodism (the Wesley brothers), and finally in a great number of sectarian movements in this country which claim for themselves the presence of the Spirit.

Pietism also had its theology, but it was generally a theology which accepted the orthodox tradition, just as the revivalist movement in America did, only making it less theologically relevant by a fundamentalist deviation and primitivization. However, Pietism fought against Orthodoxy on the ground of Orthodoxy; this was a long and often bitter fight. Let me give you an illustration of this. There was a debate on what was called the *"theologia irregenetorum,"* the theology of the unregenerate, of those who are not born again. Orthodoxy maintained the view that since theology is an objective science, it is possible to write a fully valid theology whether we are reborn or not. Pietism said, "No, that's impossible; you must be reborn with respect to everything in which you participate, in all that you talk about; you can be a theologian only if you have the experience of regeneration." The answer of the Orthodox theologians to this was: "How can you state beyond any doubt that you are regenerate? Is any emotional experience to be considered a real rebirth? Is not regeneration a process under the guidance of the divine Spirit which does not permit you to make a clear distinction between before and after?"

Of course there are some people who have a decisive experience. John Wesley had it; August Francke, the German pietist, had it, and Nicholaus von Zinzendorf had it, but these are exceptional cases. The development of the ordinary Christian does not manifest a clear-cut division between before and after, so that he could say with finality: Now I am able to be a theologian because I have really experienced rebirth. Modern theology is still discussing this point. Today we ask instead: Isn't existential participation in theological problems necessary in order to understand and solve them? I think that this way of putting the question can be a formula of union, combining the concerns of the orthodox and the pietist theologians. Existential participation indeed is necessary, but an experience of regeneration at a definite point in time is certainly not. That is impossible. It is enough that we are existentially concerned about these problems, that we participate in them existentially, even though for the moment it may be in the form of doubt. So my answer to the question which became one of the chief points of contention between Orthodoxy and Pietism is that existential participation and ultimate seriousness in dealing with theological questions is necessary. Indeed, this is a presupposition of theology, but by no means does it entail the fixing of a date and pointing to an inner experience of regeneration. The final upshot was that Pietism succeeded in bringing Orthodoxy out of its seemingly unconquerable fortress by appealing to the element of subjectivity in the Reformers themselves. That was the other side of Luther and Calvin which had been neglected in Orthodoxy. Thus Pietism was able to break open this very frozen system of thought.

C. The Rise of Rationalism

The theology of the Reformation created a special educational problem which opened the door to rationalism. In Roman Catholicism you can be saved by believing what the church believes. This is called the *fides implicita* (implicit faith). If you believe what you are taught, then implicitly you receive the truth which the Catholic Church teaches. This was one of the points on which the Reformation erupted, for in place of the *fides implicita* the Reformers taught that everyone must have an experience of grace in faith. Each individual must be able to confess his sins, to experience the meaning of repentance, and to become certain of his salvation through Christ. This became a problem in Protestantism. It meant that everyone would have to have some basic knowledge of the fundamental doctrines of the Christian Church. In teaching these doctrines, you could not carry on the instruction of ordinary people in the same way as future professors of theology are taught, with their knowledge of Latin and Greek, of the history of exegesis and theological thought. How can you teach everybody? By making the teaching extremely simple. This simplification became more and more a rationalization. You must teach what is understandable by reason in your religious education, because it is necessary that everyone should know what is said and meant in the Catechism.

The consequence of this was that the doctrines had to be made more reasonable to become more understandable. This was one of the ways in which religious education served as a preparation for the Enlightenment. Often the people of the Enlightenment had no idea that they were doing anything else than preserving the religious tradition. But they said, "We must do it in a reasonable way so that people can understand." In Protestantism we cannot have people like the masses of Roman Catholic people, who attend church, listen to the mass, perhaps go to confession, and then leave again. Protestants must have a direct personal relationship with God, whether or not they go to church. They must know for themselves, and cannot be led to priests and professors. Therefore, doctrine must be made understandable to the people. Do not forget that this is still a problem for us. Since we are all autonomous in contrast to the Roman Christians who accept what the church teaches, we must know the doctrine for ourselves, whether we are laymen or ministers. Thus liberal education in our time faces this same problem: How can these things be made understandable? That is not the whole problem, but that is the educational side which is very important for the whole development.

We have been discussing the revolt against Orthodoxy from the side of natural theology which Orthodoxy itself had made a part of its two-story system. The substructure of orthodox theology is natural theology, and natural theology is rational theology. Thus the rise of rational criticism of revealed theology came out of Orthodoxy itself. Rational theology is a theology which through arguments for the existence of God, and the like, attempts to build a universally acceptable theology by pure reason. At this point the revolt could take place, the revolt of the substructure against the superstructure. The substructure was built by the tools of rational arguments; the superstructure as revealed theology is based on the sources of revelation. In Protestantism these are virtually equated with the biblical writings, while in Catholicism the tradition of the church is included as well. The whole structure was delicately built and extremely vulnerable from the point of view of the relation between the two stories. It would be possible for reason to revolt against revelation, as it is usually phrased in traditional terminology. But this is a poor way of phrasing it, as I will show later.

This led to the struggle in the eighteenth century between a naturalistic or rationalistic and a supernaturalistic theology. This struggle brought about the weakening of the power of Orthodoxy. Now Pietism and Rationalism had one element in common. Pietism was more modern than Orthodoxy; it was nearer to the modern mind, because of the element of subjectivity in it. If the word "subjectivity" has the connotation of willfulness to you, it should not be used; rather, we should speak of existential participation. This may be a clumsy expression, but at least it avoids the bad connotation of arbitrariness which is usually connected with the word "subjectivity." The common denominator in Pietism, or revivalism as it is often called, and in Rationalism is the mystical element. This is one of the most important insights for understanding the development of Protestant theology after the Reformation to the present time. Therefore, I want to discuss now the relation between the mystical and rational elements in theology.

Rationalism and mysticism do not stand in contradiction to each other, as is so often thought. Both in Greek and modern culture rationalism is the daughter of mysticism. Rationalism developed out of the mystical experience of the "inner light" or the "inner truth" in every human being. Reason emerged within us out of mystical experience, namely, the experience of the divine presence within us. This can be seen most clearly in the Quaker movement. Quakerism in George Fox's time was an ecstatic, mystical movement, as were most of the radical movements of the Reformation and post-Reformation periods. Already in the second generation of Quakerism there developed a moral rationalism from which have come the great moral principles of modern Quaker activities. There never was the feeling on the part of Quakers that their rational, pacifist, and in certain respects, very bourgeois morality stood in conflict with their mystical experience of intuition. Therefore, it is useful to study the development of Quakerism in order to understand the relation between mystical and rational inwardness. Both of them exist within our subjectivity. The opposite of a theology of inwardness is the classical theology of the Reformers, namely, the theology of the Word of God which comes to us from the outside, stands over against us and judges us, so that we have to accept it on the authority of the revelatory experiences of the prophets and apostles.

This whole conflict is of fundamental importance to the movements of theology in the centuries that we wish to discuss. The same conflict occurred in our century, between the liberal theology of Harnack's *What Is Christianity?*[3] and Karl Barth's theology of crisis. To see this conflict you should read the classical exchange of letters between Harnack and Barth. Here we have the modern parallel to the encounter between the theologians of the Reformation and the Anabaptists and other spiritualistic movements. Unfortunately, the terms "spiritualist" and "spiritist" have been stolen by the occultists, and can no longer be used in good theology. In the third volume of my *Systematic Theology*,[4] in the part on "Life and the Spirit," I develop a theology of the Spirit, but I do not use these confusing adjectives. If by chance I do use them, I am not thinking about spiritualism in the sense of entering into communication with souls that have passed beyond death. I would not be interested in that even if it were a reality. The spiritualist movements in the Reformation period are often called "radical evangelical movements." We have this same sort of conflict between Orthodoxy and Pietism, which we have discussed, and in the nineteenth century between German classical idealism and the rebirth of Orthodoxy in the restoration theology of the mid-nineteenth century.

If for a moment I may be allowed to be personal, you see this same conflict going on between my own theology and Karl Barth's, the one approaching man by coming from the outside (Barth) and the other starting with man. Now I believe that there is one concept which can reconcile these two ways. This is the concept of the divine Spirit. It was there in the apostle Paul. Paul was the great theologian of the divine Spirit. It formed the center of his theology. The classical Protestant view has held, along with Luther, Melanchthon, Calvin, and Bucer, that Paul was a theologian of justification by grace through faith. That certainly is not wrong. But this was a defensive doctrine for Paul. He developed this doctrine in his fight against the so-called Judaizers. They wanted to transform the gospel into another law; they demanded that the pagans or Gentiles subject themselves to the Jewish law, and for them Jesus was only another interpreter of the law. Paul had to fight against this, otherwise there could be no Christian Church in the pagan

---

[3] Adolf von Harnack, *What Is Christianity?* translated by Thomas B. Saunders (New York: Harper & Brothers, 1957).

[4] The University of Chicago Press, 1963.

nations. Christianity would have remained a small Jewish sect. Nevertheless, as important as the doctrine of justification was for Paul, it was not the center of his theology. At the center was his experience and doctrine of the Spirit. Thus he is on the side of those in Protestant theology who stress inwardness. Paul goes so far as to say what many mystics have stressed since, namely, that a successful prayer is not one which obtains what we ask for, but one which attains the Spirit of God. It is God himself as Spirit who prays for us and bears witness with our spirit. You can read this in Romans 8. You will find there that Paul is indeed the theologian of the Spirit.

Although I am not a mystical theologian, I would say that I am more on the side of the theology of experience and inwardness, for I believe that the Spirit is in us. In the concept of the Spirit the highest synthesis is given between the Word of God which comes from the outside and the experience which occurs inside. Now all this has been a digression, but if a systematic theologian teaches history, he cannot help but tell you what he thinks about things. He cannot simply enumerate facts in textbook fashion. You can do that much better for yourself. The problem is the difference between the theology of the Word from the outside and the theology of inner experience, which is frequently but wrongly called "the inner Word." That is not a good term. "Inner light" is better. In modern terminology we speak of "existential experience." The point is that these two things are not mutually exclusive. The concept of the Spirit is the mediating power which overcomes the conflict between outside and inside.

I said that the principles of reason develop out of an originally ecstatic experience which produces insight. This insight can become rationalized. As the principles of reason emerge within us, the original underlying ecstasy can disappear or recede, with the result that the Spirit becomes Reason in the largest sense of the concept. We will develop this later in the lectures on the Enlightenment. Anyway, I hope that you now understand one thing: The opposite of mysticism is not rationalism, but rationalism is the daughter of mysticism. The opposite of mysticism is the theology of the Word in terms of an authority coming from the outside, to which we subject ourselves either by accepting doctrines or by fulfilling moral commands. We should also avoid the distortions of the word "mystical." A person, for instance, is said to be a bit mystical when he is somewhat foggy in his mind. That is not a serious usage of the term. Mysticism means inwardness, participation in the Ultimate Reality through inner experience. In some cases mystics have tried to produce this participation by means of asceticism, self-emptying exercises, and the like. But mysticism should not be identified with these exercises either.

Whatever we may think of abstract mysticism such as we find in Plotinus or in Hinduism, which are very similar to each other, we must nevertheless say that there is a mystical element in every religion and in every prayer. This mystical element is the inward participation in and experience of the presence of the divine. Where this is lacking we have only intellect or will; we have a system of doctrines or a system of ethics, but we do not have religion. In Protestantism, especially in some Protestant groups in this country, we see what happens when the mystical element is neglected and forgotten. Doctrines are not pushed aside, but they are put on the altar or in a box, so to speak. They are taken for granted, and no one is supposed to question them seriously. Theology is not very important. But so-called Christian morals are kept, with the result that the "teachings of Jesus" are misused and Jesus is modeled after the poor image of a teacher. Jesus was more than a teacher; his teachings were expressions of his being, and were thus not teachings in an ordinary sense. Thus Protestantism becomes an unmystical system of moral commandments, and its specifically religious basis, the presence of the Spirit of God in our spirit, is disregarded. The history of Protestant theology refutes such an attitude and shows that it is a complete deviation from the genuine experience of the divine presence.

There are many reasons why rationalism was born out of mysticism both in Greek and modern culture. But we cannot go into them. We can only observe that it happened on a large scale in the late seventeenth and eighteenth centuries. Ecstatic Protestant groups and their leaders were also the leaders of the Enlightenment. This happened in many places and can be understood only on the basis of what I have said about the relation of rationalism to mysticism. The one term which grasps their unity is the term "inner light." It comes from the Augustinian-Franciscan tradition in medieval theology, which was renewed by the sectarian movements in the Reformation period, and underlies much of Protestant theology in America. The inner light is the light which everybody has within himself because he belongs to God, and in virtue of which he is able to receive the divine Word when it is spoken to him.

CHAPTER II

The Enlightenment and Its Problems

A. THE NATURE OF ENLIGHTENMENT

Now we must go to the fundamental principles of the Enlightenment. We will not be speaking directly of the great thinkers of the eighteenth century, such as Hobbes (really seventeenth century) and Hume in England, Lessing and Kant in Germany, and Rousseau and Voltaire in France, but we will be describing the fundamental principles of the Enlightenment. Most of our academic life is based on these principles.

1. The Kantian Definition of Autonomy

We will be discussing four main concepts, without going into the details of their application. The first of these is "autonomy." In order to introduce this concept, I will indicate how Kant understood it in the latter part of the eighteenth century. Kant defined enlightenment (*Aufklärung*) as man's conquering the state of immaturity so far as he is responsible for it. Immaturity, he said, is the inability to use one's own reason without the guidance of somebody else. Immaturity of this kind is caused by ourselves. It is rooted in the lack of resoluteness and courage to use reason without the guidance of another person. The free use of reason is the essence of enlightenment. Now that is a very adequate description of what autonomy means. Kant pointed out how much more comfortably one lives if one has guardians, of whatever kind they may be, whether religious, political, philosophical, or educational ones. But it was his intention to drive men out of their security under the guidance of other people. For him this security contradicts the true nature of man.

That is the meaning of the idea of autonomy in the light of Kant's words. He could say that this is the fundamental principle of enlightenment, the autonomy of reason in every individual human being. The word "autonomy" needs some interpretation. It is derived from two Greek words, *autos,* which means "self," and *nomos,* which means "law." Autonomy means being a law to oneself. The law is not outside of us, but inside as our true being. This Greek origin of the word shows clearly that autonomy is the opposite of arbitrariness or willfulness. Autonomy is not lawless subjectivity. Kant emphasized this when he said that the essential nature of the human will is the law of reason. Every deviation from it hurts the essential nature of the will itself. It is the law implicit in man's rational structure. It has implications for the theoretical as well as for the practical side of man's activities. It refers to knowledge as well as to the arts, to the development of personality as well as to community. Everything which belongs to man's nature shares in his rational structure. Man is autonomous. The law of aesthetic fulfillment (works of art), of cognitive fulfillment (scientific inquiry), of personal fulfillment in a mature personality, of community fulfillment in principles of justice—all these belong to reason and are based on the autonomy of reason in every human being.

I must warn you about some distorted statements on autonomy. There are theological books of the neo-orthodox movement, for example, which attack autonomy as a revolt against God. They identify it with individual willfulness and arbitrariness. In doing this they distort the meaning of autonomy. Man's autonomy does not stand against the word or will of God—as if God's will were something opposed to man's created goodness and its fulfillment. We could define autonomy as the memory which man has of his own created goodness. Autonomy is man's living in the law of reason in all realms of his spiritual activity. Many philosophers of the Enlightenment identified autonomy with the divine will and were in no way critical of this identification. But for the individual man it means the courage to think; it means the courage to use one's rational powers. This becomes even more clear when we look at the opposite term, namely, "heteronomy."

The word "heteronomy" also comes from two Greek words, *heteros*, which means "strange" or "foreign," and *nomos*, which means "law." Now the whole thing is turned around. It is not autonomy but ultimately heteronomy that involves willfulness and arbitrariness. Why? Because if we should obey a strange authority, even if it were to come from God, it would go against the will of our own created goodness, and we would be subjecting ourselves to something that is not pure reason within us, such as our desires, our strivings, or the pleasure principle, and the like. Then we are looking for the security of a foreign authority which deprives us of the courage to use our reason because of the fear of punishment or of falling into insoluble problems. So we come to the surprising result that heteronomy is ultimately the attempt to escape fear, not by courage but by subjection to an authority which gives us security. In this sense heteronomy indirectly appeals to the pleasure principle and denies our own rational structure. Kant, for instance, was very much aware even before Freud and modern psychotherapy that religious heteronomy also subjects men to strange laws—whether heteronomy in relation to the church or the Bible—and that men follow these laws driven by fear. This means that ultimately they are being driven by the pleasure principle, subverting the created goodness of man's rational structure.

In this sense all religious authority can become heteronomous. Of course, the heteronomy disappears in the moment in which it is transformed into theonomy (divine law). Theonomy implies our own personal experience of the presence of the divine Spirit within us, witnessing to the Bible or to the church. It is very interesting that Calvin who sounds so heteronomously authoritarian in many of his utterances was the one who most clearly stated that the Bible can be our authority only when the divine Spirit witnesses to it (the *testimonium Sancti Spiritus internum*). Where this inner witness is lacking, the authority of the Bible has no meaning. Obedience to its authority would be mere external subjection and not inward personal experience. In autonomy one follows the natural law of God implanted in our own being, and if we experience the truth of this law in the Bible or in the church, then we are still autonomous, but with the dimension of the theonomous in us at the same time. If we do not have this experience, then we follow in authoritarian subjection as immature persons, searching for security by avoiding the anxieties of punishment and danger. Autonomy which is aware of its divine ground is theonomy; but autonomy without the theonomous dimension degenerates into mere humanism.

Heteronomy has been broken in our time, and this is a dangerous thing. Men are always looking for the security of heteronomy, especially the masses of men. The breaking up of ecclesiastical heteronomy means that the masses of people run to other heteronomies, such as the totalitarian systems, sectarian fanaticism, or fundamentalistic narrowness, thus closing themselves off from the whole development of autonomous thought in modern times.

In the light of these principles you can understand why the Enlightenment was one of the greatest of all revolutions. Socially it was a bourgeois revolution. But spiritually it was the revolution of man's autonomous potentialities over against heteronomous powers which were no longer convincing. But don't misunderstand me! As long as people in the Middle Ages lived in these traditions without criticizing them—just as we breathe air without knowing it—then it is still theonomy. But as soon as the human mind began to ask questions at the end of the Middle Ages, then the great problem arose. The church responded by using all its power heteronomously to suppress the questioning mind which was no longer at ease in the atmosphere of ecclesiastical tradition and could no longer regard it as self-evident. Something new had taken place. Man became aware of his power of radical questioning. What should then be done? Should we try to suppress autonomous thought, as the church tried to do by means of the Inquisition, or should we do something else? Should we attempt to find within autonomy the dimension of theonomy, namely, the religious dimension, without weakening autonomous thought? This is what Schleiermacher and Hegel tried to do. The problem is still alive today. We cannot surrender autonomy, but neither can we live in an empty autonomy, because then we are in danger of grasping securities given by false authorities and totalitarian powers.

* * * * * * * * * *

Question:[1] In your definition of theonomy you mentioned the experiences of the presence of the inner divine Spirit which witnesses to the Bible and church. Would you describe this Spirit more fully so that I could recognize it in myself? Or if it is self-authenticating, how does one cultivate or achieve this Spirit?

Answer: Now this is a mixture of theology and counseling. But let me say one thing. It is obvious that if we speak of the Spirit working within us, it is self-authenticating. By what else could it be authenticated? If by some other authority, why would we acknowledge that authority? Because the Spirit tells us to. Then we are back with the Spirit. This was Calvin's idea, for example, when he spoke about the authority of the Bible. The divine Spirit witnesses to the content of the Bible, and in this way the Bible can become an authority. Only through the witness of the Spirit can the Bible cease to be a merely external authority. There is, however, a problem in Calvin's theology at this point. Does the Spirit witness to the particular contents of the Bible, so that this witness is happening while reading the Bible, or does the Spirit witness to the Bible as such, so that after this the Bible becomes in itself an authority? It was the latter understanding which became predominant in Calvinistic Orthodoxy, and from there came into Lutheranism also, and thus became the principle of authority in Orthodoxy as a whole. I can repeat something I said before. If the divine Spirit witnesses to the Bible as such, without any consideration of the particular contents, then in principle anybody can write a theology. This leads us to the idea of a *theologia irregenetorum,* a theology of those who are not reborn. But if it is the particular content that is being attested by the Spirit, then you must be existentially

---

[1] Editor's Note: As was Tillich's custom, he requested that students submit questions for him to answer before the start of the lecture. His answers invariably would interweave historical and systematic aspects of the subject. The editor has selected a few of the questions and answers, both to allow Tillich to sharpen his own presentation of a subject and to retain the atmosphere of the classroom situation.

involved in the content of the Bible in every moment of reading it. You must at least be participating in such a way that the Spirit works in you and witnesses to the truth of the biblical message. But you also ask, if the Spirit is self-authenticating, what can I do to receive it? This question cannot be answered, for if I did succeed in answering it, then I would be giving you a method for forcing God upon you. But God destroys every such method even as he destroys our moral self-righteousness. The only answer which can be given is to remain open to the impacts of life—which may come from others, or from reading the Bible, or services of the church or acts of love—through which God may work upon us. In listening and waiting we may experience the Spirit, but more than this cannot be said. There is no valid method at all for forcing God upon us.

* * * * * * * * *

2. Concepts of Reason

Now we come to another equally important concept, the concept of reason. Here also much semantic clarity is needed in order to purify our image of the past. This is a very difficult concept and we can take but a few steps in attempting to interpret what this word means.

It certainly does not mean what is usually implied in all our talk about reason and/or revelation. If I can succeed in preventing you from jumping into discussions about reason against revelation before you clearly define the meaning of the terms, then this lecture will not have been in vain. In ordinary language reason is very highly respected. But it has a much narrower meaning than it had in the Enlightenment and in the previous history of the Western world. Today it means the calculation of the businessman, the analysis of the natural scientist, and the construction of the engineer. These three aspects determine the concept of reason. It would be therefore historically inaccurate to use this modern concept of reason as the model for understanding what the Enlightenment means by reason. When we speak of the "Age of Reason" we cannot restrict reason to its modern analytic and synthetic senses.

I will distinguish four different concepts of reason, and discuss them point by point.

a. Universal Reason: The first concept of reason has the meaning of the universal logos. *Logos* is the Greek word for reason. But it also means "word." In Heraclitus and in Stoicism logos means both word and reason. The Greeks asked the question how the human word and human language are able to grasp reality. Their answer was that the logos, the universal form and principle of everything created, is both in reality as a whole and in the human mind. The word is meaningful when men use it because it can grasp reality. The opposite is also true. Reality grasps the human mind, so that men can speak to and about reality.

That is the logos concept of reason. This concept appears and reappears everywhere in Christian theology as a first principle. It is a principle of order and structure in all realities. As the Fourth Gospel says, "All things were made through him [i.e., the Logos], and without him was not anything made that was made" (John 1:3, RSV). The Logos is the principle through which God created the world. This is a fundamental insight of all classical theology. Reality and mind have a logos structure. As a structure of reality and mind, logos includes our power of knowledge, our ethical awareness or conscience, and our aesthetic intuition. These are all expressions of the logos in us. (Immanuel Kant wrote the critiques of pure or theoretical reason and practical reason, and the neo-Kantian school added the aesthetic reason as a third, uniting the practical and the theoretical). Reason or logos is therefore in the tree, for instance, as well as in the man who names the tree and describes the image of tree-ness which reappears in every individual tree. This is possible only because there is a structure in the tree which man is able to grasp by his mind, or, since this is always mutual, his mind is grasped by the structure.

The universe has been created by an intelligent power, the divine ground, and since the world has been intelligently built, intelligence can grasp it. We can grasp the world intelligently because it has been created intelligently. It has a structure. This is equally valid in philosophy as well as in theology. There is no conflict here in regard to the theological or philosophical use of this concept of reason. There is a necessary logos element in all theology. Any theology which does not have an understanding of the universal character of the logos structure of the world, and that means of reason in the sense of logos, becomes barbaric and ceases to be theology. When the logos element in theo-logy disappears, theology becomes a fanatical repetition of biblical passages without endeavoring to understand their meaning.

What we have just described is a feature of that dualistic heresy which divorces creation and redemption, and sets them in contradiction to each other. Creation contains the logos, and if redemption contradicts creation, then God contradicts himself. Then we have a good God and a bad God, the good God of redemption and the bad God of creation. The church in the early centuries was almost destroyed in the fight for the goodness of creation, that is, for the logos structure of reality as a whole. The church finally overcame the temptation to accept a dualism by regarding it as a demonic temptation, demonic because the characteristic of the demonic is the split in the divinity between the good and the bad God. Yet this heresy continues to appear in Christianity. It was especially strong in the earlier period of neo-orthodoxy.[2]

But the same thing appears in other less refined or sophisticated forms. There is much of this dualistic heresy in existentialist literature which describes the "question" but does not give an "answer," leaving the world to the devil, so to speak.

b. Critical Reason: The logos concept of reason was not the most important in the eighteenth century, although it was definitely a presupposition of that piety which praised the glory of creation. Rather, the second concept of reason, namely, critical reason, was the more effective. In the name of critical reason the way was prepared for the French Revolution, which transformed the world. Before that the American Revolution occurred, uniting religious and rational dimensions in the Constitution. That is its greatness. But in the French Revolution, because of the conflict with Catholicism, reason became radical and even

---

[2] Editor's Note: Tillich expressed his delight with the apparent turn in Karl Barth's thinking represented in the little book, *The Humanity of God*. He interpreted this as a hopeful sign of a new attempt to overcome the danger of setting the God of redemption against the God of creation, and also as an emphasis which makes contact with his own thinking that always starts with the human situation.

antireligious. It brought about the destruction of the old institutions controlled by the heteronomous authorities of both church and state.

We must understand what this critical reason was. It was not a calculating reason which decides whether to do this or that, depending on which is more advantageous. Rather, it was a full, passionate, revolutionary emphasis on man's essential goodness in the name of the principle of justice. The revolutionary bourgeois fought against feudalism and the authoritarian churches. Unlike our present-day analytic and critical reason, he had a passionate belief in the logos structure of reality, and was convinced that the human mind is able to re-establish this structure by transforming society. We could therefore call it revolutionary reason as well as critical reason. Because of its religious depths this critical revolutionary reason overcame the prejudices of the feudal order, the heteronomous subjection of people both by the state and the church. It could do so because it spoke in the name of truth and justice. The philosophers of the Enlightenment were extremely passionate. They were not positivists; they were not interested in merely collecting facts which had no meaning for the revolutionary program. They became martyrs for the passion which they felt was given by the divine logos within them. It would be good if both in the East and in the West there would be more of this revolutionary reason. Both in Russia and in America it has been suppressed by the positivistic observation of facts, without that passion for the logos which is the manifestation of the divine in mind and reality.

c. Intuitive Reason: Then I come to a third concept of reason. I call it intuitive reason, which is used by all philosophers somehow or other in all periods. Formerly it was identified with Plato's idea of the intuition of the essences, and particularly of the universal essences of the good and the true. Today we have another term for it. We call it phenomenological. This is a school of philosophy which ultimately goes back to Platonism and which has many roots in the Middle Ages, perhaps especially in the Franciscan tradition. Its basic assumption is that the human mind has power to intuit essences. In looking at a red object at this moment, a red shirt or dress, the mind can experience the essence of redness. The essence of redness appears in a particular object and can be grasped by the mind. This I call intuitive reason.

Today reason and intuition are placed in contrast to each other, but they should not be. Intuitive reason is a nonanalytic reason which expresses itself in terms of descriptions. To understand the structures of life and spirit, we must use this descriptive method. Intuitive reason means looking at meanings, trying to understand them, and not analyzing objects, be it psychical or physical objects. That is another kind of reason. We use intuitive reason all the time in dealing with the world, when we see the universal in the particular, without asking analytic questions, or relational questions, etc. Whenever we are discussing meanings, as we are doing in this very lecture, we are in the realm of intuitive reason, as Plato also was in his dialogues. When he tried to discuss what virtue, courage, or fortitude are, then he used this intuitive method. This is most explicit in his early dialogues. When we want to know what fortitude is, then we look at examples, examples to which an ordinary meaning of the language leads us. We compare these examples, and from these examples we finally get a universal concept which covers the different examples and shows their point of identity.

In modern philosophy this is called the phenomenological method. This method is absolutely necessary for all the humanities. The understanding of meanings in all literature, theology, or philosophy is dependent on the use of this method. Philosophically it has been restated, but not invented, by Edmund Husserl (1859–1938) in his *Logical Investigations*[3] around 1900. He was a predecessor of existentialism. That puts us in the interesting situation that existentialism has been generally accepted, but not its predecessor. Yet we find that today some of the philosophical minds among the psychoanalysts who first accepted existentialism as the philosophical foundation of their work are now going back to phenomenology (or intuitive reason), realizing that without that method, existentialism would not be able to utter one word.

d. Technical Reason: This brings me to the last concept of reason, to its predominant meaning today, namely, to technical reason. It analyzes reality into its smallest elements, and then construes out of them other things, larger things. We see this kind of reason at work in Einstein in terms of mathematical physics. Yet there was also a strong element of

---

[3] *Logische Untersuchungen* (Halle: M. Niemeyer, 1900).

intuitive reason in Einstein. Einstein himself tried to describe the relation between the intuitive and analytic elements in his own processes of thinking. Besides these there was the critical element, exemplified in Einstein's political activities. Here he followed the eighteenth-century understanding of reason. He knew what justice means from reason, but of course he used a different kind of reason in his scientific discoveries. He also knew of the logos character of reason. In a published discussion between Einstein and myself on the idea of God,[4] Einstein said that the miracle of the structure of reality is what he called the divine. This was 50 per cent of what I would also call the logos concept.

So you see that the greatest representative of technical reason was aware of other dimensions of reason. The power of technical reason is its ability to analyze reality and to construct tools out of it. An extreme example of its use is logical positivism. What it says is merely analytic; it is a tool used mostly in order to produce other tools. We should not despise technical reason. We all live from it. Theologians especially should not despise it if they wish to remain theologians. Even the analytic form of thought used in argumentation must be kept pure. In discussions we should never replace logic by emotion or by a heteronomous acceptance of religious authorities. We must use it equally as fully and rigorously as those who are not aware of the other forms of reason, only we must use it in awareness that there are four fundamental forms of what we call reason.

3. The Concept of Nature

Next we turn to the concept of nature. This is necessary in view of the conflict that was going on throughout the eighteenth century between naturalism and supernaturalism. Supernaturalistic theology attempted to save the tradition by means of the same tools which naturalism used in trying to transform the tradition. Therefore, we must ask what this concept of nature meant during these controversies. I can tell you autobiographically that one of my first scientific inquiries into theology—which was my *Habilitationsschrift*—dealt with the concept

---

[4] Cf. Paul Tillich, "Science and Theology: A Discussion with Einstein," *Theology of Culture* (New York: Oxford University Press, 1959).

of naturalism and supernaturalism in the period before Schleiermacher.[5] Out of this study I gained insight into the intricacies of the concept of nature in these discussions, which has influenced my thinking.

There are two fundamental concepts of nature which I distinguish, the material and the formal concept of nature. The material concept refers to things in nature, usually to subhuman or nonhuman things. This is what we usually call nature, all the realities that are the subject matter of physics, biology, botany, etc. The formal concept of nature refers to human beings, but of course man's body belongs as well to the material concept; it is as natural as any animal body. But it contains a different element. It has mind or spirit. Following from man's being as mind and spirit is the fact that man has a history. So nature and history are placed into contrast.

We are using the material concept of nature when we ask questions about whether nature is also fallen, whether nature can be saved, or when we speak about going out into nature, or when we discuss whether nature is only an object of our control, subject to our technical activities, or whether nature is such that man can commune with it. In all these cases we point to the material concept of nature. But there is quite a different concept, and this one has even more theological significance. It is the concept of the natural, coming from Greek thinking, from the word *physis*, which has to do with *growth*. The opposite of this is *nomos*, which is something produced by human will, such as institutions of society, conventional rules and laws, everything that is not produced by natural growth, but produced by people who transform what is grown. This distinction helps us to understand better the social criticism which came out of the critical schools of philosophy after Socrates, the Cynics, Hedonists, and also the Stoics. Their concept of natural law as that which we have within us by birth was the basis for their criticism of all that was arbitrary in society.

In all the literature of the Western world, from the Greek to the medieval sources and perhaps up to the seventeenth century, when you

---

[5] *Der Begriff des Übernatürlichen, sein dialektischer Charakter und das Prinzip der Identität, dargestellt an der supranaturalistischen Theologie vor Schleiermacher* (1915).

see the term "natural law," it very rarely means "physical law," law as discovered by physics. Usually it means rational law, particularly the law of morals or the law of cognitive reason, that is, the rules of logic. All this is called natural law; it is man's true nature. The law of the logos of which I spoke before embraces both nature outside of man and man himself. It is given by creation, and therefore it is called natural.

In order to make meaningful theological statements about nature or naturalism, it is necessary to distinguish these two concepts of nature. Related to the concept of the natural which we have just discussed are two other concepts, the unnatural and the supernatural. The unnatural is simply the perversion of the nature of a given thing. On the other hand, the supernatural is not supposed to be unnatural. It is supposed to be higher in power and value than the natural. It is a higher sphere which can enter into and interfere with the sphere of the natural. The supernatural interferes both with nature outside and with man's mental and spiritual activities. The mind or spirit of man (spirit with a small "s" of course) belongs to the realm of the natural, not in the material but in the formal sense of nature. Man's mind transcends the material sense by the very fact he is able to use language and to create tools.

The concept of the supernatural raises a theological problem. What does it mean to say that there is a sphere higher in power and value than the human sphere? What does it mean to say that the supernatural sphere can interfere with the human sphere? In what sense is the idea of interference justified? If God interferes with the natural which exists by his act of creation, does this not lead to a demonic split in the divine nature? Does God interfere and if so, in what sense? These are problems with which all theology has to deal, including modern theology. They were the problems of Hegel and Schleiermacher, both of whom tried to develop a theology which transcended naturalism and supernaturalism. These problems are also involved in modern theology whether we are discussing the doctrine of God, christology, soteriology, or eschatology.

4. The Concept of Harmony

Now we come to a fourth concept, the concept of harmony. This concept is part of the fundamental faith of the Enlightenment. In my terminology we could call harmony its ultimate concern. All the philosophers of the Enlightenment use this concept directly or indirectly, explicitly or implicitly. All of them elaborated their systems under the guidance of this principle. Our first remark about it has to be semantic. Today harmony may have a musical connotation, which it always has had and should have. But it has also deteriorated to mean "nice," when we speak of a nice harmonious family life. Of course, harmony understood in this way was not the ultimate concern of the great philosophers of the Enlightenment.

Harmony in the philosophy of the Enlightenment is a paradoxical concept. This means that it must always be qualified by the words "in spite of." The ancient Pythagoreans spoke of a universal harmony, of a cosmic harmony, but in spite of every individual thing and every individual human being seemingly going their own way. Yet, through all there was an overarching harmony. The Greek word *cosmos* which we translate by universe originally meant beauty and harmony. The Pythagoreans discovered mathematical formulae for the musical harmonies. They believed in the harmony of the sounds produced by the movement of the stars. Therefore they spoke of a cosmic harmony of the spheres, each of which has a different sound, but all together creating a harmonious sound. If you delete the half-poetic, mythological element from such ideas, then you can say that they had a universal, ecstatic interpretation of reality. Of course, the Pythagoreans also knew that there is a split in reality, which they symbolized by the split between the even and the odd numbers. The odd numbers represent the good, the even numbers the bad, because the odd numbers are perfect. They are finished; the even numbers can be divided and are therefore unfinished. For all Greek thinking the finished is the good, the unfinished is the bad.

This concept of harmony was carried into the Platonic–Christian idea of providence. Plato was the first who philosophically made this a central concept. It is also a fundamental concept of Christian theology, and even more of Christian daily life. The daily life of the Christian believer is largely determined by providence. Ordinary Christians find in their faith in providence a kind of ultimate security in the vicissitudes of their lives. But this fundamental Christian idea of providence became secularized in the Enlightenment. Now it was formulated in terms of harmony.

The Christian idea of providence does not contain the mechanical notion that God has ordered everything once upon a time, and that now he sits on his throne and sleeps while the world goes its way. The Reformers had to fight tremendously against this distortion of the idea of providence. Rather, providence means that God is creating in every moment, and directing everything in history toward an ultimate fulfillment in the kingdom of God. Then you have the "in spite of" element. In spite of human finitude, in spite of human estrangement from God, God determines every moment so that in it an experience of the ultimate is possible, so that in the whole texture of good and evil in history the divine aim will finally come to prevail. Providence does not work mechanically, but it directs and guides. For the individual human being, providence means that in every moment of the time process, there is the possibility of reaching toward the kingdom of God. This is the Christian concept, which is so important for the personal life of the religious man and for all Christians everywhere. To anticipate things a bit—this is also a fundamental concept of the Ritschlian theology.

Even when the idea of providence is secularized in the Enlightenment, certain traits of it are preserved, especially the "in spite of" element. Christianity emphasizes that in spite of sin and error, something meaningful can be done in history by the providential guidance of God. The philosophies of the Enlightenment also maintained this aspect. It was applied by them to all realms of life. The first clear expression of this in the secular realm can be seen in the area of economics. It was expressed by Adam Smith (1723–1790) of the Manchester School of Economics in his idea of harmony. The idea is that in spite of the fact that everyone may be motivated by the profit interest, each one out for his own profit, in the end the total aims of production and consumption will be reached according to some hidden law. With many qualifications, this idea also underlies the theory of modern American capitalism. There is this basic belief in harmony. In spite of the fact that producer, seller, and buyer fight with each other, each bargaining for the greatest possible profit or for the best deal, somehow the laws of economics will be at work behind their backs in such a way that the best interests of all concerned and of the whole society will be satisfied.

Of course, history has shown that this seemingly mysterious law of the harmony of interests working behind the backs of individuals in society who act for profit in their economic life has helped to eliminate the poverty which was still existing in the eighteenth century in all Western countries. Without this belief in the hidden law of harmony, the Manchester theory would have never arisen and worked as it did.

The same principle is valid in politics. According to the philosophers of the Enlightenment, democracy presupposes that if every person follows his own reasoning, a general consensus or a majority will can be formed which is to the advantage of all. Then the minority should be prepared to acknowledge that the will of the majority was the true will of the whole, the *volonté générale*—the mystical concept of Rousseau who distinguishes the *volonté générale*, the general will, from the will of all. The majority does not represent the will of all, because there is the opposition, but it represents the general will, the true will which is driving toward the best interests of the group as a whole.

Now you can see immediately the consequence of this belief in harmony. If there is no belief in this harmony, democracy cannot work, for the minority will not accept the validity of the decision of the majority. There is plenty of evidence of this in some of the South American countries. As soon as a democratic majority appears which is disliked by the military leaders, they instigate a *putsch* to overthrow the government. This is the chief characteristic of the negation of democracy. As soon as there is no belief in harmony, that is, in the providential validity of the majority decision, then democracy is impossible.— When I was in Japan, I was often asked by Japanese intellectuals to give lectures on the religious foundations of democracy, because they have the same problem. They have a democracy too, but they know how much it is threatened when a strong minority will not accept the concept of the general will, of providential harmony.

We have the same concept applied in the field of education. Education is necessary to produce the political maturity required for people to acknowledge the principle of harmony in democracy. The belief is that education can develop the potentialities of every individual in such a way that finally a good society will come out of it. This was the belief which induced the people of the Enlightenment to create public schools, which had not existed up to that time. There had been only upper class schools or church schools where the people were subjected to the preaching and teaching of the church. But the Enlightenment created public schools which became the center of culture.—I was astonished when I came to this country to find how seriously education is taken here, much more seriously than in any European country that I know. The reason for this is that the belief in harmony is much stronger.—In any case, public schools were founded under the influence of the philosophy of the Enlightenment.

Even God was pictured as an educator. It was believed that God educates mankind in stages and that now in our great century, namely, the eighteenth century, the century of Enlightenment, the age of maturity has dawned. God has finally reached his educational aim. The classical expression of this idea was given by Gotthold Ephraim Lessing (1729–1781), the German poet, philosopher, and theologian, and the greatest representative of German Enlightenment, in his little book, *The Education of the Human Race.*[6] This book will give you more insight into the Enlightenment than perhaps anything else, from the point of view of the feeling for the meaning of life.

Another area in which the principle of harmony was applied was in epistemology, the theory of knowledge. It is very clear in John Locke (1632–1704) and is behind practically all empiricism. For here there is the belief that the chaotic impressions which come to us from reality will find a way to produce in our minds a meaningful image of reality, making knowledge and action possible. This presupposes a law of harmony working within us. It is interesting to notice how secure, how dogmatically sure many empiricists are that the law of harmony in this respect really works.

The most profound expression of this idea of harmony in philosophy is to be found in Gottfried Wilhelm Leibniz (1646–1716), the German philosopher. The whole classical period of German and European philosophy in general is to a great extent dependent on him. He was great enough at the same time so that he can now be the beloved figure of present-day analytic philosophers because he had the splendid idea of

[6] *Lessing's Theological Writings,* translated by Henry Chadwick (Stanford: Stanford University Press, 1957).

describing all reality in terms of a logical calculus! Leibniz used the term "harmony," and spoke of a pre-established harmony which makes the operations of reality in all realms possible. The philosophical background of this idea is the Cartesian (Descartes) separation of extended things or material bodies (*res extensa*) from thinking substances or the ego (soul) (*res cogitans*), raising the question of the possibility of the communication between the two. The answer was found in a third reality, which is God. In God the communication of soul with body takes place. Our soul has no direct communication with our body. Our thinking can influence our body through the medium of the transcendent unity of both body and mind in the divine ground.

Now Leibniz carried through this idea in an interesting fashion. In the history of philosophy you learned about monads, meaning "one" in Greek. Monads cannot communicate directly with each other; they are separated from each other by the body. Nevertheless, we as individual monads can talk to each other. How is this possible? Only by a pre-established harmony which goes to the divine ground of both you and me. Leibniz expressed this idea in the phrase, "Monads do not have windows and doors." This means that the individual human being is closed within himself. This theory of monads has been interpreted—rightly I think—as a symbolic expression of the dissolution of the medieval community into the atomized society of modern times.

In any case the question was: "How is communication of one being with another possible?" The answer was by a pre-established harmony behind our individual lives. Every individual monad, you and I, has the whole universe within himself. Every individual is a microcosm. But each of us embodies the universe in differing degrees of clarity. We are supposed to develop it to the highest possible clarity, but potentially we know and possess everything. The development of this potentiality is the infinite task of every monad. This is Leibniz' idea, his metaphysical formulation of the concept of harmony. This theory, however, which seems somewhat fantastic to us, had a tremendous influence on the thinking of the Enlightenment and on later philosophy.

In Protestantism we have the religious counterpart to this concept of harmony. The Protestant idea was that religion or Christianity has no need of a central authority which gives all the answers, either by councils or popes. On the other hand, the fact that the church held councils was an expression of the principle of harmony, for the assumption prevailed that the majority opinion of the council was the expression of the divine Spirit. Of course, Protestantism also had an authority, one formal principle as it was called later on, namely, the Bible. The idea that the Bible can have an impact on every individual reader through the divine Spirit is an expression of the principle of harmony. The principle of harmony is at work behind the backs of the individual Bible readers, making possible a universal harmony and the existence of the church. In spite of the numerous denominational differences and theological conflicts in Protestantism, it is believed that there is still such a thing as Protestantism. There is, to be sure, no visible form of unity, despite the World Council of Churches; Protestants are divided, and yet it is possible to distinguish Protestantism from Eastern Orthodoxy, or Roman Catholicism, or humanism, and from all other religions. There is some kind of unity; this belief is an expression of the principle of harmony, but it is always accompanied by an "in spite of" qualification.

After running through all of these applications of the principle of harmony, I hope you can see that when the central supernatural authority was removed, and the individualizaton and conflict in reality remain, then the only possible answer there can be, both in religion and culture, both in economics and politics, both in epistemology and physics, is the principle of a presupposed harmony which produces indirectly what was supposed to be produced directly by a divine interference or by an inner-historical, all-uniting authority such as existed in the medieval Roman Church. This supernatural authority was now replaced by the principle of harmony. This finally led to another question: What if the harmony does not work? This is the existentialist question which began with the second period of Romanticism in the beginning of the nineteenth century, and runs throughout the nineteenth and twentieth centuries.

We still have in the majority of our intellectuals, the bearers of our intellectual life, this kind of paradoxical optimism that is identical with the concept of harmony. We have it in Freudianism and Marxism; we have it in our ordinary democratic humanism; we have it in everything that is called liberalism in economics and politics. Yet, it is not the same as it was in the eighteenth century. Many things have happened in the meantime. The theological development of the last century and a half has been looking for an answer to the question: What if the principle of harmony does not work?

* * * * * * * * * *

Question: Please distinguish between your definition of reason in the sense of universal logos and the Enlightenment concept of harmony.

Answer: These two do not lie on the same level so it is difficult to make a distinction. But I can speak about the relation between them. The logos type of reason refers to the intelligible, meaningful structure of reality in its essential character; the concept of harmony refers to the dynamics of actual existence, that is, the way in which different tendencies in time and space are united in terms of harmony. That is, in spite of the arbitrariness of individuals, the universal outcome of the historical movement is positive and meaningful. So roughly we can say that while logos deals with the formal structure of reality in its essential nature, harmony deals with the dynamics of existence in time and space with all its ambiguities. Very simply, the one is structure, the other is dynamic movement.

Question: You have stated that one of the key doctrines of the Enlightenment was the harmony of man's mind with the eternal Logos. In what respects is this doctrine similar to or different from the romantic doctrine of the infinite within the finite? If they are similar, to what extent is the romantic movement a return to the basic Enlightenment doctrine after its destruction by Kant?

Answer: Now here there is a presupposition which is simply not factual. I have stated that one of the key doctrines of the Enlightenment was the harmony of man's mind with the eternal Logos. I think you must have misunderstood it by 180 degrees. What I really said was that the harmony of the Enlightenment is not the harmony of the mind and has nothing to do with what we call harmony today, harmony in the sense of the restfulness of the mind, of sitting in a beautiful garden, looking at the flowers and feeling harmony between oneself and nature. This question perhaps shows that I was not emphatic enough in distinguishing this concept of harmony in the Enlightenment from its sentimentalization. So I must try again.

Now harmony is a paradoxical concept. You are *not* harmonious. There is no harmony in your mind at all. You are not in harmony with God. You are in opposition to him and you fight with him. But nevertheless, behind your back destiny or providence is guiding reality in such a way that it turns out best for you in the end. This means that you are brought back to God or to yourself in spite of everything. The principle of harmony in the Enlightenment can only be understood in terms of this "in spite of." It is best to think of the Manchester School of Economics for an illustration. Both the seller and the buyer fight for their own profits. The two meet in the market, and in their struggle for their own profit, a kind of transitory equilibrium results which brings about the greatest profit for the whole society. The individual is thinking of his own advantage, but the whole society is being served "in spite of" that. Therefore we have the idea that private vices are public benefits. Although you are very greedy, and you don't want to pay a penny more to this seller than you have to, and although he has the same feeling toward you and fights against you, somehow behind your backs a harmony is brought about through the guidance of providence. This is the paradox of providence. Destiny or God, or the dialectical process in Hegel or Marx, does something of which you are not aware. Although you are greedy and disagreeable, the outcome is finally the best for all concerned. I gave you examples of this in all the other realms. In democracy, for example, despite all the name-calling in the political campaigns and all the promises made by candidates which they don't for a moment intend to fulfill, there is a *volonté générale* that emerges. Although nobody knows what the true will of society is, through the democratic process such a thing emerges. After the voting has been completed, the majority decision represents the true and general will of the society as a whole.

So the idea of harmony has nothing to do with niceness. Nor does it mean that the human mind and the eternal Logos are identical. The Enlightenment had no such idea at all. It only had the idea that reason, the logos type of reason, shows man the fundamental principles of justice. And if these fundamental principles of justice are violated, as the Enlightenment felt they were violated in the feudalistic society, then the Enlightenment fought against social abuses in the name of the principles of natural law which belong to the human mind. But there was no mystical union of man and God, no presence of the infinite in the finite as in Nicholas of Cusa.

Only one thing in this question is right, namely, that mysticism and rationalism are not contradictory, but that rationalism lives from the fundamental mystical principle of identity, the principle of the presence of the structure of truth in the depths of the human mind. This point in the question is indeed right. There is such a relationship. But no enlightened philosopher would have accepted Spinoza. They all rejected Spinoza, and Spinoza is the real heir of Nicholas of Cusa and the mystical tradition of the Western world. For Voltaire, Rousseau, and other representatives of the Enlightenment, the subject-object scheme is decisive. However, they realized that in man's natural structure there is an awareness of justice. In the name of this justice they could fight against the distortions in society.

* * * * * * * * * *

B. The Attitude of the Enlightened Man

After having dealt with four great concepts of the Enlightenment—autonomy, reason, nature, and harmony—we will discuss the attitude of the men of the Enlightenment, of the great bearers of the development of the Enlightenment and its consequences up to the present time.

1. His Bourgeois Character

First let me make a sociological statement. The enlightened man is a bourgeois. *Bourgeois* is a French word, the French equivalent of the *Bürger* in German, which means "he who lives inside the walls of the town." He is quite different from the medieval man. He is supposed to be calculating and reasonable. In the Middle Ages the self-confidence, self-consciousness, and self-evaluation of a human being were not rooted in his rational powers—reason in the largest sense—but rooted instead in his ability to deal with the situation into which he was put by a transcendent destiny. The medieval man had his particular place in society, whether as emperor or as beggar or as someone who occupied a station in life between these two extremes. Each place had a direct relationship to ultimate reality. The function of the emperor was to unite the body of Christendom all over the known world. The function of the beggar was to give the people an occasion for acts of charity and in this way help to save their souls. Everyone in between had the same feeling of having a special place. This was a hierarchical order of society—holy orders one above the other, represented both in heaven and on earth. This concept came from the great mystic, Dionysius the Areopagite (*ca* A.D.500). It was taken into the Middle Ages by the scholastics in order to describe the place where everyone stands in life, including not only the ecclesiastical hierarchy but also the secular, political, and social hierarchies. The corollary of this in the Lutheran Reformation was the concept of vocation. Everyone had his place by divine calling (*vocatio*) where God placed him. There he shall stay and not try to break out of this situation.

This vertical orientation of the totality of life in the Middle Ages stands in direct opposition to the horizontal outline of the bourgeois society of the Enlightenment. The bourgeois wants to analyze and transform the whole of reality in order to control it. The horizontal line is decisive in his work, and he wants to control it by calculation. As a businessman he must calculate. If he does not, he loses. This calculation means that he must go beyond the place where he happens to find himself now. He does not accept the status quo. This again demands knowledge of reality. Reality far beyond his limited place must be known in order to be calculated and controlled. One must presuppose that nature is regular and that reality has some calculable patterns. So the bourgeois had a calculating attitude, and to him nature and reality as a whole appeared to be made up of regular patterns on which he could rely and which make his business decisions possible.

2. *His Ideal of a Reasonable Religion*

Irrational elements which interfere with a calcuable pattern of reality must therefore be excluded. This means that the irrational elements of religion must be eliminated. The bourgeois needs a reasonable religion which views God as lying behind the whole of life's processes. God has made the world and now it follows its own laws. He does not interfere any more. Every interference would mean a loss of calculability. No such interferences are acceptable and all special revelations have to be denied.

Thus all the boundary-line concepts of life were denied because they disturb the calculating and controlling activities of man in relation to reality. For instance, death is removed as an interfering power in the progressive thought of controlling reality. The classical understanding of death in the vertical line, which views man's life as coming from eternity and going back to it, had to disappear. In the bourgeois theological preaching, even in Roman Catholicism in the early eighteenth century, the preaching on death was removed. The great conflict between Pascal and the Jesuits involved the issue of the victory of the bourgeois society in removing death and guilt and hell from preaching. The Jesuits were on the side of bourgeois society. Jesuitism at that time gave the bourgeoisie a good conscience in breaking out of the vertical line into the horizontal by removing the boundary-line situations in classical theology. Traditional threats in terms of death and ultimate judgment were omitted. They were not in good taste. It is not in good taste to speak to people about death. In modern American society too one avoids speaking of death. One does not die; one just passes away. Death is not convenient for progressive society. It means the end of man's control and calculations and the end of inner-worldly purposes.

An even stronger attack is made on the idea of original sin. There was not only the very justifiable criticism of the superstitious and literalistic way this doctrine had been preached in connection with the story of Paradise, but it was also criticized because it conflicted with the belief in the progressive improvement of the human situation on earth. Most of present-day humanism still follows the Enlightenment in this criticism. It was a great event in theology when Reinhold Niebuhr succeeded in making an inroad on this prevailing view of humanism. Of course, he received support from the existentialist style of the twentieth century in which we are living. Despite that, the humanistic assumption of a progressive improvement in the human situation is still very much alive.

The fear of hell was also dismissed. The fear of death is actually the fear of hell; therefore, this concept was removed. Its symbolic meaning disappeared. The consequence of this was that its opposite was also removed, not only the mythological symbolism of heaven, but also the idea of grace as such. Grace is an action which comes from outside man's autonomous activities, and therefore for Kant it was an expression of something heteronomous. For since it comes from outside, it undercuts the autonomous power of man. What remained then was a reasonable religion, as Kant called it.[7] In this reasonable religion prayer was also removed, because prayer relates one to that which transcends oneself. This relationship fell under strong suspicion by the enlightened people. Kant said that if someone is caught by surprise while praying, he would feel ashamed. He felt that it was not dignified for autonomous men who control the world and possess the power of reason to be found in the situation of prayer.

Thus the existential elements of finitude, despair, anxiety, as well as of grace, were set aside. What was left was the reasonable religion of progress, belief in a transcendent God who exists alongside of reality, and who does not do much in the world after he has created it. In this world left to its own powers moral demands remain, morals in terms of bourgeois righteousness and stability. Belief in the immortality of the soul also remains, namely, the ability of man to continue his improvement progressively after death.

3. His Common-sense Morality

A basic element of the morality of the enlightened man is tolerance. The enlightened bourgeois man is tolerant. His understanding of tolerance was conditioned by the religious wars. His profound disgust of the murderous and destructive forms of these wars—which in Germany killed half of the population during the Thirty Years' War (1618–1648)—caused him to deny the absolute claims of the church. The spirit of tolerance was perhaps first produced by the Reformation. But it was not until after the bloody religious wars had demonstrated the

---

7 Cf. Immanuel Kant's book, *Religion within the Limits of Reason Alone*, translated by T. M. Greene and H. H. Hudson (New York: Harper & Brothers, 1960).

impossibility of reuniting the churches that the secular powers took over and forced tolerance upon them.

A second reason for tolerance besides the political one arose out of the sectarian, spiritualistic movements of the Reformation period. They placed strong emphasis upon the belief that every individual is immediately related to God. No one type of relationship has the right to deny other possible types of relationships with God. This same feeling underlies much of American religious life. The Bible and tradition become secondary in comparison with the divine Spirit with whom each individual is immediately related.

A third reason has to do with the rise of the secular state. The state became increasingly secular because it had to transcend the split between the churches. It could not succeed in identifying itself with one of them. Now an interesting problem arose, which is stated clearly by John Locke. Could there be a complete tolerance? Can one be tolerant of the Catholics, for example, when they are on principle intolerant, especially when they possess the power? John Locke said no. Catholics should not be tolerated. Nor should atheists be tolerated, he thought. For the whole system of morality in society is based on the belief in God as the moral lawgiver and judge. If this belief disappears then the whole system collapses. Here we see that basic limits are set to tolerance even by its champions.

We were discussing tolerance as an element in the attitude of eighteenth-century bourgeois society, classically expressed in Locke's writings on tolerance. We pointed out that tolerance has its background in the experience of the seventeenth century, the century of the terrible religious wars which almost destroyed Europe. When it was seen that neither the Protestants nor the Catholics could gain a decisive victory, the secularized state had to intervene, identifying itself with neither religious group. Tolerance toward different religious traditions grew out of this experience of the cruel and destructive religious wars. Such wars are always the most bloody because in them an unconditional concern expresses itself in a particular way, and this particular way then assumes the ultimacy which is supposed to be expressed by that concern, but which is not identical with it. This results in the demonization of religion in its worst form.

We have the same phenomenon in our century, the struggle of the quasireligions with their tendency of totally eradicating the enemy on account of an absolute, unconditional faith in the concrete and particular expressions of their ultimate concern. The wars between Nazism and Communism within the nations and between the nations, as well as the spirit of absolutism which runs through the cold war between liberal humanism in the West and totalitarianism in parts of the East—these are modern forms of this phenomenon. We see the horror resulting from the demonic elevation of something finite to absolute validity. I call it demonic because individuals and nations become possessed and are driven to destroy everything which stands in their way. And since this is done on a finite basis, they are themselves ultimately led to self-destruction. These are the dialectics of the demonic. The demonic expresses itself first in the realm of the concrete religions, in France between the Catholics and the Huguenots and in all the rest of Europe between Catholics and Protestants. Each side is unaware of the fact that God is greater than any particular form in which his manifestation appears. Against this situation it is understandable that the idea of tolerance should arise, and be championed by the secular power. In a Europe which was almost destroyed, the secular state brought salvation from religious fanaticism, and was supported in this principle of tolerance by the religious mystical idea of the immediacy of each individual before God. So much for the idea of tolerance, which was not an unlimited tolerance, as we said, because, at least for Locke, the Catholics and the atheists had to be excluded, the Catholics because they were intolerant on principle, and the atheists because they denied the religious foundations of tolerance.

We come now to another characteristic of the bourgeois moral life, the element of discipline. The whole bourgeois culture is based on the repression of those elements which were allowed in the aristocratic society of feudal times. In part this sense of moral discipline goes back to Calvinism. Calvinism itself came from a city, Geneva, in which the factor of discipline was fundamental. In the aristocratic society, at least in the upper classes—but also among the peasants as the works of the Dutch painters of peasant scenes in the seventeenth century show— there was an acceptance of enjoyment in life, an expression of vitality in the more primitive directions of erotic play, the desire for intoxication to elevate the feeling of vitality, but also the sense of beauty in the arts and the glory of nature as in ancient Greece. The more aristocratic a position someone held, the greater possibility he had of expressing all forms of heightened vitality. The aristocrats were not only the big land owners, but also the patricians in the medieval and late medieval cities.

In bourgeois society all this was denied, partly in the name of religion and partly—and these are always interdependent—in the name of the needs of the sociological and economic structure of the bourgeois order. All this had to be restricted and repressed for the sake of the purpose of transforming reality through work. This work required discipline and self-control. This is connected with Protestantism also in another way. Protestantism had abolished the monastic form of asceticism. It was the monumental attack on monasticism by Luther and Calvin and all the Reformers which destroyed the monastic form of asceticism as a valid religious order of life. But now in Protestantism a different form of asceticism arose, an inner-worldly—not extra-worldly as in monasticism —asceticism of labor and of laboring people who produce the technical means for transforming reality in the service of mankind. It was Max Weber (1864–1920), the great German sociologist, who described this inner-worldly form of Protestant asceticism.[8] The idea of the kingdom of God, so important for Calvinistic thinking, took on the connotation of working for the transformation of nature for the sake of mankind.

In this light we can understand such things as the fourteen-hour workday, both by those workers who received only the minimum of subsistence and by the owners who worked even harder and longer but received the profits. Thus work, discipline, and self-control formed the heart of the ethical principles of bourgeois society. The forms of economic existence of bourgeois society were undergirded by this inner-worldly asceticism for the sake of the kingdom of God.

It is instructive to study those cases where this type of bourgeois self-discipline disintegrates. As soon as it starts to disintegrate, the whole system begins to crumble. We have economic-historical inquiries into nineteenth-century Germany showing what happens with the gradual

[8] *The Protestant Ethic and the Spirit of Capitalism* (New York: Charles Scribner's Sons, 1930).

victory of the bourgeois society. This victory was delayed in Germany, for Germany was under feudal power much longer than France, England, Holland, and Belgium, but finally toward the end of the nineteenth century the bourgeoisie became victorious also in Germany. There one can see the following sociological law at work, although such laws are never strict because human freedom can change them. First of all, the producers of the great corporations and enterprises were as a rule subjected to a strict discipline of work. In the second generation this discipline was continued, but now on a more luxurious basis. Then the third generation, enjoying a much higher standard of living, became what is known as playboys in this country. In Germany they sought the luxuries of life, giving expression both to the sensual and artistic forms of vitality. Perhaps they collected paintings or built great mansions. This law of the three generations which helps to analyze bourgeois society shows that when repression is not enforced any more and when there exists simultaneously an ascetic form of dedication to labor, you have the beginning of the disintegration of the pillars of this society.

4. His Subjective Feeling

One of the words we meet most often in the literature of the eighteenth century is the word "tears." Everybody weeps; everybody cries in ecstasy of despair or happiness. Whenever scenes of happiness are described, people shed tears; they cannot help it. What does this mean? This was the century of reason, and yet there was sentimentality. How are they related to each other? There is an alliance of two poles. People wept about everything which remained after the principles of reason were actualized. Rationalism says that emotional elements should be excluded from rationality. Emotions are irrelevant to the serious things of life, such as the production and merchandising of bourgeois industry. So when the emotions are excluded from reason and are not subject to the criteria of logic, the result is that they run wild and end in all kinds of uncontrolled emotionalism. This happens in human beings of the twentieth century too. People who are complete rationalists in the realm of thought fall into uncontrolled emotionalism in their personal life. If man is split into two parts, into the rational and the emotional, the result will be the absence of reason from his emotions. A dangerous situation develops when emotionalism is connected with ignorance. One of the dangers in this country is all of the ignorant emotionalism that has been created by the cold war propaganda, for one day it may explode in the wrong way and destroy many of the democratic institutions. This is the danger of all the fascist movements from McCarthyism to its current forms. We should also realize that if the philosophers remain in their closed spheres of mere logical inquiry of logic, and do not go into the relevant problems of life, then they abandon the reality of our existence to movements which unite emotionalism and ignorance.

C. Intrinsic Conflicts of Enlightenment

Now we must deal with conflict within the Enlightenment itself. It is important to see these to understand the concurrent theological development. There are conflicts in the Enlightenment, and our usual gray image of the period is not at all true. In reality the period of the Enlightenment is infinitely more rich than our gray image of it would indicate. Actually no period in history should be seen as monolithic. If we look at the Renaissance and think that every peasant in southern Bavaria was a bearer of the sixteenth-century Renaissance, then we are imagining a ridiculous thing. There were only a few thousand people in all Europe who brought about the Renaissance. But these were the people who were conscious of the situation and who became the intellectual leaders of the future. So neither the Renaissance nor any of the following periods was monolithic.

In the period of the Enlightenment there were continually underground movements, underground because only occasionally did they come clearly to the surface and revolt against the surface situation. But these reactive movements never became really dominant; they were never able to prevent the final victory of the bourgeoisie, either in the intellectual life or in the economic life, which was the most important in bourgeois society, either in political revolutions or in religious consequences. They did not overcome the optimistic and progressivistic attitude of the Enlightenment. Nevertheless, they were there and made their appearance when the victorious bourgeoisie suffered internal conflicts, preparing the way for the new situation of the twentieth century. We must mention them also because they played a tremendous role in later theological discussions.

1. Cosmic Pessimism

The first one I want to mention is the underground of cosmic pessimism in the whole Enlightenment. This was the reaction to natural events of catastrophic proportions. What was the attitude of the eighteenth-century theologians? It was what I would call teleological optimism. *Telos* means aim or purpose in Greek. There was a basic optimism toward the divine purpose in creating the world. What was the purpose of God? It was to make the universe in such a way that all things would work together for the good of man. The descriptions of the Enlightenment theologians of the divine wisdom always portrayed God as a wonderful technician who made the best possible machine for the glory and well-being of man. For this purpose he created the sun and the moon. He took care that the sun does not shine at night so man can sleep. In every least little thing one saw the wisdom and goodness of God in creating the best possible world for man's purpose. Everything was teleological and had a purpose for the human race. Why should one not be optimistic and progressivistic and enjoy everything that God in his wisdom created for man's good?

But then something happened. That was the earthquake of Lisbon in the middle of the eighteenth century which killed quite a number of people. Compared with the horrors of the twentieth century that perhaps cannot mean very much to us. But at that time, when there were fewer human beings and a higher culture, that is, a higher evaluation of human beings, it came as a tremendous shock. Sixty thousand people were killed by this earthquake in Lisbon. This was a catastrophe of unimaginable dimensions to a period in which God was considered as having created the world for the purpose of serving man. This event was in part responsible for the shaking of the optimism and progressivism of the eighteenth century. Also it symbolized in a dramatic way what everyone knew can happen at any time, but which can easily be glossed over.

It is interesting to see how the philosophers were shaken. It was an event which greatly influenced Goethe (1740–1832) in the early years of his life. It was after this earthquake that Voltaire (1694–1778), the classical representative of the French Enlightenment, wrote the deeply pessimistic novel, *Candide,* which ends with the advice to retire to one's garden and withdraw from the horrors of world history.

Such things were not able to inhibit the continuing progress of bourgeois society out of which later came the evolutionary ideas of the nineteenth century. In any case this pessimism was latent and could come into the foreground as a powerful philosophical movement, as it did in the later Schelling (1775–1854) and Schopenhauer (1788–1860). But the dominant philosophy of the Enlightenment was basically optimistic, and was most characteristically expressed by Leibniz in his principle of theodicy. The word "theodicy" comes from the two Greek words, *theos* meaning God and *dike* meaning justice. Theodicy thus means "justifying God for the evils in the world."

Leibniz' theodicy was, however, much more profound than the use of it by the optimistic philosophy of the Enlightenment. His idea was that if God would create a finite world, he would not be able to overcome the limits connected with finitude. God had to accept these limits of finitude and the various types of evil that go along with it. This is a risk he had to take. Assuming then that God was to create a world at all, it would naturally be—as our world actually is—the best of all possible worlds. This phrase became a slogan, and when the pessimistic reactions set in, this phrase was used ironically. Look at Lisbon and the sixty thousand dead people, and who will speak of the best of all possible worlds? This was the reaction. But of course it was unfair to a great philosophy. This often happens. The same thing happened to Hegel. What Leibniz really meant was not that the world was all good, but that if there is to be a world at all, then this is the least evil or the best possible world, because God cannot make a finite world absolutely good. That is to say, finitude has within itself the necessity of evil.

This fundamental philosophical problem will reflect itself in all the theologians of the nineteenth century. They will deal with the problem of theodicy. The world that God created is good, but because it is finite, the world cannot be perfect. Leibniz' phrase was singled out, distorted and placed against him with bitter irony.

2. *Cultural Vices*

Another question: How does progress come about in bourgeois society? Here a very interesting paradox was seen by some of the philosophers of the Enlightenment, and in particular by Rousseau (1712–1778). In his first book[9] Rousseau dealt with the question: Have the sciences and the arts contributed in a positive way to the morals of society? The question itself was formulated by the Academy of Sciences for a literary contest, and Rousseau won the prize. The question itself indicated that some skepticism about the glory of civilization had cropped up among the intellectuals of French society. Rousseau's answer was, No, the arts and sciences have not contributed either to the morality or to the happiness of mankind. What they really do is to advance immorality, not in the narrow sense in which we often use it, but in the wider sense of ethical development and sensitivity, or rather, their opposites, antiethical development and insensitivity.

Rousseau alleged that in the new state of society the increase in the pleasure of a few has become the basis for the misery of the many. He did not have in mind only the bourgeois society, but instead the whole development of civilization since primitive times. The advance of the sciences and technical productivity has produced a much sharper division in society between the "haves" and the "have nots" in comparison with the earlier period. The earlier period becomes the "lost paradise" for Rousseau, and the seemingly progressive culture becomes the negative state. This situation has been brought about by the establishment of private property, which is something that did not exist in the earlier period. So Rousseau gave a vivid description of the eighteenth-century political and economic situation before the French Revolution, namely, on the one hand luxury and laziness, and on the other hand exploitation and misery. Therefore Rousseau questioned the belief in the progressive development of morality through civilization. Is cultural progress good?

[9] *Discours sur les sciences et les arts* (1750).

No! Is modern progressive society better because it has the arts and sciences in comparison with the natural state of the savages, the noble savages as they were later called? And many answered with Rousseau, No! So let us go back to the primitive state of nature.

In these views Rousseau proved to be a double prophet. In his political writings he was the father of the French Revolution and the spokesman of the bourgeois society. Nobody foreshadowed the French Revolution so powerfully and representatively as Rousseau. But with his critical attitude toward progress in civilization, he became the predecessor of Romanticism, the period which followed the Enlightenment and which fought to overcome it. The interesting thing is that Rousseau represented both at the same time. Indeed, the great fulfillers of the Enlightenment were at the same time the conquerors of it. There was David Hume in England, Immanuel Kant in Germany, and Rousseau in France. As great representatives and fulfillers of the Enlightenment, they were somehow at the same time its conquerors. Therefore, we have been speaking of the intrinsic conflicts of the Enlightenment. It is especially clear in the case of Rousseau. The father of the French Revolution was at the same time the predecessor of Romanticism.

3. Personal Vices

Then another problem arose. If we have a society of economic exchange that is dependent on selling and buying, it happens that human desires must be aroused to make such selling and buying possible. Thus an antipuritan principle developed in the midst of the Enlightenment and bourgeois discipline. If everybody should work and no one should buy and use the products of industry, there would soon be no work to do and the whole system would collapse. Therefore, it is not only good but essential to arouse in people the desire for goods. This resulted in the introduction of the pleasure principle as a dynamic into bourgeois society in opposition to the original Calvinistic and early bourgeois principle of work with its ascetic character. To put it in a formula one can say that *private vices are public goods*. We will see how this was exhibited in England by Mandeville.

We must say something about the philosophical presupposition of the ethics of eudaemonism which developed after the ascetic period of bourgeois society. Often we use the word "materialism." It is used today in cold war propaganda, for the Communists are considered to be materialists. The people who use this term in propaganda do not bother with its meaning, otherwise their passion for propaganda might decrease—and that would be a pity! But here in an academic room we must try to find out what materialism really means.

There are many different forms of materialism. Marxist materialism, for example, is entirely different from the French materialism of the eighteenth century. This latter is a particular type, namely, an ontological or metaphysical materialism—one of the ideas against which Marx fought most ardently. But there was an eighteenth-century philosopher very much worth studying because theological ethics up to today has tried so hard to refute ideas like his. This man's name is Helvétius (1715–1771), which in Latin simply means "Swiss." Helvétius was a Frenchman and a representative of materialism. He had the idea that the only principle by which man acts is that of self-love. He does not try very hard to analyze what this self-love is, but basically it means that nobody desires objects for their own sake. Helvétius' psychology was that every person loves things only for his own pleasure. There is no foundation for the idea of a moral conscience which distinguishes between good and bad. The conscience is the result of punishment. So he formulated the thesis: "Remorse begins where impunity ends." That means that you repent for what you have done only if you are punished, but if you get away with it, there is no remorse. Psychologically, this is true to a great extent, but it is not always true, and it is not true as a matter of principle. According to Helvétius the greatest men are those with the greatest passions and with the power to satisfy them. Even if everything were equal in education, opportunity, and talent, there would remain the difference in passion. This power of passion would make all the difference in the world.

This element of power is one of the most important underground elements of the Enlightenment. It was largely repressed and kept underground. Machiavelli (1469–1527) was taboo in the eighteenth century as in the two preceding centuries, not because he was wrong but because those who acted according to his principles suppressed his theory. All possible forms of power were allowed, even poison and murder, with recourse to the ideological consolation that it is good for the state. All of the politicians were Machiavellian, but his ideas were not expressed. If they had expressed his ideas, they would have undercut their own power. It is only effective when it is done without talking about it. So the struggle for power was a real underground element of the eighteenth century. A nineteenth-century philosopher came along and did what Machiavelli did, not in a diplomatic political form, but in a more universal metaphysical form. This was Friedrich Nietzsche with his idea of "will to power." Nietzsche blew the lid off the Enlightenment and brought this power element out into the open. He was one of the main forerunners of the existentialist philosophy of the twentieth century.

Of course, on this basis religion was denied. The power of the priest is based on the stupid credulity of the masses. Nietzsche also had to deny the church because it condemned passion as sin; whereas for him the great passions are what accomplish the most. The really great virtues which finally do the most for everybody are virtues of passion. Religion contradicts these passions and pleasures which are accessible to everyone; religion demands repression, so drop religion.

4. Progress Based on Immorality

Out of the underground of the Enlightenment a demonic naturalism arose, but could not come to the surface before the end of the eighteenth century. A large part of it was expressed in sexual ideas. In England it was expressed in a more philosophical way: Progress is based on immorality, on the negation of ethical principles. This idea was also in Helvétius, but it was formulated philosophically by Bernard de Mandeville (1670–1733). Like the Manchester theory of economics he held that because of necessity of economic exchange, it is best for the whole society if everyone follows his own pleasure instincts. Progress depends on those people who have a great desire for luxury and who are able to buy items of luxury for themselves. If we keep in mind that these ideas developed on the soil of English puritanism which for a long time had suppressed pleasure, we can appreciate the intrinsic conflict which resulted from now glorifying the strivings for luxury out of economic necessities. If the groups which indulged in luxury were to be eliminated, all social progress would break down. If privilege and status were negated, economy would be retarded. Thus the proposition was advanced that the private vices of the powerful individuals who desired luxury, glory, and social status are the forces which keep the whole machinery of capitalistic society moving.

If we study these things, we see that the eighteenth-century society was anything but monolithic. The problems which we have come to know under the label of the existentialist analysis of the human predicament were part of the underground of the Enlightenment, and were there ready to come to the foreground later.

D. THE FULFILLERS AND CRITICS OF ENLIGHTENMENT

Now let us deal with the three men to whom we referred earlier as the fulfillers and conquerors of the Enlightenment, Rousseau, Hume, and Kant.

1. Rousseau, the French Revolution, and Romanticism

I do not think I need to say much more about Rousseau as the father of the French Revolution. His principles led both to the American and to the French Revolution. They were the principles of natural reason. It was the use of critical reason, as I called it, derived ultimately from the Stoics, which made Rousseau the philosopher of the French Revolution. It was the application of the belief in harmony, that the will of the majority is the true will of society and the best for it. But in Rousseau we also have the other concept of nature. You remember that I spoke of the two concepts of nature, the material and the formal. The material concept of nature refers to nature outside of man, but includes man's physical body. The formal concept refers, for instance, to man's natural spirit. Rousseau as the father of the French Revolution was using the formal concept of nature when he identified nature with reason. He derived his notion of the natural or the rational from the idea of an original paradisiacal state of mankind, the state of original communism. He did not use the word "communism" but spoke rather of the "absence of private property" among the savages. Here nature existed in prerational form, in the form of the natural community of all beings together —a nature-produced ecology, as it is called today, where man is a part of the whole nature. This notion was intensified by the sentimentality about which I spoke, this longing to go back to nature. You can see this illustrated in Versailles if you visit the Petit Trianon which was built in order to play shepherd and shepherdess. This is a mixture of frivolity and a longing to escape civilization. It was Rousseauism that was expressed in these impressive buildings. One can see a strange combination of the two concepts of reason. There is the critical reason which laid the foundation for the revolutionary philosophy of the French Revolution, as well as for some of the fundamental principles of the American Constitution, and alongside of this there is the romantic sentimental longing for nature outside of men in which, as he believed, the "natural" was embodied thousands of years ago before the beginning of civilization. With this second aspect of Rousseau's thinking, the Enlightenment philosophy which undergirded the French Revolution was conquered by the Romanticism of the following period. So we have in Rousseau both the fulfillment and the conquest of the principle of reason in the eighteenth century.

2. Hume, the History of Religion, and Positivism

Now we come to the second thinker in whom I see the fulfillment and conquest of the Enlightenment. He is David Hume in England (1711–1776). The trends of the Enlightenment which were expressed in classic form by John Locke came to an end in Hume. In his epistemology he criticized the confidence of the Enlightenment in its rational principles. He undercut the certainty of belief in the validity of what we have called the intuitive and critical concepts of reason. And along with this he undercut the metaphysical foundations of natural law on which the Enlightenment depended.

The main religious concepts of the Enlightenment theology were God, freedom, and immortality. Hume undercut them by his fundamental epistemological skepticism. He represented a way of criticizing the rational certainty of the Enlightenment, which in England was felt like a death blow. Hume defeated the great attempt of modern men to treat all the problems of life on the basis of reason in its different meanings. In this respect he can be considered an important point of departure for what we call positivism in modern philosophy.

The bourgeoisie had conquered its foes in the various revolutions and was now increasing its position of power. If the principles by which the bourgeoisie gained power would still be valid in this situation, they could become threatening to the victorious bourgeoisie itself. Therefore, critical reason was replaced by a positivistic acceptance of observing and calculating reason. This signifies the great change from the critical passion of the great thinkers of the Enlightenment to the positivism of nominalistic philosophy in modern times. What does positivism mean after all? It means accepting what is positively given as such, observing and describing it without trying to criticize it or without trying to make a constructive system out of it. We have then in Hume a great change which became important also for the continent of Europe through Hume's impact on Kant.

This changed orientation is significant for the situation in the three countries which were the leading contexts of modern philosophical development: France, Great Britain, and Germany. In the France of Rousseau's time we have reason fighting and struggling against tradition up to the French Revolution. France was Catholic and the Enlightenment was nourished in part by the critical attitude of Freemasonry. Even today it splits the French mind into those who follow the Catholic Church and those who fight against it. The great struggles in the beginning of this century between church and state in France, the radical separation in every respect, and the inner division of the whole nation are understandable only on the basis of the leading ideas of the Enlightenment which conflicted with the authoritarian system of the Roman Church, and not only with its authority, but also with its content. There are not many symptoms in the last fifty years of French history which suggest that this tremendous split can be overcome through a synthesis. That is the French situation even today.

The British situation is determined by Hume's positivistic attitude. Hume never attacked the established church, but he did attack the belief that you can justify it by reason. From the point of view of reason there was a thoroughgoing skepticism over against all the symbols of Christianity, but without that radical and hateful attack which took place in France. This also characterizes the situation in England today. We have there two attitudes which do not openly fight against each other, but which run beside each other, almost without touching each other. On the one hand, there is the established church with all its traditions and symbolism guarded over by the Queen, the symbol of the empire, of the past, but not a real power. On the other hand, there is the majority of the intelligentsia which goes its own way without really attacking the established church but also without uniting with any of its traditional symbols. No synthesis is attempted. That is why the contribution of the established church in Great Britain to systematic theology is almost nonexistent. For some reason this does not apply equally to the Scottish Church. But in French Catholicism, especially in some of its apologetic works, a great contribution was made to theology. Also nineteenth-century German theology made a great contribution because of its urgent need to find a synthesis.

Now in these days there is an interesting thing happening in England, something which I have become aware of recently because in a way I am involved in it. A book has appeared written by Bishop John Robinson of Woolwich, with the title *Honest to God*.[10] Those of you who read the section on religion in *Time* magazine have no doubt heard of it. This was also the way in which I first heard of it before the Bishop sent me the book. He develops theological thoughts which were born in the German situation and which seek an answer to the conflicts between the religious tradition and the modern secular mind. Robinson refers a great deal to my writings and to the writings of Bonhoeffer, the theologian martyred by the Nazis, who wrote letters from prison.[11] In these letters Bonhoeffer dealt with the same problem that I have dealt with in all my books, namely, the problem of seeking a solution to the conflicts between the religious tradition and the modern mind. Robinson's formulations provoked much resistance because they undercut the traditionalism of the church. The church never took seriously the prob-

[10] Philadelphia: The Westminster Press, 1963.
[11] Dietrich Bonhoeffer, *Letters and Papers from Prison,* translated by Reginald H. Fuller (New York: The Macmillan Company, 1953).

lem of finding a union of tradition with the modern mind and of showing the significance of the traditional symbols to modern man. And so a great shock was produced in the church by this book. Of course, in the British situation there have been some rare exceptions, like Archbishop Temple, who tried to take in some of the basic ideas of continental theology. But on the whole what has been characteristic of the British situation is the unwillingness to sacrifice the security of its liturgically founded tradition for the sake of radical theological thought. Therefore, it has not given answers to the questions implied in the existence of modern man.

3. Kant, Moral Religion, and Radical Evil

I must now concentrate on Germany which has done far more than any other country for Protestant theology in the nineteenth and twentieth centuries. Of course, I must include Switzerland because linguistically and theologically it belongs to the same situation. Karl Barth, for example, was for many years a professor of theology in Germany before he went back to Switzerland.

The man who was decisive for the theology of the nineteenth century, perhaps even more than Hegel or Schleiermacher, is Kant (1724–1804). He is the third of these three great figures who fulfilled and conquered the Enlightenment.

Kant followed Hume in his epistemological criticism of a philosophy which assumes that the religious ideas of God, freedom, and immortality can be established by rational arguments. This is impossible for the basic reason that man is finite. The finite mind is not able to reach the infinite. Almost everyone in the nineteenth and twentieth centuries accepted this criticism as a presupposition. You will not find a theologian who has not accepted it, or modified it, and attempted to save what could be saved of natural theology after Kant's tremendous attack on it. Even a man like Karl Barth who is so firmly rooted in the classical tradition has fully accepted the Kantian criticism of natural theology.

The basis of this criticism of natural theology is Kant's doctrine of the categorical structure of the human mind. The categories of thought and the forms of intuition, time and space, constitute the structure of man's finitude, and therefore these categories are valid only for the understanding of the interrelations of finite things. If one transcends the finite things and their interrelations, then the categories of causality, substance, quantity and quality, etc., are not valid. The immediate consequence of this is that you cannot make God a first cause or a universal substance. These categories are valid for physical or other scientific calculations; they must be presupposed. In fact, they are presupposed by everybody. Even Hume who criticizes them presupposes them in his criticism. Nevertheless, you cannot go beyond them. The category of causality, for example, is a description of the interrelation of finite experiences. Time is the main form of finitude by its transitoriness, by the impossibility of fixing it in one moment. If you fix this moment, time is already gone. If the categories are not used in the realm of phenomena, those things which appear in time and space, they cannot be used at all. This means that the use of the concepts of God, freedom, and immortality is impossible in terms of rational structure, as natural theology tried to do.

This criticism is so fundamental and radical that Kant has been called the destroyer of the whole rational theology of the Enlightenment. But there is another implication in it. The first philosophical lecture I heard in my life was delivered by Julius Kaftan (1848–1926), the systematic theologian of the University of Berlin. I was perhaps sixteen years old and still in the *Gymnasium*. In Germany there is no college, but there is a *Gymnasium* which takes you till the eighteenth year, and then you go directly into the university. I was fascinated by this lecture and never forgot it. It was an oversimplification, but a very impressive one which had a great deal of truth in it. Kaftan at this time was the leading authority of the Kantian-Ritschlian school of theology. He said that there are three great philosophers and there are three great Christian groups: The Greek Orthodox whose philosopher's name is Plato; the Roman Catholics whose philosopher's name is Aristotle; and the Protestants whose philosopher's name is Kant. Now this alone would be very interesting because now in the ecumenical movement Plato, Aristotle, and Kant may come together to join in a heavenly disputation. However this may be, what is the basis for the statement that Kant is the philosopher of Protestantism? The real basis is the fact that he is the philosopher who saw most clearly and sharply the finitude of man and man's inability of breaking through the limits of his finitude to that which transcends it, namely, to the infinite.

Kant's doctrine of categories and of time and space as the structure of man's mind, a structure which construes the world of the finite for him but beyond which man cannot go, is what gives him a certain kind of humility before reality. This humility is also found in empirical philosophy which accepts the empirically given phenomena. But in Kant it goes much deeper existentially than in ordinary empirical philosophy.

We are finite and must therefore accept our finitude. The Protestant idea that we can come to God only through God, that only grace can overcome guilt, sin, and our estrangement from God, and not we ourselves, and no good works can help us, this idea can be extended also to the realm of thought. We cannot break through to God even in the realm of thought. He must come to us. This was a very fundamental change in contrast to the metaphysical arrogance of the Enlightenment which believed in the power of reason—all the different forms of reason —to place man immediately in the presence of the Divine. Now men were in a prison, so to speak. Kant had placed man in the prison of finitude. All attempts to escape—which characterize both mysticism and rationalism—are in vain. The only thing we can do is to accept our finitude. Certainly in this way Kant represents to a great extent the attitude of Protestantism.

But could this be all? Is man nothing more than finite? Can philosophy even speak of finitude if there is not a point at which man transcends it? Animals are finite, but they do not know it. They are not above finitude at any point. Then Kant wrote his second critique, the critique of practical reason. This dealt with the idea of the moral imperative. He called it the categorical or unconditional imperative. Here there is a breakthrough, not in the realm of theoretical thought but in terms of the experience of the unconditional command of the moral imperative. The breakthrough does not go directly to God. Kant gave an argument for the existence of God which falls under his own criticism and was never really accepted. But he showed one thing, that in the finite structure of our being there is a point of unconditional validity.

This point is the moral imperative and the experience of its unconditional character.

So we have no certainty about God or freedom or eternal life, but we have the certainty of belonging to something unconditional which we can experience as such. It is obvious that Kant did not have in mind particular contents of the moral imperative. He was educated enough in terms of ethnology to know the vast differences of content in the moral imperative from culture to culture. But the commanding form of this imperative, its unconditional character, is independent of any particular content. Thus not the content of the moral imperative but its radical form is what gives Kant the feeling of a breakthrough to that which transcends the prison of finitude in which the human mind has been placed by theoretical reason.

Another thing appeared in Kant's philosophy which came as a shock to his contemporaries, even to people who, like Goethe, had transcended the Enlightenment. The unconditional command of the moral imperative is given to us. But we who live in time and space have not taken it into our actual will. Although it is our essential will, that which makes our will the true will, our actual will is perverted. The principle of action or the maxim, as Kant called it, according to which we act is perverted. This he called the radical evil in man. Now remember that the most passionate point of attack of the Enlightenment against Christianity dealt with the doctrine of original sin, or of radical evil, as Kant called it, or of universal tragic estrangement, as I prefer to call it. Radical evil means that evil goes to the *radix,* meaning "root" in Latin. Radical evil means that in the root of human existence there is a perversion of man's essential will.

Kant's idea of radical evil was an unforgivable sin from the point of view of the Enlightenment. Kant was attacked very much because he said this. But Kant was followed later on by several who even deepened it and carried it through to the early sources of existentialism, namely, the second period of Schelling the philosopher. Here we find in Kant a deviation from the Enlightenment that is very radical. Kant elaborated these ideas in his book, *Religion within the Limits of Reason Alone,* into a whole philosophy of religion. Or I would simply call it a little systematic theology. This systematic theology underlies much of what is going on in America even today, for Kant's ideas were developed further by Ritschl and his school and were transmitted into American theology by Walter Rauschenbusch (1861–1918) and the Social Gospel movement. This movement was still very powerful up to the years before the second World War when Reinhold Niebuhr attacked it.

We must now briefly present a picture of Kant's theological ideas. Kant conceives of history as the ongoing struggle between evil, radical evil, and good. The good principle is present in mankind; it is identical with man's essential nature, which is good. It has appeared in the Christ who represents this essential goodness of men over against its perversion by radical evil. In the Christ the perversion was overcome; the unity of God and man was re-established. The victory over the evil principle by Jesus is the beginning of the kingdom of God on earth. The church is the invisible body of those who are determined by essential reason and who take into themselves the power of reunion with God. The transition from the invisible church to something very mixed in the empirical churches is unavoidable. But the empirical church must always be criticized by the standard of the essential church of pure reason. For Kant this criticism is very radical, so radical that it is actually a negation of the empirical church. The empirical church is seen by him as a group ruled by superstitions and subjected to ecclesiastical authorities. Therefore every individual belonging to the essential church should try to overcome this visible church which destroys autonomy by heteronomous authority and destroys reason by superstitions. Everybody should try, and the church as a whole should try, to overcome these elements.

The sharpest attack was made against the priestly rule of the church. This for Kant was the absolute opposite of the autonomous rule of reason. From Kant's point of view all elements of immediacy between God and man were to be eliminated. I indicated this already when I spoke of his criticism of the arguments for the existence of God. Now we can see that there is a certain religious type which expresses itself here in Kant. He allows no room for the presence of the divine Spirit in the human spirit with its ecstatic implications. The mystical presence of the divine is radically denied. In the Ritschlian school which was influenced by Kant, the most radical attack on mysticism ever made in the history of Christianity was carried out by Ritschl and his disciples, including Harnack, the greatest figure of this school. What we are left with is a consistent type of finitude in which only the moral imperative elevates man above animal existence. Morality gives him dignity, and the struggle between good and evil is a moral one in which elements like grace and prayer are denied.

Grace supposedly devaluates man's autonomous freedom for good and evil, and prayer is an ecstatic experience of which one would be ashamed if someone caught him in the act by surprise. This was Kant's fundamental feeling. And, of course, ecstasy in nature itself, for which we have the word miracle, is an encroachment upon the universal essential structure of reality. What remains is a philosophy of the kingdom of God. This kingdom is identical with the establishment of the moral man on earth. This notion includes not only individual morality, but also social justice and peace on earth. Kant wrote a classic little book on eternal peace which became the basis of the religion which influenced the Social Gospel movement at the end of the last and the beginning of this century.

Kant wrote a third critique, the *Critique of Judgment*. Here he tried with great caution to escape the prison of finitude. His followers in the classical period of German philosophy took it as a way out. From Kant's point of view it would be better to say that he was only enlarging and beautifying the prison, but not really breaking through it. But his followers considered it a breakthrough. In this *Critique of Judgment* Kant tried to bring together the two divergent critiques of reason, theoretical and practical reason. He showed possible unions between the two. These cannot, however, be affirmed assertively, but only in terms of possibility, or better, as a human vision of realities without knowing that the realities really correspond to the vision.

In this *Critique* Kant developed his notion of nature. Thereby he became the father of modern *Gestalt* theory reflected in all forms of organicism, and in the arts. In these two realms Kant saw that judgments are possible, the judgment that nature is an organism as a whole and in the organic structures and the judgment that in art there is an inner aim in every representation of meaning. Kant did not say that nature is actually like this, but always added a qualification in terms of an "as if" (*als ob*). He was completely overwhelmed by the Newtonian natural laws, by the mathematical, scientific approach to nature. But he said that although the real nature with which we have to deal is the nature of Newtonian physics, we can nevertheless consider nature *as if* there were structures, meaningful structures, or organisms, and *as if* the whole universe had the character of an organic structure of this kind.

So Kant, with caution and great restriction, introduced a principle which was picked up by Romantic philosophy as a main principle for its philosophy of nature, only minus the "as if." That is the big difference. From the presuppositions of Kant's prison of finitude you can only say "as if," but if at several points you can break through this prison, then you might be able to say what nature or reality really is like. This was the watershed between critical philosophy and later ontological philosophy.

Thus Kant stands like Rousseau and Hume as a fulfiller and critic of German Enlightenment. His greatness is that he understood man's creaturely finitude, of course, on the basis of his half-pietistic Protestantism. The pietistic element was removed, but existentialism and pietism have much to do with each other. I am reminded of the atheistic sermon which Heidegger once gave us in his pietistic categories. At any rate Kant was praised by all the theologians of the nineteenth century for establishing the insight into man's creaturely finitude, or as we would say today, into man's existential situation. But the human mind and the human soul could not remain on this level. Therefore, all movements of the nineteenth century, although based on Kant, would try to go beyond him. In my student years there was a slogan often repeated: Understanding Kant means transcending Kant. We all try to do this, and I will be showing you various ways in which theology has tried to do it.

CHAPTER III

The Classic-Romantic Reaction

against the Enlightenment

We have discussed two figures from France, Voltaire, the classical representative, and Rousseau, the fulfiller and conqueror of the Enlightenment; and two from England, the classical figure, John Locke, and then the fulfiller and conqueror, David Hume. From Germany I have presented only the fulfiller and conqueror of the Enlightenment, Kant, but not the classical figure, Gotthold Ephraim Lessing.

A. LESSING, HISTORICAL CRITICISM, AND THE REDISCOVERY OF SPINOZA

Lessing's was a very universal mind. He was a poet, dramatist, philosopher, and theologian. He stirred up one of the greatest storms in the history of Protestant theology, when as a librarian in a small German town he edited a book written by a historian, Reimarus.[1] Reimarus started this modern search for the historical Jesus. Lessing, the librarian, published certain of Reimarus' fragments of research on the

---

[1] Hermann Samuel Reimarus' studies were published by Lessing after the death of Reimarus in 1768, in a collection called the *Wolfenbüttel Fragments*. The English translation is entitled *The Object of Jesus and His Disciples, as Seen in the New Testament*, edited by A. Voysey (1879). Cf. also Albert Schweitzer's book, *The Quest of the Historical Jesus*, the original German title of which is *Von Reimarus zu Wrede*.

life of Jesus which he had conducted by applying radical historical criticism. It was very dangerous to publish them. Reimarus had already died, but his manuscript was in the hands of Lessing. The storm was tremendous when these fragments were published. The chief pastor of Hamburg, Goetze, tried to defend orthodoxy, with some good and some bad arguments. But the whole intellectual climate was irreversibly changed. No theologian could thereafter approach the documents of the story of Jesus without being aware of the questions asked by Reimarus concerning the reliability of the Synoptic Gospels.

Thus the fundamental problem of historical criticism arose in the middle of the eighteenth century. People were shocked in that time just as many lay people were shocked today when the Dead Sea Scrolls were published. Except for the fact that we know more about first-century Palestine, the situation is not basically different so far as theology is concerned. Lessing's courage to edit these radical fragments of research was one of the things which made him great.

Another important thing about Lessing is his classic expression of progressivistic thought about philosophy and religion in his little book, *The Education of the Human Race.* His idea was that mankind has arrived at the age of reason. The description of this reason as autonomous is very similar to the idea of the great prophet of the twelfth century, Joachim de Fiore, who prophesied the coming of an age of the divine Spirit in which everyone will be taught directly by the Spirit and no authorities will be needed any more. I told you about the intimate relation between this kind of spirit-mysticism and rationalism. Well, Lessing is a great representative of this unity. The age of reason is for Lessing the actualization of the age of the Spirit. He refers directly to the movement of Joachim de Fiore as among his predecessors.

Another fascinating idea comes up in Lessing, as in other enlightened people of that age. That is the idea of reincarnation of men. People who had died before the age of reason had dawned would return so that they could participate in the fulfillment of true humanity. What seems to be a very irrational idea is used to answer a difficult problem for all progressivistic thinking. If we say that in the future sometime there will be an age of reason and peace and justice etc., we must ask about those who die before the coming of that age. Are they excluded from fulfillment?

If there is no transcendent fulfillment, they are excluded. And for the people of the Enlightenment, of course, there was no fulfillment. At least, it was not as unambiguous as it was in the Christian tradition. So they had to answer in terms of time and space. The idea of rebirth or reincarnation was the only one which could help them.

Perhaps we can add still another thing about Lessing. He wrote a play, *Nathan the Wise*, which has been translated and often performed. In this play he describes the encounter between Islam, Christianity, and Judaism. The wise Jew is the hero of the whole play. The theme of the play is the relativism of religions. In the history of Christianity it was the encounter with Islam which brought the question of the relativism of Christianity itself to the fore. Christianity became fanatical because now it was threatened. Paganism did not represent a real religious threat, but Islam did, and conquered the eastern half of Christianity. This raised the question of the relation between these two historical religions.

Then a last point. On his deathbed, Lessing had a conversation with the philosopher Jacobi (1743–1819)[2] who played an important role at that time. After Lessing's death Jacobi published that in this conversation Lessing had acknowledged a great admiration for Spinoza. According to this report Lessing even went so far as to call himself a Spinozist. This was a scandal. At that time spiritual things were taken so seriously that the idea that a man like Lessing, the great figure of the Enlightenment, should have been a Spinozist came as a great shock. Spinoza was taboo, not only to Christian and Jewish Orthodoxy—he had been thrown out by the Jewish congregation in Amsterdam—but also to the Enlightenment, because the innermost center of Spinoza's thought, the volcano beneath his frozen geometrical system, was Jewish mysticism of the Middle Ages. This can be traced historically. If you read Spinoza's ethics not in terms of the validity of his definitions and conclusions which were given *more geometrico* (in geometrical fashion), as he called it, but in terms of the underlying passion, in terms of the highest aim which is placed before man, namely, to participate in the eternal love with which God loves himself, then you see how pertinent it is to

[2] F. H. Jacobi followed Kant in removing religious certainty from the sphere of reason to that of faith. He is often quoted for claiming to have been a "pagan with his head, but with his heart a Christian."

speak of a mystical volcano hidden beneath a geometrically frozen surface.

The eventual result was that Spinoza was received more and more widely. Schleiermacher even wrote a hymn to Saint Spinoza. He really was a "saint" in his life as much as any Catholic saint ever was. Schleiermacher asked his contemporaries to sacrifice in thought and in feeling to this saint who was a lonely man, and in his loneliness was one of the deepest and greatest thinkers of all times. Yet all these men were Kantians. Kant's Copernican revolution, as he himself called it, had shaken all the philosophical foundations. How could Spinoza then be received on a Kantian basis?

B. The Synthesis of Spinoza and Kant

The relation between Spinoza and Kant became the philosophical and theological problem. Why should this be so difficult? Well, on the one side is Spinoza's mystical pantheism, as it has sometimes been called. This is the idea that there is one eternal substance, and that everything that exists is but a mode of this substance. This universal substance has innumerable attributes, but we know only two of them, mind and extension, as Descartes, Spinoza's teacher, had said. This one substance is present in everything. Here we have what I would call the principle of identity. Everything has a point of identity in the eternal divine substance which underlies everything. The identity between the finite and the infinite is complete. It was this mystical background which accounts for the fascination which thinkers in the following periods up to today have had in Spinoza's philosophy. This is true of Goethe who was perhaps even closer to Spinoza than Lessing was.

Now against this mystical pantheistic system stands Kant's philosophy, which emphasizes the principle of distance, the principle of finitude which man must accept, the transcendence of the divine beyond man's grasp and lying outside his center. This finitude of man and his inability of ever reaching the infinite is the motive in all Kant's criticisms. So all of Kant's followers and the whole continental philosophy faced this problem: How to unite mysticism and the Protestant principle; how to unite the principle of identity, the participation of the divine in each of us, and the principle of detachment, of moral obedience, without participation in the divine.

My doctoral dissertation was about this tension. It focused on one particular man, Schelling, the predecessor, friend, and later enemy of Hegel. I tried to discover how Schelling sought to solve the problem of this tension. The title of my book was *Mystik und Schuldbewusstsein in Schellings philosophischer Entwicklung*, 1912.[3] Here you see these two things. More abstractly you can express it by the principle of identity in relation to the principle of contrast, or even of contradiction, in a moral sense at least. Here we have the fundamental motives in attempting to create the great synthesis following Kant. It started in part already during his lifetime, and then was fully developed after his death, coming to its conclusion in Hegel and Schleiermacher. Later the great synthesis was destroyed, partly at least in the name of the slogan "back to Kant." The slogan meant that we should give up the principle of identity, accept finitude and have a religion of moral obedience.

I call this the great synthesis of Kant and Spinoza, a synthesis which, of course, includes many other things. This is the synthesis of the principle of identity and the principle of detachment or contrast. The philosophers of Romanticism, and above all Schleiermacher, the great theologian of Romanticism, are all characterized by this attempt at synthesis. They were Protestant theologians; they had learned about Kant's destruction of natural theology; nobody doubted this any more. On the other hand they came from mystical traditions. For instance, Schleiermacher came from the tradition of Zinzendorfian pietism. All these theologians had the task of uniting these seemingly irreconcilable contrasts.

The dynamo of the history of theology ever since, going through the whole nineteenth century, is the tension between these two things. If you take a seminar on Karl Barth, you will see again the protest against mysticism, against any form of the principle of identity. But there are also theologies which come from the union of Kant and Spinoza.

[3] *Mysticism and Guilt-Consciousness in Schelling's Philosophical Development* (1912). This book has not been translated into English.

C. The Nature of Romanticism

Before we deal with Schleiermacher, we have to discuss what Romanticism is, in order to understand what people mean when they speak of Schleiermacher as a romantic philosopher. Karl Barth, who dislikes Romanticism very much, has said that we are all romantics. That means that he was fair enough to acknowledge even his own dependence on the great anti-Enlightenment romantic tradition of the nineteenth and twentieth centuries.

In order to speak about the nature of Romanticism I first need, as always, to make a semantic statement. When I came to America, I heard Reinhold Niebuhr, my friend and colleague at Union Theological Seminary in New York speak of Romanticism in terms of what I usually called utopianism. Utopianism is the idea of a fulfilled society in the future and of an original, just society along the lines of Rousseau's idea of the noble savages. Niebuhr called this Romanticism. In continental Europe nobody would have referred to utopianism by the term Romanticism, although certain elements in Rousseau, such as the sentimental desire of returning to nature, had a relation to actual Romanticism. But the Romanticism of the main countries in which it appeared, of France, England, and Germany, is really quite different. Now I want to show you what some of the constitutive elements of Romanticism are, by asking, what made theologians and philosophers like Schelling, Schleiermacher, Schlegel, and Rothe all romanticists? What produced the great romantic poetry in Germany? How did Romanticism influence the naturalistic philosophy of the late nineteenth century of men like Nietzsche? And—this should not be forgotten—what produced the romantic music in people like Schubert and Schumann and up to Brahms?

1. The Infinite and Finite

Our first consideration has to do with the relation of the infinite to the finite. Here we have to go back to the early Renaissance, to Nicholas of Cusa, cardinal of high standing in the Roman Catholic Church, who was born in 1401 at Cues (Cusa) on the Moselle. He is a very important man, but better known in the twentieth century than in the nineteenth. In the nineteenth century under the power of neo-Kantian philosophy, Descartes was almost exclusively regarded as the founder of modern philosophy. But in our century it has become clear that we need to know more than merely the creator of the method of modern philosophy, namely, Descartes, who influenced both empiricism and rationalism. We also need to know the one who represents the metaphysical foundations of the modern mind, and this man is Nicholas of Cusa.

The philosopher who helped to rediscover Nicholas of Cusa is Ernst Cassirer,[4] who also came to this country with the help of Hitler. I myself learned of Nicholas of Cusa very early in my thinking through the influence he had on the line of thought which led to Schelling.

Very much like Descartes, this man was basically mathematically minded, but he used his mathematical education not in a methodological but in an ontological direction. His main principle was the *coincidentia oppositorum* (the coincidence of opposites), the coincidence of the finite and the infinite. In everything finite the infinite is present, namely, that power which is the creative unity of the universe as a whole. And in the same way the finite is in the infinite as a potentiality. In the world the divine is developed; in God the world is enveloped. The finite is in the infinite potentially; the infinite is in the finite actually. They are within each other. He expresses this in geometrical terms by saying that God, or better, the divine, is the center and the periphery of everything. He is in everything as the center, although he transcends everything; but he is also the periphery because he embraces everything. They are removed from him and at the same time he is in them.

It is very interesting that Martin Luther in his discussions of the presence of the divine in the sacramental materials of bread and wine used similar formulations, probably without any dependence on Nicholas of Cusa. It is doubtful that Luther knew him, but he had similar earlier sources available to him, that is, in German and ultimately neo-

---

[4] Ernst Cassirer's books on the Renaissance and the Enlightenment are entitled: *Individual and Cosmos in the Philosophy of the Renaissance* (1927); *The Platonic Renaissance in England* (1932); and *The Philosophy of the Enlightenment* (1932).

Platonic mysticism. Luther said that God is nearer to everything than anything is to itself. He is fully in every grain of sand, but the whole world cannot comprehend him. He transcends everything finite, although being in it. So we have here a common development and this common development underlies the modern mind in its ultimate concern, so to speak, in the fundamental principles of interpreting God and the world.

This represents a tremendous change from the common view that God is in heaven, but only his active powers are on earth. For Nicholas and for Luther on his mystical side—a mysticism which at first was open, but later hidden—they are within each other. The modern mind overleaps the strict dualism of a divine sphere in heaven and a human sphere on earth which developed in the later ancient world. The divine is not in some place alongside of the world or above the world, but is present in everything human and natural. In some respects one can say that modern naturalism was born out of the mystical idea of the coincidence of opposites. This was not simply a methodological approach to reality, rationalistic or empiricistic. Behind it was an experience that nature is not outside of creative reality, but is potentially before the creation in God—of course this is not meant temporally but logically—and then after the creation the divine is within it. This means that the finite is not only finite, but in some dimension it is also infinite and has the divine as its center and ground.

This principle of the relation between the finite and the infinite is the first principle of Romanticism on which everything else is dependent. Without it Romanticism and a theologian like Schleiermacher become completely unintelligible.

Now let me briefly indicate the line of thought coming from the early Renaissance (Nicholas of Cusa) and going into the eighteenth and nineteenth centuries. The next person whom we must mention is Giordano Bruno (1548–1600), the martyr of this Renaissance naturalism. His was an ecstatic naturalism, not a calculating naturalism of subjecting nature to analysis and technology. Bruno repeatedly spoke about the enthusiasm for the universe, and this brought him to his death by the Inquisition. This could happen because the whole system of authority was based on the principle of detachment, of nonparticipation, the principle of authority, of mediation between God and man. The mystical inwardness of Nicholas of Cusa was not accepted.

Nicholas of Cusa was able to be one of the most influential cardinals in Rome without being attacked, although he wrote something which was even more dangerous than almost anything that Giordano Bruno wrote, namely, *De Pace Fidei*.[5] In this book he wrote about the peace of faith in heaven where there is an assembly in which it is taught that the Logos, the divine word, is present in every religion—in accordance with the interpretation of Paul—and that therefore the struggle between the religions is unnecessary. This idea of a peace based on something that transcends the particular expressions of the religions was a dangerous idea. It touched on an issue which had become burning ever since the encounter with Islam and the continuing theological discussion with Judaism in medieval Christianity. Nicholas could get away with holding such ideas in the early Renaissance, but Bruno became a victim of the counter-Reformation, perhaps because the church felt that his enthusiastic naturalism would remove the divine out of reality.

In England we have Shaftesbury (1671–1713), a great representative of the principle of harmony, who applied it to an organismic interpretation of nature. In Germany the most representative of this line of thought was not the philosopher Schelling, but the poet Goethe. Here again we see an enthusiasm for nature. Goethe expressed this not only in his poetry but also in his natural scientific inquiries which anticipated to a large extent the modern *Gestalt* theory. According to this theory nature is not a causal assemblage of isolated atoms, but is composed of structures. One must look for these structures, these original phenomena, in nature. In the psychological realm these are the archetypes of Hume. Both these original phenomena of Goethe and the archetypes of Hume go back to Plato's ideas or essences which transcend every empirical reality.

So we can say that in Goethe the motifs of Nicholas of Cusa, Giordano Bruno, and the Earl of Shaftesbury were combined to form an image of reality which was overcome in the second half of the nineteenth century by the empirical sciences. But there were continual reac-

[5] *On the Peace of Faith.*

tions to the empirical sciences in the nineteenth and twentieth centuries. There was Nietzsche, for example, an ecstatic naturalist like Giordano Bruno, but without the mystical elements.

In Goethe the idea of the infinite in nature was certainly present, but it was present in a balance between the infinite and the finite. We call this the classical attitude of Goethe, a development which is altogether against the Enlightenment. In Goethe's attitude toward nature the Greek spirit is still alive, namely, the balance of elements in the classical form. Of course, in one sense this was not possible any more. All attempts on the basis of Christianity to return to Greece have proved to be failures. You cannot return. Modern humanism is and remains Christian humanism, and the most anti-Christian of the humanists, people like Nietzsche, often happen to be sons of Protestant clergymen, as Nietzsche actually was. The Christian substance cannot be wholly lost. It is not by chance that many of the classical thinkers, like Schelling and others, came from the homes of Protestant ministers. The Protestant ministers in the rather barbaric Protestant countries in Northern Europe were the bearers of the higher culture. Often they were grasped by the spirit of Greece to such a degree that they wanted simply to return. But this is never possible.

In any case, the problem of the infinite and the finite was solved during Goethe's brief classical period. This was not the period of the later or early Goethe, but the middle-aged Goethe. It is an interesting thing that the classical periods are always like the upper edge of a roof; there is much which goes on before they can appear. There must be Enlightenment as in Greek sophism; there must be *Sturm und Drang* (storm and stress), a youth movement, then an intellectual movement. Only after these stages could Goethe come to his classical period. The same thing was true of Plato. The classical Plato is to be found in the middle dialogues. We find the same thing in Greek sculpture. The classical period endures only a short time between the archaic and the naturalistic period. Thus the classical period was represented only during a short period of Goethe's life. Then Romanticism broke through. Romanticism broke the classical balance of the infinite and the finite, by the dynamic power of the infinite which transcends every finite form.

Here we have another characteristic of fully developed Romanticism. In this sense we are all romantics, because our thinking is dynamic and does not want to bind itself to any given form. Behind this is Kant's doctrine of freedom which had a great influence on Romanticism, especially in the form in which it was interpreted by Fichte (1762–1814) in his philosophy of the absolute ego. The ego is creative, and everything in the world is only a limit to the ego; but the innermost nature of reality is freedom. This he learned from Kant and his doctrine of practical reason. Fichte construed the whole world as a fight between the principle of freedom in every individual self and the resistance of a nonego, an "id" as Freud would call it, against that freedom. This fight is going on all the time. Here you have the romantic dynamics breaking through every particular form. This has certain implications. Take, for instance, a social structure in which one lives today, a suburban structure in America in the 1960's. How can one get beyond this structure? By imagination. Romanticism is a philosophy of imagination. He who is not able to transcend the given situation in which he lives through his own imagination finds himself imprisoned in that situation.

America never had a real period of Romanticism. It imported something from England, but very little of Romanticism influenced the whole life of the educated people. This has had the consequence of underestimating the imagination, of drying out the imagination which alone can transcend the given state of things and conceive the infinite potentialities given in every moment. So you have here another consequence of the victory of the infinite over the finite. But this infinite was not, as it still was in Nicholas of Cusa, in the dimension of going up and going down, with the presence of the divine in the individual in a more or less static way, even if there was an enthusiasm for the cosmos. But modern Romanticism has behind itself the baroque period of the modern world, which had the dynamics which drive into the horizontal line. So this is not only the infinite *above*, but also the infinite *ahead*, presenting in each new moment an infinite variety of possibilities for new creativity. The idea of creativity, of cultural creativity, is a romantic element which has entered this country also. It is the Fichtean and generally romantic idea that culture is human creativity, and that this creativity is infinite in the horizontal line.

We have here then the breaking through of the infinite against the balance it had in the classical criticism or negation of the Enlightenment, the romantic breakthrough of the balance into the horizontal line. This must be understood if we are to understand the basis for the rediscovery of history in Romanticism. The whole understanding of history is something which has to do with Romanticism. Before dealing with this we must deal with another point, the emotional and aesthetic elements in Romanticism.

2. The Emotional and the Aesthetic Elements in Romanticism

Romanticism is, as I said, against the Enlightenment. There is no lack of emotion in the Enlightenment, but it is subjective or sentimental emotion. We have the tears which are shed all the time. Romanticism is not sentimental because it does not have to complement, so to speak, the rationality of Enlightenment, the calculating and fighting critical reason. If the infinite is in everything finite, then the awareness of the infinite in the finite is intuitive. This is complete mysticism, or natural mysticism. Mystical intuition is not divorced from emotion; it objectifies emotion by taking it into the very act of intuition. In Romanticism there is the emotion which is not sentimental, but which is revealing and has the character of the Platonic *eros*. It is no mere coincidence that Schleiermacher was the great romantic translator of Plato. If you read this, you will see that it is a romantic interpretation of Plato. It is a sound translation, but translation is always interpretation.—Probably you have to be born German in order to feel this in the language which Schleiermacher uses.—It is the language of *eros* which runs through all of Schleiermacher's translation of Plato. It is the creative *eros* in which the emotional and the cognitive elements are united in the intuition of the infinite in the finite.

This has immediate consequences for the aesthetic element in Romanticism. Romanticism looks at the world through aesthetic categories. Kant had the natural scientific analysis of nature together with the moral imperative with its categorical or unconditional character. In his third critique, the *Critique of Judgment,* Kant found a principle for uniting the theoretical and the practical reason in the aesthetic intuition of reality. In this he found that which transcends the scientific consideration of nature, the Newtonian as it was called at that time, as well as the moral principles. The moral always commands while the theoretical analyzes. Is there a union between them? Is there something in nature which, so to speak, fulfills the commands of the moral imperative and transcends the mere scientific analysis of nature? He discovered, as I told you, the organic in nature and the aesthetic in culture. It is what at that time could still be called the beautiful, but I would call it the expressive, in which the two are united.

Romanticism, therefore, used Kant's *Critique of Judgment* more than anything else because there Kant offered the possibility of accepting the fundamental restrictions of his previous *Critiques* and at the same time of going beyond them.

This means that romantic philosophy replaced religion by aesthetic intuition. Whenever you find the statement made by artists or in works on art that art is religion itself, you are in the sphere of the romantic tradition. For Schelling, in his aesthetic period, art is the great miracle, the unique miracle in all history. It is a miracle which would have to appear only once in the world to convince us of the presence of the ultimate. He calls this the identity transcending subject and object, transcending the theoretical and the practical. We find the same aesthetic intuition of the universe in Schleiermacher's *Speeches on Religion*. Aesthetic intuition as participating intuition takes art seriously as revelatory.

3. *The Turn to the Past and the Valuation of Tradition*

The idea of the presence of the infinite in the finite gave Romanticism the possibility of a new relationship to the past. Here the conflict with Enlightenment was especially great. For the Enlightenment the past was more or less in bondage to superstition. Now that the age of reason has appeared the superstitions of the Middle Ages have disappeared. This was the Enlightenment's view of history. If you read Lessing's little writing on the education of mankind, you will find this idea that at the present time the age in which reason is victorious has begun. Romanticism, on the other hand, had a very different attitude toward the past. The infinite was also present in the past periods of history through expressive forms of life and their great symbols. They had their revelatory character also. This means that history, the historical past, be taken seriously. Tradition could be important for Romanticism, whereas the Enlightenment was merely the critic of tradition, as Protestantism also was in some respects.

This new attitude toward history was very important for historiography. The great nineteenth-century historians were influenced by these romantic ideas. In the past the infinite is present; it has revealed itself in the Middle Ages as well as in Greece, and therefore the idea of a totally new beginning now in the age of reason appears fantastic. Goethe ridiculed this idea in his *Faust,* and so did all the romantics. Many of them tried to go back to the Middle Ages to re-establish its culture. They also applied their philosophical concept of the organic to society. They had the idea of an organic society. The French religious socialist, Saint-Simon (1760–1825), distinguished critical and organic periods in history. It was very easy to show that the Middle Ages formed an organic period. Everything had its special place and function in the organism. The eighteenth-century Enlightenment, on the other hand, formed a critical period in which the organic structures were attacked, because of their deterioration in terms of tyranny, superstition, etc. Saint-Simon and the religious socialists expected the coming of a new organic period. Most of the later European religious socialist movements—and there have been many of them—have been dependent on this idea of an organic society over against the atomized mass society. This was the idea of Saint-Simon and his school; this was the idea of the later religious socialists in the various European countries, including the religious socialist movement in which I participated.[6]

Without the rediscovery of the organic in society and the presence of the divine in the past periods of history, these developments could not have happened. Here again I see something characteristic for the American situation which has had an almost unbroken tradition of Enlightenment up to today. Romanticism never really broke through into the American tradition. It has appeared in some literary manifestations, but it has never been a transforming power as in Europe. What in

[6] See below, for a discussion of Religious Socialism, pp. 234–239.

Europe was seen as politically conservative is here extreme liberalism, and what is here called liberalism is closer to socialism in Europe. The terminology and the feeling toward life are different. One of the consequences of this is that history has not been taken as seriously as it has been in Europe. Even the empirical historians of today do not take it very seriously; seriously means existentially significant for our own existence here and now. When the romantic historians dealt with classical Greece or the Middle Ages, they of course also wanted to discover the facts, but this was not their main interest. Their chief interest was in the meaning of past history for the self-interpretation of man today.

If these existential questions are not asked, the study of history merely deals with the facts of the past instead of dealing with our own situation in terms of the past. I believe that the resistance of American students against taking history seriously is due in part to the fact that Romanticism has never had a profound influence in this country. The American Constitution is a great political document of the Enlightenment; you do not find many romantic elements in it. This is not by chance. The Enlightenment feeling that a new beginning has been inaugurated is part of the American experience.

Therefore, the concept of conservatism is very ambiguous. In Europe conservatism is always associated with a romantic affirmation of the past. It means keeping the traditions, finding the infinite in the religious and cultural traditions of the past, longing for the Middle Ages, for primitive Christianity or Greek culture. The word "conservatism" in this country, on the other hand, does not have the same traditional meaning. It has more to do with the individualism of the capitalistic society. This would never be called conservatism in Europe. Thus it can happen that the term "conservatism" can be used for simple fascist movements, like the John Birch Society, as I learned during my two months in California. These movements have nothing to do with conservatism. They are based on the mass culture of the present and wish to exclude all liberal elements, not for the sake of the Middle Ages, or some similar epoch in the past, but for the sake of maintaining the rule of the upper classes in capitalistic society. It helps to know history to understand the meaning of terms we use so freely.

4. The Quest for Unity and Authority

I said that Romanticism is a longing to return to the Middle Ages and its organic structure, but this organic structure is always identical with a hierarchical structure. It is interesting that there is some degree of nonauthoritarianism in the organic character of the larger cities, and only to a limited extent could we call it organic. On the whole the organic has a hierarchical character, which can easily be derived from the concept of the organic in nature. Man as an organism is also hierarchically construed; his centered self is the top of the hierarchy which directs everything. So the idea of the re-establishment of authority was a powerful element in Romanticism, and out of this came the reaction against the democratic tendencies of the American and French Revolutions. We see that reaction very clearly in the German type of Romanticism, but also in France. If you want to understand a figure like Charles de Gaulle, you must understand the romantic traditions and the desire for a hierarchically ruled organism which have broken out again and again in France.

The hierarchy was understood not so much as an isolated political hierarchy, but as a religious political hierarchy, a return to the reunion of the political and religious realms. Richard Rothe (1799–1867), for instance, a pupil of Schleiermacher, was very much interested in the idea of a culture in which church and state become identical again, just the opposite of the American principle of separation of church and state. The state would become the comprehensive form of all culture. We have the same thing in Hegel when he called the state the divine on earth. But this must not be misunderstood. If such men speak of the state as the divine on earth, or if Bonhoeffer speaks of the secular world and not the religious sphere as the real manifestation of the divine, then they are not thinking of the state as an administration in the hands of politicians. That is the liberal democratic concept of the state, presupposing a separation of church and state. Instead they are thinking of the state as the unity of all cultural activities. This is a cultural concept of the state. The political side is less decisive than the religio-cultural side.

Obviously, if you have this concept of state in mind, you can go back romantically to the Greek city-state in which there was no religion alongside political life. The whole political life was permeated with the presence of the gods and the functionaries of the city were also the priests. If you read the early fragments of Hegel, you will find a romantic description of the Greek city-state, involving the identity of state and church as a most important part of the whole idea. Novalis (1772–1801), one of the romantic poets, wrote a famous pamphlet or essay entitled *Die Christenheit oder Europa*[7] in which he described this reunion of everything cultural within the religious in all Europe, overcoming the boundary lines separating European countries, and the re-establishment of a Europe in terms of a religio-political authority similar to the pope. Here in this essay Novalis described the image a romantic man had of the future society.

5. *The Negative and the Demonic in Romanticism*

Now let me say a few things about the negative and demonic side of Romanticism. The first thing that we must emphasize is that there are two periods in Romanticism. I learned this very early through my study of Schelling who in his own development is the prototype of these two lines. Schleiermacher and the early Schelling belong entirely to the first part, but then the later Schelling and Kierkegaard belong to the second part. Perhaps one can say that in the twenties of the nineteenth century the transition from the first to the second half occurred. The first period of Romanticism stressed the presence of the infinite in the finite. We will see what that means for Schleiermacher's development. In the second period something else happened. The depth dimension, the dimension of the infinite, reaches not only up to the divine, but also down to the demonic. This discovery by romantic poets and philosophers is extremely important for our situation because in this second period of Romanticism we have the pre-formation of almost all the ideas of twentieth-century existentialism.

The existentialism of the twentieth century lives not only in terms of

---

[7] *Christianity or Europe,* untranslated.

Kierkegaard, but also and primarily in terms of the second period of Schelling, who had a decisive influence on Kierkegaard and many others. Here the darkness in man's understanding and in the human situation becomes manifest. The concept of the unconscious is of decisive importance for the whole following century into our time. This concept is not an invention of Freud, as I think all of you know. It is actually older than the second period of Romanticism. We have it indirectly in people like Jacob Boehme and Franz Baader and others, but most important perhaps was its rediscovery and expression in Schelling's philosophy of nature. He construed the whole philosophy of nature as a conflict between an unconscious and a conscious principle. From this point much of Schopenhauer's philosophy of the unconscious will developed, and Freud discovered this category of the unconscious in Eduard von Hartmann (1842–1906), Schopenhauer's pupil. Then Freud developed it further in his psychological and empirical methods, bringing it into the center of our attention today. But the real discovery of the unconscious, and its expression in powerful philosophical terms against the Cartesian philosophy of consciousness, were the work of the second period of Romanticism.

Now the negative element became in Romanticism a demonic element. It reveals the demonic depths of the human soul, something of which the Enlightenment was only dimly aware. After the presence of the infinite in the finite was formulated, then the presence of the demonic in the finite was expressed. The struggle between the good and the bad principles in Kant's philosophy of religion now became the struggle between the divine and the demonic. In spite of all the naturalism which runs through the whole nineteenth century, we have a tremendously intense awareness of the demonic forces in reality during this same period, often in a way that was prophetic of the radical outbreak of these forces in our century.

* * * * * * * * * *

Question: You spoke of Romanticism as the breaking-through of the infinite against the classical balance in the horizontal line. What do you mean by the horizontal line?

Answer: This question reminds me of the fact that I neglected to speak on one particular aspect of the romantic thinking, namely, the concept of irony. There is especially one man who is important for this. His name is Friedrich Schlegel (1772–1829), a friend of Schelling and a member of the Berlin circle of romanticists. Something typical of the romantic period was expressed in his attitude. That was irony. The word "irony" means that the infinite is superior to any finite concretion and drives beyond to another finite concretion. The ego of the romanticist in Schlegel's sense is free from bondage to the concrete situation. A concrete situation means both the spiritual situation, a concrete form of faith, and the situation in relation to human beings, for instance, sexual relations which played a great role in the romantic attitude, or the experience of ecstatically transcending any particular finite situation. All these things were implied in the romantic concept of irony. It must be understood in terms of the fundamental principle of the relation between the infinite and the finite. I said that in Goethe's classical period we have a balance, the desire to have a form in which the infinite is actualized in the finite, whereas Romanticism drives beyond any particular actualization of the infinite in a finite situation.

Now this romantic irony breaks through the sociological forms, for instance, the traditional Lutheran paternalism, the idea of the family, the relation of parents to children, the political stability, etc. All these forms now became questionable. Every special content in the traditions of the European countries became a matter of "yes" and "no." Irony does not mean simply an attack; there is a "yes" in it, but the "no" is predominant. It always says "no" as well to a concrete solution to life's problems.

In these avant-garde romantic groups there was an ironical transcending, a going beyond, the given forms of social existence. A consequence of this was the dissolution of traditional ethics. Wherever you find this, it has to do with this romantic ironical elevation of the individual subject beyond the given forms. But if this happens, then with the loss of concreteness a sense of emptiness sets in. Schlegel had the feeling that by undercutting the forms of life, the beliefs, the ethical ties to family, etc., a situation arises in which there is no content, no obligatory contents. This results in a feeling of emptiness with respect to the meaning of life. You see now that the central problem of the twentieth century, namely, the question of the meaning of life, the problem of emptiness in the younger generation, is not as original in our century as we are inclined to believe. It also came out very strongly in the second period of Romanticism. I can formulate the result in one sentence. Schlegel, the most refined critical representative of romantic irony, became a Roman Catholic. This means that out of the feeling of emptiness he gained the desire to subject himself to an authoritarian system in which the contents were already given to him. This is a radical situation which has been repeated again and again among the European intelligentsia, both in the nineteenth and twentieth centuries, especially after the World Wars, after the great catastrophes in Europe. Many people out of a sense of meaninglessness or lack of any contents which are normative, binding, and productive of community, etc., returned to the Roman Catholic Church as the embracing and protecting mother. This is what I meant by the breakthrough of Romanticism into the horizontal line. It is this dissatisfaction with any concrete situation, this ironical undercutting of everything, not in terms of a direct revolutionary attack, and not in order to transform reality as bourgeois society tried to do, but in terms of questioning, undercutting, etc., in terms of "yes" and "no."

We have much of this in Kierkegaard too. He was far from being a revolutionary. Politically he was conservative. But his ability to question every state of life he learned from the basic ironic attitude of Romanticism.

* * * * * * * * * *

D. The Classical Theological Synthesis: Friedrich Schleiermacher

We will devote a lecture or more to the discussion of Friedrich Schleiermacher (1768–1834). Everything we have lectured on so far is a necessary presupposition for understanding him. If you do not have this presupposition firmly in mind, but simply pick up some phrases from the textbooks, it would be better for you to forget about him altogether. Then it is meaningless; you cannot defend him and you cannot attack him either. If you attack him, it is all wrong, and if you try to defend him, you have no power to do so. You must understand an idea out of the sources from which it comes. You must know the negative implications, the struggle in which a person was involved, the enemies against which he fought, and the presuppositions which he accepted. If you do not know these things, everything becomes distorted when dealing with an important figure like Schleiermacher. That is the reason I did not begin with him in lecturing on Protestant theology in the nineteenth and twentieth centuries. He is the father of modern Protestant theology. This is his official title during the nineteenth and twentieth centuries, until neo-orthodox theology tried to disinherit him, deprive him of his fatherhood, and make out of him a distorter of theology.

Now this is a serious problem, because in this conflict over Schleiermacher which took place during and after my student years, theology was faced with having to make a basic decision, whether the attempt to construct a synthesis out of all the elements in theology we have described is the right way, or whether a return to the orthodox tradition with some modernizations is the right way. If the latter method is followed, then of course Schleiermacher has to be abolished; but if the former, then Schleiermacher remains the founder of modern Protestant theology. So you have to make a decision about this. My decision, if I may anticipate, is thoroughly on the side of Schleiermacher, but with one qualification. Neither he nor Hegel, who was even greater and who tried the same thing, really succeeded. From their failure the orthodox groups of the nineteenth century and the neo-orthodox groups of the twentieth century have drawn the conclusion that it is impossible. But I draw the conclusion that it must be tried again, and if it cannot be tried again, then we had better abandon theology as a systematic enterprise and stick to the repetition of Bible passages, or at best, limiting theology to an interpretation of the Old and New Testaments.

But if systematic theology is to have any meaning, we must try again after the breakdown of the syntheses of both Schleiermacher and Hegel. In fact, it has been tried again, both later in the nineteenth century and now in the twentieth century, and even if we have here a continuous history of failures, that is no argument against systematic theology. This is part of the human situation which implies failure wherever there is risk and courage. Besides, out of these failures more insight has come than through the unfailing repetition of orthodox phraseologies. This is not said against Barth who has written a beautiful book about the theology of the nineteenth century, and also about philosophy and music in the eighteenth century. In this book he has wonderful sections on both Mozart and Schleiermacher. He is much more fair than all his neo-orthodox pupils and opponents. So this is not directly against Barth, but indirectly it is, because he has produced those pupils who do not share his greatness and have only inherited some elements of his earlier dictatorial attitude.

1. *The Background of Schleiermacher's Thought*

Schleiermacher represents what I call the great synthesis in the theological realm. Out of this attempt proceeded the whole of later Protestant theology, including its failures. But there is only one alternative to life with failure, that is lifelessness without failure. Schleiermacher is supposed to be the victor over the Enlightenment in the theological realm. He did not deny the enlightened philosophy, but tried to overcome it on another level. For instance, he said that a true philosopher can be a true believer. He can combine piety and philosophy, and there was much piety in Schleiermacher from his early Moravian associations. He can combine piety with the courage of digging into the depths of philosophical thought. Or another word: The deepest philosophical thoughts are completely identical with my most intimate religious feeling.

This means that when we speak of him as the conqueror of the Enlightenment, we are not to think that he separated theology from philosophy, that he despised philosophy and excluded it from the theological enterprise. Enlightenment had reduced religion to the knowledge of God in terms of the arguments for his existence, or more exactly, to natural theology and to morality. The moral side was still very strong in Kant. Kant's philosophy of religion is an appendix to his philosophy of morals, and is determined by his practical philosophy. Religion is only a tool for the fulfillment of the moral imperative. Also the emphasis on knowledge in religion, the emphasis on natural theology, is an element which contributed finally to the failure of Hegel's great and embracing synthesis.

The basis of the theology of the Enlightenment was the separation of God and the world, God and man. This was foreshadowed by English deism. The deism of the early eighteenth century in England followed the philosophy of John Locke. Deism was a philosophy of religion in which the existence of God was established by natural theology, but in such a way that he would not interfere with the activities of the bourgeois society. This was a necessary prerequisite for admitting the existence of God at all. If God interfered in some way, he could not be acknowledged. So he was placed alongside the world as the creator or as the watchmaker—to use other imagery—and after the watch has been made, it runs by itself without the continual intervention of the maker. The deists left men—that means the intellectual representatives of the producing and trading bourgeois society—to their own reason, and in particular to their calculating reason. If this is done, it is possible that by means of calculating and critical reason, the Christian tradition can be criticized. This they did in a radical way, even before Rousseau and Voltaire did it in France. Deism preceded them; it also preceded Hume's positivistic attitude of placing religion as the established church and the critical mind beside each other without scarcely ever touching.

These deists were a very interesting bunch of people, bunch, I say, because that is the way they were considered in England by the representatives of the aristocratic groups which cooperated with the high bourgeoisie and which did not like this kind of critical attitude. They were considered vulgar. It is still vulgar in England to criticize religion in the name of reason. You accept it as something positively given; perhaps you describe it sociologically, but you do not criticize it. It is not noble and aristocratic to do so. The consequence of this attitude was that the deistic thinkers, Toland and Tindal *et. al.*, were considered to be operating on a lower level of reason, of reason that has run wild. And they did run wild. The title of one of the main deistic books, for instance, is *Christianity Not Mysterious* (1696) which removes all supernaturalistic and miraculous elements. They criticized the biblical literature and in a way were the inaugurators of historical criticism, producing results which anticipated much of the historical-critical theology in the modern time. Reimarus, for example, the man whose fragments Lessing published, was dependent on the English deists, and he created the revolution in thinking about the biblical sources in Germany. The rational idea of God in Voltaire and the French Enlightenment also came from the English deists. These deists were part of the background of Schleiermacher's theology. So you will find that he quite often refers to such typical theologians of the Enlightenment.

But there was another side. We spoke about this in connection with Spinoza. The fundamental principle that God exists alongside the world is shared by both the consistent rationalists and the supernaturalists. Against the deistic principle of God existing beside the world, either never interfering with it, as the rationalists said, or occasionally interfering with it, as the supernaturalists said, we now have the principle of *deus sive natura* (God or nature) coming from John Scotus Eriugena, the great theologian of the ninth century who mediated mystical theology to later medieval theology. This principle reintroduced a quite different form of thinking about religion, the real antithesis to the Enlightenment. In discussing Romanticism we called it the principle of the infinite within the finite, the principle of the mutual within-each-otherness.

Spinoza, of course, was modified. It was not the geometrical Spinoza. Those who know a little about Spinoza know that he called his main work *Ethics*,[8] but ethics *more geometrico*, ethics written by the use of the geometrical method. As a title this is in itself of greatest interest. He tried to use the all-powerful mathematical methods in discussing such subjects as metaphysics, ethics, and politics. All of this is presented in a way which makes the world into a geometrically describable whole. This was a very static concept of the world and of the divine ground of the world. He called this "the substance." In any case, this idea was founded on the principle of identity over against the principle of detachment and separation in the Enlightenment. God is here and now. He is in the depths of everything. He is not *everything*, as this much abused term "pantheism" says. Nobody has ever said that. It is absolute nonsense to say such a thing. It is better to avoid the term itself, but if it means

[8] Edited with an introduction by James Gutman (New York: Hafner Publishing Co., 1949).

anything at all, it means that the power of the divine is present in everything, that he is the ground and unity of everything, not that he is the sum of all particulars. I do not know any philosopher in the whole history of philosophy who has ever said that. Therefore the word "pantheism," which you can translate as "God is everything," is downright misleading. I would wish that those who accuse Luther or myself of pantheism would define the term before using it. And, of course, Nicholas of Cusa, Schelling, Hegel and Nietzsche, and many others, are accused of pantheism. As if everybody who is not a supernaturalistic deist or a theist—and theism as the term is used in America today is nothing else than a supernaturalistic form of deism—is a pantheist. Whenever some people hear about the principle of identity, they say this is pantheism, which supposedly holds that God is this desk.

Now, of course, Luther would say that God is nearer to everything than it is to itself. He would say this even about the desk. You cannot deny that God is the creative ground of the desk, but to say that God is the combination of all desks and in addition all pens and men—this is absolute nonsense. The principle of identity means that God is the creative ground of everything. What I dislike is the easy way in which these phrases are used: theism is so wonderful and pantheism so horrible. This makes the understanding of the whole history of theology impossible.

2. His Concept of Religion as Feeling

The principle of identity in contrast to the principle of duality gave Schleiermacher the possibility of creating a new understanding of religion. This new understanding was first expressed in his famous book, *On Religion, Speeches to Its Cultured Despisers.*[9] This book is apologetic theology of the clearest kind. "Apologize" in Greek means answering, answering before the court. For instance, if you are accused, an apology is what you say in your own defense. So apologetic theology is answering theology. I would say that every theology must somehow answer the questions in the human mind in every period, and the

[9] Translated by John Oman (New York: Frederick Ungar Publishing Co., 1955).

apologetic element should never be neglected. Historically, Christian theology was created out of the apologetic needs of the church in the Roman Empire, politically answering the attacks of the pagans during the persecution of the Christians, and theologically answering the criticisms of the philosophers. This was answering theology, and the apologists who formed a particular school of theology in the second century represent more than a particular school. They represent the answering character of all Christian theology up to Augustine.

That is what Schleiermacher also did. He answered the despisers of religion among the cultured people, as the title of his book states. Then out of this apologetic theology new systematic possibilities arose. The argument of Schleiermacher's *Speeches* is as follows: Theoretical knowledge of the deistic type—whether rationalistic or supernatural-istic—and moral obedience of the Kantian type presuppose a disjunction between subject and object. Here I am, the subject, and over there is God, the object. He is merely an object for me, and I am an object for him. There is difference, detachment, and distance. But this difference has to be overcome in the power of the principle of identity. This identity is present within us. But now Schleiermacher made a great mistake. The term he used for the experience of this identity was "feeling." Religion is not theoretical knowledge; it is not moral action; religion is feeling, feeling of absolute dependence. This was a very questionable term, because immediately the psychologists came along and interpreted Schleiermacher's concept of feeling as a psychological function.

But "feeling" in Schleiermacher should not really be understood as subjective emotion. Rather, it is the impact of the universe upon us in the depths of our being which transcends subject and object. It is obvious that he means it in this sense. Therefore, instead of speaking of feeling, he could also speak of intuition of the universe, and this intui-tion he could describe as divination. This term is derived, of course, from "divine" and means awareness of the divine immediately. It means that there is an immediate awareness of that which is beyond subject and object, of the ground of everything within us. He made the great mistake of calling this feeling. And it is regrettable that a man like Hegel should misunderstand him, in view of the fact that both he and

Schleiermacher were pupils of Schelling and both had experienced the meaning of the principle of identity. Hegel and Schleiermacher, who were both at the University of Berlin, did not like each other. Hegel did what German philosophers and theologians have done so often: they interpret the foe, the one whom they attack, *in pejorem partem,* which means according to the worst possible meaning of what a man has said.

In this country, on the other hand, I have had the impression that the moderateness of the British spirit in theoretical discussion has produced the desire to understand the one with whom we disagree *in meliorem partem,* that is, in the best possible light. For this reason it is much easier to be a member of a theological faculty in America than in Germany. But it does have some shortcomings. Occasionally one has the feeling that theological matters are not taken as seriously as in Germany. This is perhaps the single qualification I have to make, but I would say, from the point of view of *agape,* I prefer the American attitude.

At any rate, the best evidence that when Schleiermacher spoke of feeling he did not mean subjective emotion is the fact that in his systematic theology, in *The Christian Faith,* he uses the expression "feeling of unconditional dependence." In the moment that these words are combined, the feeling of unconditional dependence, the psychological realm has been transcended. For everything in our feeling, understood in the psychological sense, is conditioned. It is a continuous stream of feelings, emotions, thoughts, wills, experiences. On the other hand, the element of the unconditional, wherever it appears, is quite different from subjective feeling.

Therefore, his own phrase, feeling of unconditional dependence,[10] is a phrase which makes it quite apparent that this feeling is not the subjective feeling of the individual and that Hegel's criticism is unfair. The consequence of this in the German churches was an unfortunate misunderstanding also, for when religion was preached as feeling, the male section of the German congregations stopped going to church. When they were told that religion is not a matter of clear knowledge and moral action, but of feeling, they reacted. I can tell you this from my own participation in the nineteenth-century situation. The churches

[10] In German, *"das Gefühl der schlechthinnigen Abhängigkeit."*

became empty. Neither the youth nor the men were satisfied with feeling. They looked for sharp thought and moral significance in the sermons. When religion was reduced to feeling and weakened by sentimental hymns—instead of the great old hymns which had religious power of the presence of the divine—people lost interest in the churches.

Schleiermacher's concept of religion as feeling had unfortunate consequences in this country too. When I discuss theology with antitheological colleagues, they are very happy if they can quote somebody who puts religion into a dark corner of mere subjective feeling. Religion is not dangerous there. They can use their scientific and political words, their ethical and logical analysis, etc., without regard to religion, and the churches can be removed to one side. They do not have to be taken very seriously for they deal with the realm of subjective feelings. We do not participate in such things, but if there are people who do have such desires, let them go to church. We do not mind. But in the moment in which they are confronted by a theology which interferes very much—not from the outside but from the inside—with the scientific process, political movements, and moral principles, and which wants to show that within all of them there is an ultimate concern, as I call it, or an unconditional dependence, as Schleiermacher called it, then these people react. Then they want to put religion back into the realm of feeling. And if theology itself, or religion itself, allows them to do this, they are doing a disservice. Such a preaching of religious feeling does a great disservice to religion.

Schleiermacher did not sufficiently protect himself from the criticism that this feeling is merely, as Freud called it, an oceanic feeling, that is, the feeling of the indefinite. It is really much more than this, and Schleiermacher has another point which makes this as clear as possible. He distinguishes two forms of unconditional dependence. The one is causal, which simply means being dependent on someone as a baby is dependent on its mother, or as we are dependent on the weather to some extent; the other is teleological dependence, which means, from the Greek *telos,* directed toward an aim, namely, the moral fulfillment of the moral imperative. This is important inasmuch as he classifies Christianity as a teleological type of religion, and not the ontological type like the mystical religions of Asia. Teleological dependence has the unconditional character of the moral imperative. Now both elements are present, but according to Schleiermacher the dominant element in Western religion is the teleological-moral element. Here the Kantian influence is quite visible, and thus it is even more unfair to say that Schleiermacher's "feeling" is indefinite. It is very definite in the moral sense; it is also definite in the mystical sense. It is not subjective oceanic feeling.

This is the essence of what is called religious experience, the presence of something unconditional beyond the knowing and acting of which we are aware. Of course, it also has an emotional element in it as everything does when a total person is involved, but this emotional element does not define the character of religion.

On this new basis Schleiermacher proposed that the discussion between the Enlightenment and Orthodoxy, between rationalism and supernaturalism, which was the modified form of Orthodoxy, could come to an end. Both sides are wrong on the basis of this new principle. Supernaturalism is wrong. Things like miraculous interventions of God, special inspirations and revelations are beneath the level of real religious experience. Those are objective events which can be looked at from the outside concerning the existence or nonexistence of which one can debate, but religion itself is immediacy, an immediate relation to the divine. Such external, objective events do not add anything to this fundamental experience of unconditional dependence or divination of the divine in the universe.

Consequently, the authorities which guarantee such supernatural interferences are also unnecessary. Every authority in religion, whether biblical or ecclesiastical, which makes such statements about interferences is removed. This liberates modern science from religious interferences. The supernaturalistic statement about the suspension of the laws of nature for the sake of miracles collapses completely.

But other things also collapse on this basis. The idea of an existing person called "God" and the idea of a continuation of life after the death of a conscious person, or the idea of immortality, collapse as well. This whole supernaturalistic heritage is denied by Schleiermacher in his *Speeches*. The way in which he restates the essence of this heritage in *The Christian Faith* is a question to which we will return later.

The first radical and fundamental apologetic statement made by

Schleiermacher is the following. The unity with God, participation in him, is not a matter of immortal life after death; it is not a matter of accepting a heavenly lawgiver; instead it is a matter of present participation in eternal life. This is decisive. Here he follows the fourth Gospel. The classical German philosophers called this the true Gospel, not because they thought this Gospel contained, historically speaking, reliable reports about Jesus—very soon they learned that this was not the case at all—but because the Gospel of John came closest to expressing principles which could overcome the conflict between rationalism and supernaturalism. This idea that eternal life is here and now, and not a continuation of life after death, is one of the main points they stressed. It is participation in eternity before time, in time, and after time, and that means also beyond time.

This same criticism turned against all mediators between God and man. The principle of identity and all mysticism were always very dangerous for the hierarchical systems, for priestly mediation between God and man. This was the case both in Catholicism and Protestantism. The Protestant Churches were just as hostile as the Roman Church was to the mystical groups, to the Quakers, for example, in whom the principle of identity was affirmed in some way. They were suspicious of mysticism because it offered men the possibility of immediate unity with the divine apart from the mediation of the church. So Schleiermacher reacted against priests and authorities; they were not necessary, because everybody is called to become a priest and to be filled with the divine Spirit. From this point of view you can understand the resistance of the church against all spirit-movements, against the movements in which the individual is immediate to God and driven by the Spirit himself. You can also understand the reason for the subjection of the Spirit, wherever it appears, to the letter of the Bible. The Reformers who originally fought against the Roman Church in the power of the Spirit soon had great difficulties of their own in their struggle against the spirit-movements of the Reformation period. It is a good thing there were countries like Great Britain, the Netherlands, and America to which these representatives could flee from the severe persecutions of both the Roman and Reformation Churches.

Instead of seeing religion as something mediated by the functions of the church, Schleiermacher saw it as the musical accompaniment of the special melodies of every life. In this poetic way he expresses the presence of the religious concern, the ultimate concern, in every moment of life. It is, one may say, the typical idealistic anticipation of eternal life in which there is certainly no religion but in which God is present in every moment. He expresses the ideal which in the New Testament is spoken of as "praying without ceasing." If this is taken literally, it is nonsense. But if it is taken as it is meant, it makes a lot of sense. It means considering every moment of our secular life as filled with the divine presence, not pushing the presence into a Sunday service and otherwise forgetting it.

In order to experience the presence of the divine in the universe as Pythagoras did when he spoke of the harmony of the spheres in musical terms, each of which, while making a different tone, contributes symphonically to the harmony of the cosmos, we must first find that presence in ourselves. Humanity, of which each individual is a special and unique mirror, is the key to the universe. Without having the universe in ourselves we would never understand it. The center of the universe and of ourselves is divine, and with the presence of the infinite in ourselves we can *re*-cognize (I purposely underline the first syllable) in the universe the infinite which is within us. And what is the key to this in ourselves? He says it is love, but not love in the sense of *agape*, the Christian concept of love, but love in the Platonic sense of *eros*. Eros is the love which unites us with the good and the true and the beautiful and which drives us beyond the finite into the infinite.

Every period of human history expresses this encounter between the infinite in ourselves and in the whole universe in different images. The uniqueness of every individual and every period makes it necessary that there be many religions. The manifoldness of religions and the differences in the same religious tradition during its different periods in history are basically the result of the infinite mirroring itself in ourselves and in the universe in always different ways. So the romantic spirit of Schleiermacher caused him to emphasize the concreteness of the historical religions. This was a tremendous step beyond the enlightened idea of natural religion which reduced all religions to three principles: God, freedom, and immortality. The deistic views, whether of the rationalistic or supernaturalistic types, were overcome through the rediscovery of the richness, concreteness, and fullness of the particular religions. In this way Schleiermacher conquered by his principle of the immanence of the infinite in the finite the naturalistic, rationalistic, and supernaturalistic ways of abstracting from the concrete religions some principle which is supposed to be valid for all religions and which obliterates everything concrete in them.

Without the valuation of individuality in the Renaissance and without the element of ecstatic intuition in Romanticism, all this would not have been possible. This is what enabled religious thought to find its way back to the positive religions. The whole Enlightenment was an extinction of the meaningfulness of the concrete or positive religion. Only abstract religious principles were left. On the basis of this rediscovery of the concrete, positive religions—positive means "historically given"—Schleiermacher proceeded further to emphasize a positive Christianity.

Schleiermacher's *Speeches on Religion* (1799) were so successful that when the third edition (1821) was issued, he wrote in his introduction that instead of having to defend himself any more against the enlightened despisers of religion, he now had to fend off the orthodox fanatics who in the name of his defense of Christianity returned to the pre-Enlightenment orthodox tradition, and tried to extinguish the whole development on which Schleiermacher had based his work.

3. *His Positivistic Definition of Theology*

Romanticism generally speaking was the bridge to an appreciation of the positively given. This was quite different from the English type of positivism. David Hume was a positivist out of empirical scientific considerations, out of a critical epistemology in which he thought that we have only given data or sense impressions. In continental Europe positivism was a child of Romanticism which valued the historically and traditionally given. When Schleiermacher wrote his book, *The Christian Faith*, it is significant that he called it *Glaubenslehre* (the doctrine of faith). He did not call it "doctrine of God" which is what "theology" means. He did not dare to give it such a title, for what is positively given is the Christian faith as such. That is a given reality. You can find it in Zinzendorf's Moravian groups of piety to which he belonged for a period in his life, and you can find it in the churches everywhere. Thus systematic theology is the description of the faith as it is present in the Christian churches. That is a positivist foundation of theology. You do not first have to decide about the truths or untruths of religion in general or of Christianity in particular. You find Christianity given as an empirical fact in history, and then you have to describe the meaning of the symbols within it.

Theology is then positive knowledge of a historical reality. Schleiermacher made a very sharp distinction between this empirical positive theology and the so-called rational theology of the Enlightenment. And he goes even further. He says that Christian theology is the totality of those theoretical insights and practical rules without the possession and use of which no church government is possible. Now this definition is something unheard of in the development of theology. It is the clear transition from all kinds of rational theology to positive theology. In this definition the question of truth is completely absent. It is a highly positivistic conception of theology. I would call it a positivistic description of some group which you find in history, whose existence you cannot deny. You can describe the ideas which are important in it and the rules which are accepted. Then you can educate young theologians who are called to be leaders in the church in the knowledge of those things which they are to practice later on. This is a positivism in which the question of truth is left out.

This positivistic character of theology becomes even more pronounced in the following idea. He distinguished philosophical, historical, and practical theology even as we do today, but with one difference. The difference is that dogmatics and ethics belong to historical theology, not to philosophical theology. They belong to historical theology because they are the systematic development of the doctrine which exists in the church or in a particular denomination at a given time. You cannot be more positivistic than that. This doctrine exists today, and the historian has only to describe it. This he calls systematic theology. This is a most conspicuous expression of positivism, and I can add that although it has not survived, it has been very influential. Now we have both philosophical theology and systematic theology, and both are distinguished from historical and practical theology. We have these four, or else we may take philosophical theology into systematic theology.

* * * * * * * * * *

Question: Granted that by feeling Schleiermacher did not mean subjective emotion, nevertheless, his *Speeches* are not unemotional in character, and having emotion is an undeniable part of being human. What is the role of the emotions in the religious life for you and Schleiermacher?

Answer: This is a very valid question in view of the ambiguity of the term "feeling" in Schleiermacher and much theology later on. Nevertheless, it is obvious that Schleiermacher is here in the same situation as we all are. Nobody can exclude the element of feeling in any experience in which the total personality is involved, and in religion this is perhaps more true than in any other realm. It is certainly true that the response of our whole being in immediacy—which might be the right definition of feeling—can be seen in an earnest prayer or in the worship service of a community, or in listening to the prophetic word. This emotional element is there. Let us take an example from the arts. You are deeply grasped by a painting at which you are looking while visiting an art gallery; you are taken into it; you live in it and your emotions are strongly awakened. But if someone should say that your aesthetic experience is only an emotion, you would answer that it is more than that. If it were only emotion, it would not have this definite character which is given through this kind of painting. I recognize, in this moment in which I am emotionally moved, a dimension of reality of which otherwise I would never be aware, and a dimension in myself would never be opened up except through participation in the painting.

I would say the same thing about music. Music is often said to be completely in the realm of feeling. This is true, but it is a very special kind of feeling which is related to the particular musical figures and forms which make music a work of art. This also reveals to you a dimension of being, including your being, which would otherwise not be revealed if there were no musical impact on you. So we can say that although the emotional element is always present in experience of whatever kind, you cannot say that a certain experience is only emotion. Take the experience of love. You cannot say that love *is* emotion. Love has an element of emotion in it and very much so, but it is not an emotion. It is a reunion, as I would call it, of separated entities that belong to each other eternally. This experience cannot be identified with the personal reaction which we call feeling.

What Schleiermacher calls unconditional dependence in religion is certainly connected with a strong element of feeling. This feeling has been described by Rudolf Otto (1869–1937) in his *The Idea of the Holy*[11] as a feeling of being both fascinated and overwrought at the same time. These contrasting feelings are present. But they do not constitute the religious act as such. The appearing of the unconditional to you in the religious act is what constitutes the religious act. Usually I call it the unconditional concern in your very existence. This is a concern also of your mind; you ask about the truth of it; it is a concern of your will; you must do something if you experience it. It changes your whole existence. All these dimensions are implied. If it were only a feeling, it would be a detached aesthetic pleasure, and that would be all. Sometimes Schleiermacher has been misunderstood in this way, but that is not the real Schleiermacher.

In answering the question about Schleiermacher, I also answered the question about my own thinking, because I believe that his "unconditional dependence" is only a slightly narrower way of saying "unconditional concern." Unconditional concern does not emphasize the element of dependence in the way Schleiermacher does. However, it also tries to go beyond the subject-object scheme. It has the same basic motives and is an expression of a total experience, the experience of the holy. There is not a dogmatic difference, but chiefly a difference of connotation, between ultimate concern and feeling of absolute dependence.

* * * * * * * * *

In our last discussion about Schleiermacher we dealt with his positivistic conception of Christian theology. We pointed out the astonishing fact that he subsumed dogmatics and ethics under historical theology

[11] Translated by J. W. Harvey (New York: Oxford University Press, 1923).

because they are the systematic development of the doctrine as it exists in a particular church at a particular time. This we call positivism; it is theology as a description of the empirically given reality of the Christian religion. But if this were all, then Schleiermacher would not have been a systematic theologian; he would have been a church historian dealing with the present conditions of the church.

But this positivistic feature is counterbalanced—in a logically unclear way—by the fact that Schleiermacher begins with a general concept of religious community as it is manifested universally in the history of humanity. From this he derives a concept of the essence of religion. This is no longer positivism. It is a philosophical analysis of the essence of a thing. This presupposes constructive judgment about what is essential and what is not. His concept of the feeling of unconditional dependence is certainly a concept of a universal and philosophical type. He subjects Christianity to a concept of religion which at least by intent was not derived from Christianity but from the whole panorama of the world's religions. Actually, of course, the derivation which a philosopher of religion makes is always largely determined by the door through which he enters this panorama of religious reality in the world. In his case it is pietistic Christianity. In every philosophical concept of religion we can observe the traces of this entry way, namely, the philosopher's own religion. Nobody can abstract this subjective element from his definition, for in order to derive a concept from reality, one must be able to participate in the life of this reality. For example, one cannot develop a concept of the arts without being able to experience works of art.

The consequence of this is that Christianity becomes a religion among the religions. There are other religions besides Christianity. Usually, then, on this basis Christianity is described by Christian theologians as the highest, the truest, the most fulfilling of all religions. This is a very important point which has been to the fore in theological discussions during the last fifty years because of the Barthian challenge. When we look back into the history of Protestantism we find a book by Zwingli, the Swiss reformer, entitled *De vera et falsa religione*[12] in which he describes Christianity as the true religion over against the false religions which have distorted the divine revelation (cf. Romans 1). But Paul in

[12] Huldreich Zwingli, *On the True and False Religion*.

Romans did not speak of the Christian religion. He spoke of Christ. He would not say that the Christian religion is the decisive thing. It would be well to read Paul's letters to see how he attacked the Christian religion as it existed in his time. He attacked the Jewish-Christian (legalism) as well as the Gnostic distortions (lawlessness). This means that while Paul criticized all religions, he does not exempt Christianity from criticism. He does not put Christianity against the other religions. Rather, he puts Christ against every religion, even against the actual Christian religion as this was expressed in the congregations which he founded.

Now in Zwingli, also in the Reformers in general and in most orthodox theology, we find that this distinction between Christ and Christianity is not clearly carried out. If Christianity is put on the top, then one is bound to ask whether it does not stand under the same judgment as all other religions, in view of its own distortions. If we look at the history of idolatry, we will find that much of it has occurred in the name of Christianity. Actually, the absoluteness of Christianity, as Troeltsch called it, is not the absoluteness of the Christian religion, but of the Christ over against all religion. The superiority of Christianity lies in its witnessing against itself and all other religions in the name of the Christ. Barth has seen this difficulty, and for this reason he tends to avoid the concept of religion and does not want to apply it to Christianity. But if this is done, it is another way of elevating the Christian religion, and not only the Christ above the other religions. I doubt that Barth really intends to do that.

However that may be, the concept of religion is needed because there is the empirical religious reality; there is a great similarity in all the actual religions. If you reject the word "religion," you must simply find another one in naming the given religious reality, the word "piety" or something like that. The term "religion" is, however, unavoidable. I can tell you of my own experience. In the early twenties I wrote an article with the title "The Conquest of the Concept of Religion in the Philosophy of Religion."[13] This was very much in line with Barth's thinking, but even at that time I was aware that this can be done only if Chris-

[13] "Die Überwindung des Religionsbegriffs in der Religionsphilosophie," *Kant-Studien*. Berlin, XXVII, No. 3/4, 1922, 446–469.

tianity also is conquered as a religion in the philosophy of religion, and if there is something in religion which stands against religion. If this is not seen there is no real conquest. But the impact of Barth on Germany was so great that when I returned to Germany in 1948, I was immediately criticized by my friends for still using the word "religion." It had been, so to speak, eradicated from the theological discussion in Germany.

This situation has changed but there is still a resentment against the concept. I believe that this resentment is a self-deception, for then other terms are only substituted for the term "religion." What we need, however, is to be aware of the fact that the method of Schleiermacher, Troeltsch, Harnack, and others, is not sufficient, namely, first defining Christianity as a religion, and then saying it is the highest or absolute religion. What the Barthians do is equally wrong, to say that Christianity is a revealed religion over against the others which are merely human attempts to come to God and are not based on revelation at all.

If we are to try to conquer the concept of religion which seems to relativize Christianity, we have to do it by putting the Christ against every religion, or God as manifesting his judgment in the cross against every religion, but not by elevating Christianity as a particular religion.

Now we have to deal with Schleiermacher's understanding of the essence of religion. In all histories of theology he is regarded as the conqueror of the Enlightenment distortion of religion, where it was intellectualized and moralized. The negative side of Schleiermacher's definition of religion was that it is not essentially a thinking and an acting. The positive side is that religion is the feeling of unconditional dependence, the immediate consciousness of the unconditional in one's self, the immediate existential relation prior to the act of reflection, the immediacy of the awareness of the unconditional in our consciousness. All these terms point to the same reality of religious experience. Knowledge and action are consequences. Religious knowledge and religious action follow from this immediate awareness, but they are not the essence of religion. The immediate awareness of unconditional dependence transcends the mixed feelings of partial freedom and partial dependence which we have in our relation to the world. In all our relations to the world and to others there is this mixed feeling of freedom and dependence. If we are vitally powerful, we feel very much free in dealing with reality; if this feeling of freedom is reduced, then we feel our dependence on others and on all kinds of finite things. Now this whole realm of the experience of the finite is transcended in the awareness of the unconditional. If we speak of God, we can only say that this is the name for the whence of our unconditional dependence. Then God is not conceived of as an objectively given reality as another galaxy of stars. He transcends every finite relation and he is the ground of all of them. They are all unconditionally dependent on him.

If God were an object besides other objects, we could act upon him in terms of knowing and acting. This would mean that God could be proved. Such proofs could be verified and God could be moved by our activity. But God is not an object besides other objects. He is present in our immediate consciousness and all that we say about him are expressions of this immediacy. Schleiermacher is afraid that the term "person" as applied to God would make him an object subject to our cognitive and active dealings. So he uses the term "spirituality" instead of "personality." Of course, in spirituality the personal element is implied. There is no spirit which is not at the same time the bearer of the person. But the concept of spirituality is better suited than personality in removing the danger of an objectifying distortion of the idea of God.

4. His Interpretation of Christianity

That is the philosophical concept of religion which underlies Schleiermacher's whole description of Christianity. In the long run this proved to be stronger than the positivistic element, that is, the mere acceptance of Christianity as an empirical reality to be described. Now we come to a section in his thought where he breaks through the positivistic element. This is his christology. When he explains why he thinks Christianity is the highest manifestation of the essence of religion, he says it is because Christianity has two characteristics which distinguish it from other religions. The first is what he calls ethical monotheism. This means that the unconditional dependence in religion is not primarily a physical dependence thought of in materialistic terms. It is not a mechanical dependence as in some of the distortions of the idea of predestination in Calvinist theology in which the religious symbol of predestination is confused with mechanical causality. This is not Schleiermacher's idea, although his idea of dependence has been clearly traced to Calvinistic influences. Christianity is not a religion in which the relation to God is that of physical or mechanical dependence, but is that of teleological dependence, a dependence on God as the giver of the law and showing the goal toward which we have to go. This teleological dependence means that God is the whence of our unconditional moral imperative. Here you see clearly the Kantian element in him. It is not as in Schelling's philosophy of nature where men are dependent on the ultimate through nature.

The other thing which makes Christianity the highest religion is that everything is related to the salvation by Jesus of Nazareth. Salvation has a very definite meaning for him. It is the transformation of a limited, inhibited, or distorted religious consciousness into a fully developed religious consciousness. That person is saved who has a fully developed religious consciousness. He is in continuous conscious communion with God. This is salvation. All eschatological symbolism is removed or must be reinterpreted. This work of salvation, this liberation of our religious consciousness from inhibition, limitation, and distortion, is done by Christ, who himself has the fully developed religious consciousness. Since he does not need salvation, he can become the Savior.

This does not mean that Jesus is a mere example for man. Rather, he is the *Urbild*, the archetype, the original image, the representative of what man essentially is in unity with God. Here we have surprisingly high christological statements in Schleiermacher when we consider the universal concept of religion from which he started. This was possible because his own personal piety and his positivistic affirmation of Christianity came to fulfillment. It is interesting that Emil Brunner in his book on Schleiermacher[14] says that Schleiermacher's christological thinking is an interlude in his dogmatics; it does not fit into the whole system. It is a case of his piety breaking through his systematic principles. I do not think this is true because the positivistic element in Schleiermacher is genuine. It is one of the ways of escaping the

[14] *Die Mystik und das Wort. Der Gegensatz zwischen moderner Religionsauffassung und christlichem Glauben* (Tübingen: J. C. B. Mohr, 1924).

problems of philosophy of religion which, on the other hand, are inescapable. Brunner is right only insofar as one can say generally of all Schleiermacher's thinking that there is a tension between the purely philosophical and the more positivistic approaches to Christianity. All the later schools had the same difficulty. The whole Ritschlian school, which was dependent on Schleiermacher, was strongly positivistic and biblical, on the one hand, and yet dependent on Kant's epistemology, on the Kantian philosophy of religion, on the other hand.

Without going into details concerning the individual doctrines of Schleiermacher, we can say a few words about the method which permeated the whole system. His theological method was to describe the content of the religious consciousness of the Christian as it is determined by the appearance of the Christ. Systematic theology or the system of doctrine is rational insofar as it creates a consistent system of thoughts which do not contradict each other, but are interdependent. He does this with all the means of refined theological dialectics. When he deals with special problems, such as Bible, Christ, sin, salvation, atonement, or whatever it may be, he first discusses the two opposing views, the one which is given in the classical tradition which he knew as well as a Protestant theologian must know it, and the other which is the Enlightenment criticism of seventeenth-century Orthodoxy. Then he tries to find a solution to the problem by looking at the Christian consciousness, which is of course determined by his own concept of religion.

The methodologically decisive thing is that theological propositions about God or the world or man are derived from man's existential participation in the ultimate, that is, from man's religious consciousness. These are valid statements, but not in the sense that everybody could make such statements about the latest discovery in physics or astronomy. The form of the statements is quite different. The difference in form arises from the fact of existential participation, as we would say today. This means that the qualities or characteristics which we attribute to God are expressions of our relation to him. As a follower of Calvin, he said that we cannot say anything about the *essentia dei,* God in his true essence. We can say something only on the basis of his relation to us which is manifest through revelatory experiences. This has implications for the doctrine of the trinity. A doctrine of an objective trinity as a transcendent object is impossible. The doctrine of the trinity is the fullest expression of man's relation to God. Each of the *personae—you* should not say *persons* because that means something else—is a representation of a certain way in which God is related to man and the world. Only in this way do the *personae* make any sense. Therefore he places the trinitarian symbols at the end of the whole system. The doctrine of the trinity stands at the end as the completed doctrine of God, after all particular relations—such as those dealing with sin and forgiveness, creation and death and eternal life, the presence of the Spirit in the church and in the individual Christian, etc.—have been positively described from the religious consciousness of Christians. After this has been done, the lines can be drawn up to the divine as such, which yields to us trinitarian statements.

I follow the same method as Schleiermacher, but with one difference. I have two stages in drawing these trinitarian lines to God. The first is from the doctrine of the living God. The living God is always the trinitarian God, even before christology is possible, before the Christ has appeared. He who speaks of the living God is trinitarian even though he calls himself unitarian. In discussions with Unitarian students and colleagues at Harvard, I did not start with christology, but with the symbol of the living God. He is not a dead oneness in himself, a dead identity, but he goes out and returns. This defines the process of life everywhere. If we apply this symbolically to God, we are involved in trinitarian thinking. The numbers two or three or four—all of them appear in the history of Christian theology—are not decisive. But the movement of the divine, going out and returning to himself—this is decisive if we speak of a living God.

Now Schleiermacher did not use this possibility. He saw trinity only in relation to christology. But I believe that if one does not see it in connection with the idea of a living God, then the trinitarian symbolism, because it would be applied too late, becomes almost impossible to use. In being bound to the single event it easily becomes superstitious; in being related only to the historical Jesus it becomes only something to be observed.

I will give you an example of why this is significant. If we today imagine the possibility of spiritual beings existing in other parts of the universe, the question arises as to the meaning of Christ for them. Then people who have an exclusively christologically oriented conception of the trinity would say that we must bring them the message of Jesus of Nazareth as the Christ. This seems to me absurd. Instead, I would say that the divine Logos, the eternal Logos, the principle of God going out and manifesting himself, appears wherever there are spiritual beings, appears in their history as he has appeared in the center of human history. But what appears precedes human history. "Before Abraham was, I am."[15] This means that the universal Logos, the principle of the divine self-manifestation, is present in Jesus of Nazareth.

In spite of this limited criticism of Schleiermacher, I would say that the fundamental methodological notion that the trinity is not an *a priori* speculation about God is valid. The experience of the living God and the experience of the saving God both give rise to the trinitarian idea. This idea follows from the revelatory experience and cannot precede it. My main criticism of the Barthian method in his *Church Dogmatics*[16] is that he jumps, so to speak, directly into the doctrine of the trinity without starting from the human question. Here I am on the side of Schleiermacher in spite of my limited criticism.

Another point that must be mentioned is Schleiermacher's doctrine of sin. This was very influential. In this he followed the general trend of German classical philosophy and certainly of the Enlightenment. According to this trend, sin is a shortcoming. It is not a "no" but a "not yet." Sin arises because of the discrepancy between the great speed of the evolutionary process in the biological development of mankind and the slower pace of moral and spiritual development of man. The biological development is far ahead of man's spiritual development. Sin is the "not yet" of man's spiritual development within an already fully developed bodily organism. The distance or the gap between these two processes is what we call sin. This condition is universal. It is the state of mankind universally. The Christ is then an anticipation of a state which lies ahead for all mankind. This makes sin in some way necessary and unavoidable. The idea of the fall is swallowed up by the idea of the

15 John 8:58.
16 Karl Barth, *Church Dogmatics*, Vol. I, Pts. 1 and 2 (New York: Charles Scribner's Sons, 1936).

evolutionary necessity of estrangement or sin. At this point later theologians went back instead to Kant's idea of the original transcendent fall and the existentialists developed this on the basis of Schelling's doctrine of freedom.

In many later developments, however, Schleiermacher's relativization of sin was predominant. I said that for Schleiermacher salvation is the presence of God in man, in man's consciousness, which is determined by the divine presence in all its relativities. Here we see the mystical background in Schleiermacher's philosophy, mystical not in the sense of "foggy" but in the sense of the presence of the infinite within the finite. So the Savior takes the faithful, those who belong to him and participate in him, into the strength of his consciousness of God. And the church is the community in which this consciousness of God is the determining power. However relative it is, however distorted and limited, the church has this as its principle. This brings us to the end of our discussion of Schleiermacher's theology. Of course, it would be very interesting to go point by point into his various doctrines, but then this would be a course on Schleiermacher and not on the history of Protestant theology.

E. The Universal Synthesis: Georg W. F. Hegel

I must now come to the man who produced the great synthesis in philosophical terms. Schleiermacher is the great synthesis in theological terms. His colleague, Hegel, at the University of Berlin in the beginning of the nineteenth century, was the fulfillment of the synthesis in the philosophical realm. Both of these in their appearance and in their effects were immediately supraprovincial. Of course, their roots were in the German development, but the effects they had on others transcended the German limits and provincialisms. Schleiermacher's influence on all Protestant theology is also visible in this country, and Hegel's influence extended not only into religion but into the political transformation of the world in the twentieth century; even the rise of existentialism against him bears the imprint of his thinking. So we can say that his great synthesis is the turning point for many of the actual problems of today, including world revolution and the East-West conflict. Neither Marx, nor Nietzsche, nor Kierkegaard, nor existentialism, nor the revolutionary movements, are understandable apart from seeing their direct or indirect dependence on Hegel. Even those who opposed him used his categories in their attacks on him. So Hegel is in some sense the center and the turning point, not of an inner-philosophical school or an inner-theological way of thinking about religion, but of a world-historical movement which has directly or indirectly influenced our whole century.

1. The Greatness and the Tragic Hybris of Hegel's System

When we speak of Hegel's great synthesis in the realm of philosophy, this can be understood in two ways: first, the great synthesis of the cultural elements present in Western culture, and secondly, the synthesis of the conflicting polarities present in religious thought. I will describe him in both ways.

Before I can do that, however, the distorted image of Hegel must be removed. It would be far better for you to know nothing of Hegel than simply to know the usual caricature. If you have only this image of the noisy mill whose wheels are turning all the time—thesis, antithesis, synthesis—then it would be better not to know anything about him. When I gave my first lecture course in Frankfurt on Hegel, I spent the whole academic year, four hours a week, and got through only half of the material. At that time the early fragments of Hegel were discovered.[17] These fragments offer the best help in purging our minds of the distorted image of Hegel. In Frankfurt at that time I tried to show my students that every great philosophy combines two elements. The one is its vitality, its lifeblood, its inner character; the other is the emergency situation out of which the philosophy grows. No great philosopher simply sat behind his desk, and said, "Let me now philosophize a bit between breakfast and lunch time." All philosophy has been a terrible struggle between divine and demonic forces, skepticism and faith, the possibility of affirming and of negating life. The question of

[17] G. W. F. Hegel, *Early Theological Writings*, translated by T. M. Knox, with an introduction, and fragments, translated by Richard Kroner (Chicago: University of Chicago Press, 1948).

the mystery of existence stands behind all who became creative philosophers and were not merely analysts or historians of philosophy.

In Hegel's fragments one thing stands out quite clearly, namely, that religion and politics formed the lifeblood of Hegel's thinking. It was religion of a supernatural kind in conflict with rationalism which he found disrupting the souls of students of theology and philosophy while he was a seminary student living in the *Stift* in Tübingen, Württemberg. Besides religion there was the political situation determined by the French Revolution, on the one hand, and the tyranny of the German princes, on the other hand. And across the Channel there were the democratic beginnings of the British constitution.

These two things, religion and politics, came together very early in Hegel's philosophy of life. If you want to know what "philosophy of life" means in continental terminology—*Lebensphilosophie* in German can hardly be translated into English—you can read Hegel's fragments. Here among others you have a fragment on love which offers one of the deepest insights into the dynamics of the love relationship, not only on the human level, but in all living reality.

That is the one side in Hegel's thinking. But there was another element in Hegel as in every philosopher, namely, the method which became more and more predominant. His work on logic was in itself great, but its consequence was that gradually the earlier "philosophy of life" was covered over by a logical mechanism of thesis, antithesis, synthesis. It is a great tragedy in the history of philosophy that this logical element became the decisive thing. For instance, in his encyclopedia we have the impression of a mill which always makes the same noise and goes through the same rhythm so that if a concept goes into the mill you know ahead of time what will come out of it. This is a strong element, and a disagreeable one, in Hegel. And I do not wish to hide it. But it is also fair to see what is the lifeblood and its consequences in a man's thinking. For Hegel this was in the religious and political realms.

After these introductory words we will discuss the different periods which he wanted to unite in a great synthesis. Coming from the Enlightenment he witnessed the great struggle between the tradition of Orthodox Protestantism and the rationalistic criticism of it. So he had the problem of uniting traditional Christianity and the Enlightenment. But this was by no means all. He was also living in the period which we called the classical period. We spoke about it in connection with Goethe. It was a direct attempt to return to classical Greece both in the arts and in philosophy, and then indirectly in theology. This element of classicism was very strong in the early writings of Hegel when he described, for example, the ideal political system. He always described the ideal of the Greek *polis*, the city-state, in which religion and culture were united and in which the individual participated democratically in the whole life. So this had to be put into the right place in the great synthesis.

Then he went to the romantic period. He himself was strongly romantic in the beginning and dependent on Schelling. But because of his sober mind, he very soon separated himself from many of the emotional elements of Romanticism and even criticized them in his greatest published work, *The Phenomenology of Mind*.[18] This title is an unfortunate translation of *Die Phänomenologie des Geistes*, for *Geist* in German means "spirit." There we see another element being introduced, namely, the cause of the French Revolution. The students of the theological school in Tübingen participated in the French Revolution to the great anger of the ruling prince of Württemberg. Yet, they did not become revolutionaries because that is not the German temperament. Only in spirit did they become revolutionary, but not in a political way. Later on the revolutionaries came from another world, but using Hegelian categories.

If you look at all of these elements, you see how much is involved: Christian tradition, classical Greece, the Enlightenment, the movement of Romanticism. All these things had to be united into a universal synthesis. Nobody has attempted this so radically and with such a power of synthesis as Hegel. Although Kant was a more profound thinker in his critical way—this is a difficult judgment to make, but still possible— than Hegel, it was Hegel who more than Kant created an epoch in the history of philosophy, in the history of religion, and in politics.

Therefore, the breakdown of this great synthesis was a historic event. It was not simply an inner struggle between philosophical schools. This

18 Translated by J. B. Baillie (New York: The Macmillan Company, 1910).

happens all the time, but sometimes such struggles can become of world-historical importance, as did the theological controversies of the fourth and fifth centuries. The events which surround the rise and fall of Hegel's system transcend the situation of a conflict between schools. This is the greatness of Hegel's system, but often greatness and *hybris* go together. *Hybris* is a Greek word which is often translated as pride. But it should not be so translated because pride is a particular moral or antimoral attitude. It is possible to be without pride and full of *hybris*, extremely humble but in this humility remain in a state of *hybris*. The best translation is "self-elevation toward the realm of the divine." That is what it means in Greek tragedy. The great heroes are those who fall into *hybris*, who try to elevate themselves to the life of the gods, and who then are cast down by the tragic reaction of the divine powers.

This is the case with Hegel's system. It does not have primarily to do with the personal character of Hegel. There are others who have much more of this *hybris*, Schelling, for instance. It is in his fundamental idea itself in which the *hybris* is expressed, the idea that world history can possibly come to an end with one's own existence. The reason that Hegel was attacked from all sides and removed from the throne of providence on which he had placed himself was that the finished system cut off all openness to the future. Only God is on that throne and only God is able both to understand the past and to create the future. When Hegel tried to do both, then he was in the state of *hybris*, and this *hybris* was followed by the tragedy of his system.

Here you see that the history of philosophy is more than the history of some interesting ideas which people find to contradict in each other. The history of philosophy is the history of man's self-interpretation, and any such self-interpretation stands not only under the judgment of logic but also under the judgment of the meaning of existence as a whole. This is the responsibility of thinking and at the same time its greatness.

2. *The Synthesis of God and Man (Mind and Person)*

The synthesis of the divine and the human in Hegel's system is expressed in the doctrine of the absolute and the relative mind or *Geist*. Mind is a poor translation of *Geist*, but the word "spirit" is also full of difficulties. The word "spirit" has been reserved for religion and attributed to God and divine things alone. Man has been deprived of spirit, and has been divided into mind and body. This mutilation of the doctrine of man has had tremendous practical and theoretical consequences, making almost impossible a sound doctrine of man. We have psychology, we have biology, but we have no doctrine of man. And generally anthropology is—at least when I came to this country—a doctrine about the bones which have been left by the human race on the surface of the earth. Now we have in addition cultural anthropology. But this does not say anything about the essence of man, but only about the stages through which our former ancestors passed. It is also characterized by an especially disagreeable dogmatism regarding the concept of culture itself. Everything which man has created is explained in terms of a particular given culture. Since man is only a product of his culture, we cannot say anything about man universally nor anything about what distinguishes men from animals. But no cultural anthropologist tells you who has produced the culture, why cultures have changed, and what has happened in the context of the culture. So on the doctrine of man as man we are faced with special difficulties today.

Perhaps one of the ways in which we can try to overcome such difficulties is by reintroducing the concept of spirit, with a small "s" and not use this term for God alone with a capital "S." For if you cannot experience what spirit is in yourself, you cannot apply it symbolically or analogically to God either. When we have a doctrine of man as spirit, we must define spirit as the unity of mind and power, the unity of creativity—which makes human culture possible—and vitality—which is the life-power of man. Spirit is a dynamic concept. If you take away the power element of spirit, as you do by using only the concept of mind, what is left is simply intellectual movement. The intellectualization of the mental side of man results in placing the emotional element outside the intellect, in depriving us of what we find in Plato's doctrine of *eros,* namely, the unity of the emotional, the volitional, and the intellectual elements in the person as a whole; it results also in a loss of what is meant in the Christian concept of *gnosis,* as Paul used it, which means both knowledge and union. Knowing God means a union of man's spirit with the divine Spirit. It does not mean *episteme,* that is, detached scientific knowledge, inquiry into the structure of finite things. *Gnosis* always means union, and if the word were not so distorted today, we could say, mystical union, as Protestant Orthodoxy was still able to do. Mysticism means the experience of the union of the divine and the human.

So although Hegel's phenomenology of *Geist* has been translated as phenomenology of *mind*, we will, despite the terminological difficulties, translate *Geist* as *spirit*. For Hegel God is absolute spirit and man is relative spirit; or God is infinite spirit and man is finite spirit. To say that God is Spirit means that he is creative power, not creative power in a naturalistic sense of a mere objective process, but creative power united with mind, or perhaps better, with meaning. This creative power in union with meaning produces in men personal self-consciousness and creates through men culture, language, the arts, the state, philosophy, and religion. All these things are implied in the concept of the spirit. But if you speak of absolute mind, then you have to think of some highest intellect somewhere, a bodiless intellect, so to speak, a mind without power. However, according to the religious tradition, both Jewish and Christian, as well as many other religions, God is first of all the Almighty. He is power. He is unrestricted. He is infinite power. He is the power in all other powers, and he gives them the power to be. This element of power belongs to the concept of spirit. If you take this away by translating *Geist* with mind, it becomes impossible to understand the history of Protestant theology, or Hegel's system and his theological successors.

I have often said that I am a crusader for the rescuing of the word "spirit" with a small "s." We need the word. All other languages have it. In French we have *esprit*, in German *Geist*, in Hebrew *ruach*, in Latin *spiritus*, and in Greek *pneuma*, but in English this word has been more or less lost, in part due to British empiricism and in part due to Descartes' division of man into intellect and body. In spite of all Descartes' greatness in creating the method of modern scientific and philosophical analysis, we must say that from the standpoint of the doctrine of man he has omitted the real center of man, which is between mind and body. Formerly this was called "soul"—a word which is now forbidden by the watchdogs of language in every university, because this word is connected with sentimentality and has no scientific value; this despite the fact that it is the central concept in Aristotle's doctrine of man, namely, *psyche,* which must be translated by *anima* (Latin) or soul.

In any case, this is the bad situation in which we find ourselves, which makes it difficult to understand Hegel at this central point. Spirit is the creator of man as personality and of everything which through man as person can be created in culture, religion, and morality. This human spirit is the self-manifestation of the divine Spirit, and God is the absolute Spirit which is present and works through every finite spirit. To understand this we must go back to what I said about Hegel as a philosopher of life, of life processes. All life processes are manifestations of the divine life, only they appear in time and space whereas in God they are in their essential nature. God actualizes his own potentialities in time and space, through nature, through history, and through men. God finds himself in his personal character in man and his history, in the different forms of his historical actualization. God is not a person besides other persons. The absolute Spirit of which Hegel speaks is not a being beside the finite spirit, but in God its essential reality is given. In time and space it becomes actualized, yet at the same time estranged from its essential character.

Here we have the whole vision of the world as a process of the self-actualization of the divine essences in time and space. Therefore, everything in its essential nature is the self-expression of the divine life. This world process goes through nature and through the various actualizations of spirit. In man's spirit, particularly in man's artistic, religious, and philosophical creativity, God finds himself as he essentially is. God does not find himself in himself, but he comes to himself, to what he essentially is, through the world process, and finally through man and through man's consciousness of God. Here we have the old mystical idea that in man's knowledge of God, God knows himself, and in man's love of God, God loves himself. We found these ideas also in Spinoza, and therefore I emphasize so much that Spinoza is a geometricized Jewish mystic. In Hegel, however, we have these mystical ideas in a dynamic creative form and not in Spinoza's static geometrical form.

Hegel sees God as the bearer of the essential structures of all things. This makes him the great representative of essentialist philosophy, a philosophy which tries to understand the essences in all things as expressions of the divine self-manifestation in time and space. The later existentialist protest can only be understood as the reaction to this essentialist philosophy. Modern existentialism was born as a protest against Hegel's essentialism. Therefore, we must understand Hegel's essentialism, the essences as manifestations of the divine life. God in himself is the essence of every species of plants and animals, of the structures of the atoms and stars, of the nature of man in which his innermost center is manifest. All these are manifestations of the divine life as it is manifest in time and space.

Hegel cannot, therefore, conceive of God as a person beside other persons. Then he would be less than God. Then the world process, the structure of being, would be more than he, would be above him. God would then have a fate; he would be thrown into reality like the Greek gods who are subject to fate, who come and go, who are immortal with respect to a special structure of the cosmos, but who are born and die with this cosmos. But the God of Christianity is not less than the structure of reality. He has it in himself; it is his life. This fundamental change liberates the Christian man from the anxiety of destiny. You can observe the fight against this idea already in the Greek tragedians who were fighting against gods who themselves were subject to fate and who therefore were inferior to man, because man is able to resist the universal fate in the power of the logos. Man is beyond the fate and therefore beyond the gods. So God is not a person. He is spiritual, as I told you in connection with Schleiermacher, but he is not a person because that would subject him again to the fate of the Greek gods.

There is a point of identity between God and man insofar as God comes to self-consciousness in man, and insofar as man in his essential nature is contained together with everything in the inner life of God as potentiality. The process in which God creates the world and fulfills himself in the world is the means whereby the infinite abundance of the divine life grows in time and space. God is not a separate entity, something finished in himself, but he belongs to the world, not as a part of it, but as the ground from which and to which all things exist. This is the synthesis of the divine and the human spirit. It was the point most attacked by the nineteenth-century theology of religious revivalism, which wanted to emphasize the person-to-person relationship and the difference between God and the world.

3. The Synthesis of Religion and Culture (Thought and Imagination)

Another synthesis which Hegel constructs is the synthesis between religion and culture. As a result of the basic idea of the relation of the absolute and the relative spirit, religion has a double meaning in Hegel. In one sense everything in its essential nature is rooted in the divine. In order to understand Hegel's synthesis of religion and culture, we must know what "nature" meant to him. Nicholas of Cusa's basic idea of the coincidence of the divine and the human in everything was certainly present in all of Hegel's philosophy. In nature the absolute Spirit is present. But it is present in terms of estrangement. Here we come to the very important twentieth-century concept of estrangement. It is the existentialist concept for what in religious symbolism is called the fall. This idea is applied by Hegel to nature. Nature is spirit, but estranged spirit, spirit not yet having achieved its true nature. God leaves himself, so to speak, in order to go over into estrangement. The important thing historically is that this concept which Hegel created was later used by his pupils against him. For Hegel developed a philosophy of reconciliation, as we shall see, but his pupils said that there is no reconciliation. This statement that there is no reconciliation is the basic statement of existentialism. The world is not reconciled. The greatness of Hegel is that he created the categories in terms of which others could attack him. The tremendous importance of the concept of estrangement in Karl Marx's interpretation of capitalism is derived from Hegel, but then used against him. You cannot understand Marxism and its significance for the philosophical spirit of the nineteenth and twentieth centuries without knowing that he took the concept of estrangement from Hegel only to attack him by means of it. Against Hegel he said, estrangement, yes, but reconciliation, no! The class situation shows that there is no reconciliation. Hegel said that in the state (Prussia) the political reconciliation and the social reconciliation do exist. Against this the existentialist revolt began.

Now in Hegel's system there is a transition from natural philosophy to logic. In Hegel's logic something interesting happens, which you must know in order to understand Kierkegaard's attack on Hegel's system. In his logic Hegel develops the essences of reality in terms of their logical abstraction. He does not speak of men, but man as an essence appears in Hegel's logic. He does not speak of quantities in reality, but the category of quantity appears in his logic. He does not speak of animals, but the category of animal life appears in his logic. So he has in his logic a fully developed system of the essential structure of reality without going into the actualization of these essences in time, space, and history. It is, so to speak, the description of the inner divine life. For this he even uses the symbolism of the trinity, God going out and returning to himself in his eternal life, in the life of the eternal essences, before anything has happened in time and space, before the categories and essences became actuality.

It is clear that we have here a philosophy of the inner divine life under the name of logic. Logic is here not semantics; it is not analytic logic, that is, a subjective power of man's mind. But like Aristotle's logic, it is a description of the structure of reality. However, in Aristotle as in all Greek thinking, it was a static description—the hierarchy of abstractions, and then the conclusions. Hegel's logic describes the structure of the dynamic process of the inner divine life in which all realities in their essence are present, before they are actually in time and space.

Then the question arose: How does this all come to actuality? Here Hegel unites the idea of creation with the idea of the fall, and speaks of nature as the alienated or estranged spirit. The two words "alienation" and "estrangement" went on to play a great role in existentialist philosophy. In my opinion the two words mean the same thing, but I know that some philosophers prefer the word "alienation," perhaps because it is a bit more abstract. I myself have preferred to use the word "estrangement" because it contains the imagery of the stranger and the separation of people who once loved each other and belong essentially to each other. I think it is a more powerful term.

When Hegel says that nature is estranged spirit, estranged does not mean annihilated or altered. So the whole world process is seen by Hegel as a process of divine self-estrangement. This divine self-estrangement reminds us very much of the risk God took, according to Christian theology, when he created the world with the possibility of man's fall. Christian theology would say that God created the world in spite of the fact that he foresaw its estrangement and fall. In Calvinist theology God is said to have even decreed the fall. At any rate, this is the religious substance of Hegel's more logical statement of the alienation of the divine Spirit in nature.

Man's spirit develops out of nature going through many processes. In his encyclopedia Hegel presents a lengthy philosophy of nature. This is largely dependent on Schelling who on the basis of the synthesis of Kant and Spinoza, of which I spoke, developed the romantic element of nature. Schelling showed the inner powers of nature, the conscious and the unconscious. He was the first to use the term "unconscious" in philosophy, and through a special line of thought Freud received this term, and used it for empirical psychological purposes. But actually it comes from Schelling's philosophy of nature. What the romantic philosophers of nature wanted to show is that in nature spirit is struggling for its full actualization in man. You have the same idea in Teilhard de Chardin, the Jesuit, who wrote *The Phenomenon of Man*.[19] It has many analogies to the romantic philosophy of nature and even to the classical if we consider Goethe a representative of the classical philosophy of nature. The great problem of this philosophy of nature was to show its relation to scientific research which had been going on vigorously ever since Galileo and Newton, first in astronomy, then in biology and physics. Hegel tried to take the results of scientific research into his system, as did also Schelling, who personally knew many of the best scientists of his time. But the danger is that if a preliminary result of scientific research is used in the formation of philosophical or theological statements, it tends to become fixed as something metaphysically true. Then the scientists resent this use of their scientific results because they know of the preliminary and tentative character of these results. The same day on which the philosopher writes down his philosophical interpretations of physics or biology, new insights are already being discovered in some laboratory which upon publication will make the philosopher's interpretations

[19] Translated by Bernard Wall, with an Introduction by Julian Huxley (New York: Harper & Row, 1959).

obsolete and invalid. This difficulty is always present. On the other hand, I know from personal encounter with physicists that they desire very much to have a philosophical evaluation and interpretation of what they are doing. So philosophy has a difficult task, but most contemporary philosophers settle for logical analysis of the scientific method, so as not to prejudice any results. But even this is precarious, for it may be that some new result will make necessary a change in method. So the only thing we can do is to say that the vision of a special level of considering nature must remain independent of the progress of natural sciences. This is what Teilhard de Chardin has done. He himself was a member of the expedition which discovered the skull of Pekin man or Sinanthropus, one of these prehistoric beings not yet man but in the series of development toward man. In spite of his very strict scientific training and work, he dared to have such a vision. In the third volume of my *Systematic Theology* I have tried something like this from the philosophical point of view, but I am aware of how precarious and dangerous it is. If, on the other hand, we do not try this, we remove God from nature, and if God is removed from nature, he gradually disappears altogether, because we are nature. We come from nature. If God has nothing to do with nature, he finally has nothing to do with our total being.

For Hegel man is born out of nature, and in man another phenomenon occurs; spirit comes to itself. In man God finds what he essentially is, namely, absolute spirit himself in a relative being, in a being which is biologically conditioned, but with the dimension of the spirit, of self-consciousness. Hegel distinguishes three dimensions or levels of spirit: (a) the subjective spirit, which is man's personal inner life. Psychology, for example, belongs to the doctrine of the subjective spirit; (b) the objective spirit, which is society, state, and family. The subject of ethics belongs here; (c) the absolute spirit, which is the full manifestation of God on the human level. Art, religion, and philosophy belong here.

This is very interesting in many respects. One dangerous thing in it is that ethics appears as philosophy of society. Ethics is connected with family, society, and state. Hegel's ethics is an objectivist ethics. It was at this point that Kierkegaard's most radical attack occurred, for Hegel understood ethics only from the point of view of the essential structure of man in society. He did not understand it as the decision of the individual personality with relation to himself and his society. Against this Kierkegaard placed his concept of the ethically deciding individual person. Because Hegel had no personal ethics in his system, Kierkegaard emphasized so much the decision of the individual personality. Hegel had only a system of social ethics in which the ethical relations of the individual person were developed, but the free, deciding individual did not appear in the system.

The next point has to do with the relation of religion to philosophy. Religion stands between aesthetics and philosophy. This also is important. In a special period of Schelling's development, the aesthetic was the great miracle of the divine self-manifestation. In the aesthetic vision the Kantian dualism between theoretical and practical reason was overcome. Even the state for Schelling was the great work of art, and the artistic creation was regarded as the real manifestation of the divine. Hegel saw that this is impossible because in all art there is an element of unreality. There is a seeming reconciliation, but only in the image, not in reality itself. So Hegel places art as a stage prior to religion, and religion beyond it as the substance. In his philosophy of religion—which was unfortunately never published by Hegel but is available only through several transcripts made by students of Hegel—we find one of the greatest evaluations of religion. Religion is for him the substance and center of life, that which makes everything sacred and gives everything its depths and heights.

But now something interesting happens. Philosophy is put above religion. To understand in what sense, you must first understand one thing in Hegel. In Hegel's hierarchy of natural philosophy—the subjective spirit, the objective spirit, the absolute spirit—the higher level never abolishes the lower one. Man as spirit is still under the law of physics, the law of chemistry, the law of biology. These are three forms which he also distinguishes. You can see immediately how impossible this is from the point of view of modern atomic physics in which the distinction between the chemical and the physical is almost extinguished. Be that as it may, for Hegel the higher does not abolish the lower. But the higher is an expression of the more perfect actualization of the absolute spirit in time and space. And so, if philosophy is higher than religion, it does not abolish religion. Religion remains for Hegel the substance of spiritual reality, that is, the relation to the absolute mind. Here he develops a whole history of religion in which all religions are put in their right place, and Christianity as the revealed religion is given the highest place.

What then is the difference between religion and philosophy? The difference lies in the form of our awareness of the relation to the absolute. In religion we think in images, in *Vorstellungen*, as he called them. Today we would speak rather of myths and symbols. Philosophy is able to interpret these images or symbols in terms of concepts (*Begriffe*.) The conceptualization of the religious contents is the highest aim of philosophy. In this respect Hegel is very near to the way in which Western philosophy has always developed. We can follow this development with marvelous clarity in early Greek philosophy. First there were the myths, theogonies, stories of the genesis of the gods, then cosmogony, the genesis of the world, and then out of these religious myths the first great philosophical concepts were born. The history of philosophy shows this. So Hegel also believed that the philosophical concepts were universally born out of the mythological symbols of religion. In a real sense his own philosophy is philosophy of religion; but in a narrower sense philosophy of religion, connected with the church tradition, symbols and myths, has a special place in his system. In this way he unites the critical mind of philosophy with the intuitive symbolizing mind of religion by having philosophy provide the conceptual form for the symbols of religion.

4. *The Synthesis of State and Church*

The third synthesis of which I want to speak is in the political realm, the synthesis of state and church. If you hear the word "state" used by Hegel and in romantic philosophy generally, you should not think of what is called "state" today in liberal democracy, that is, an abstract system of government. Therefore, the idea of keeping the state away from the economic and cultural contents of life is in this country quite different from what it was for all European countries. In Hegel's understanding state is the synthetic unity of all communal activities in a nation. It is the directing center of education, the arts, religion, economy, defense, administration, law, and of all things which belong to the realm of culture. If you take state in this sense you can better understand the expression Hegel once used that the state is the divine on earth. If you identify state, however, with the central administration, then this is almost blasphemy. It is an unfortunate expression, and has often been used against Hegel. What it means is the presence of God's self-realization in all cultural realms in time and space. The centered unity of this is the state, in the largest sense. If you take it in this sense too, the state is actually the church, because the state is not merely the administration, but the cultural life in all directions, including religion. Then it can be called the body of God on earth, so to speak.

But this expression is so unfortunate because it has been used consciously or unconsciously by the totalitarian ideologies as they developed in Germany, Russia, Italy, and elsewhere. So Hegel is often referred to in order to justify a centralist control of all political and economic life. This is not what Hegel meant at all. Administration is only one of the functions, and law is another, but none of them is meant in a totalitarian way, although there lurked this danger in his formulation. For us the most important is the relation to the church. If we take Hegel's definition of state, then of course church and state are identical. Some of the theologians who followed Hegel thought it was clear that there should not be a particular church at all. The life of the nation and of the church should be identical. The influence of classicism is clear here because in the Greek city-states there was no independent "church" or cult separated from the life of the *polis*. So this became the ideal both for the philosophers and the theologians. One of the theologians, Wilhelm De Wette (1780–1849), said that the destiny of Christianity is no longer dependent on the church, but on the substance given in society and expressed in the form of the state. Substance stands here for spiritual substance, the creative ground out of which the life of a nation grows. Therefore state and church are no longer separated.

These ideas should not sound so strange. In public addresses in America we often hear, "We are a Christian nation." What does this mean? Certainly we are not a Christian nation in any empirical sense. We are extremely unchristian, as every nation is. Perhaps it means that in all our secular life and in the several expressions of our national life, there is a substance which has been shaped by Christianity. If understood in this sense, it can be right, but it is also very dangerous, especially when used in our anti-Communist propaganda. Then it is wrong, for no nation is ever simply Christian or godless, whatever theory its leaders may hold. Neither the one nor the other is true.

We are still involved in this problem as is most evident in some of the statements that Bonhoeffer made in his letters from prison. In these letters he stated that man has come to maturity, that the separation of the religious and cultural spheres should not be maintained any longer, that the church should know that it is not the only representative of the divine in history, but that the secular culture has an equal claim, and perhaps a more genuine claim in our time. This is the Hegelian concern repeated in these ideas. Is culture something which stands beside the church? Shall the church stand aside from the autonomous development of culture? Should it be pushed into a corner where it loses its relevance for all of culture? Or should we instead understand the religious element in culture and the cultural element in religion, and attempt to drive toward a new unity as this existed in former centuries and cultures. This is the deeper meaning of the expression that the state is the divine on earth or of the identity of state and church.

5. Providence, History, and Theodicy

There is another point, a very important and decisive one, at which Hegel tries the great synthesis. That is the interpretation of history in terms of providence and theodicy, which is justification of God for the kind of world this is. Hegel followed Leibniz and the Enlightenment with their concept of the harmony of the universe. Harmony is a paradoxical concept also in Hegel. In spite of the contradictions of reality, in spite of individual willfulness and irrationality, the ultimate outcome of history is positive and is in line with the divine purpose. One can say that Hegel's interpretation of history is the application of the idea of providence in a secularized form, in a form in which the philosopher, so to speak, sits on the throne of God, looking into his providential activities and describing them. In everything which happens Hegel can see the self-actualization of the absolute spirit, the divine ground of being itself. This means that somehow everything in history is divine revelation. He can say that history is reasonable, but reasonable according to the logos concept of reason, according to the principle of the divine self-manifestation in history, according to the universal principle of form in which the divine ground manifests itself.

On this basis Hegel made a statement which has been very much abused, misunderstood, and attacked by very clever philosophers. This is the statement that everything real is rational. Now every eight-year-old boy knows that not everything that is real is rational, but it took sixty-year-old philosophers at the end of the nineteenth century to show with their immense wisdom how to refute Hegel. Then they could express with great feeling how superior they were to Hegel because they knew that there are many things in reality which are not reasonable. But they were not superior; they were only unable to understand the profound thought of the great mind. What Hegel said must first of all be thought of as a paradox. It is the paradox that in spite of the immense irrationality in reality, of which he could speak again and again, there is nevertheless a hidden providential activity, namely, the self-manifestation of the absolute Spirit through the irrational attitudes of all creatures and especially of people. This providential power in history works behind human activity, willing, and planning, and through man's rationality and irrationality. This idea has the same paradoxical character as the Christian doctrine of providence. In spite of tragic occurrences which Hegel also knew about, he did not despair of providence; nor did the early Christians under horrible persecutions. It is only if you speak of providence unparadoxically that you must despair. If you speak of it paradoxically, you can say that in spite of this or that, the mystery of life is behind everything that happens. Every individual is immediate to God in every moment and in every situation, and can reach his own fulfillment in time and above time.

But while the paradoxical element in Hegel's statement is obviously there, Hegel did not accept the mystery in the way in which Christianity has always accepted it. Hegel *knew* why things happened as they did. He *knew* how the process of history unfolds. Therefore, he missed the one element in the Christian affirmation of the paradox of providence, the mystery about the particulars. He did not even discuss the particulars, but he believed he knew the general process as such. He constructed history as the actualization of the eternal essences or potentialities which are the divine life in their inner dialectical movement, the play of God within himself, so to speak. Here he developed the trinitarian symbolism within the divine life. These eternal essences are actualized in the historical process in time and space.

But how are they actualized? Here Hegel's almost tragic feeling in regard to history comes out in a way usually overlooked by his interpreters. He said history is not the place for the happiness of the individual. The individual cannot be happy in history. History does not care about the individual. History goes its grand way from one idea or essence or potentiality within the divine life, actualizing itself, to the others. The bearers of these ideas are the social groups, the nations, and the states. Each nation, each cultural group, has its time in which a particular eternal idea, as it has been spelled out in Hegel's logic, becomes actual in time and space.

He said all this happens by passion and interest. Nothing in history happens without passion and interest. Here we have an insight of the existentialists which they received from Hegel and by means of which they attacked him. The term "interest" was used especially by Kierkegaard in his attack against Hegel, while "passion" and, in the larger sense, will-to-power and economic will, were used by anti-Hegelians like the early Marx and Nietzsche. They were all dependent on the one against whom they fought, even in their use of terminology.

Hegel had a concept which gives strong expression to the "in spite of" character of his doctrine of history. This concept is "the cunning of the idea," a very mythological-sounding phrase. The cunning of the idea is the divine trick, so to speak, working behind the backs of those who are acting in history and bringing into existence something that is in line with a meaningful development of history. This idea makes it possible to understand figures like Hitler. In this respect Hegel is very near to Luther who understood figures like Attila the Hun and the leaders of the Turks during the invasions at the time of the Reformation as the "masks of God." They are the masks through whom God works out his purposes in history. This is also mythological imagery, similar to the cunning of the idea. Both point to the paradoxical character of the divine activity. By paradox we mean it in its original Greek sense, namely, against all expectation, contrary to our normal belief and opinion. In this sense Hegel's cunning of the idea and Luther's masks of God in world history are in the same line. So Hegel could say that he views history as the divine theodicy, the justification of God for the horrors of world history. Hegel said that there is no easy explanation of the negativities in history. We are not able to justify God, but the historical process justifies him. Or God justifies himself by the historical process in spite of the fact that this historical process is full of events which seem to contradict the divine purpose.

There is another important point in Hegel's interpretation of history, of the world process, and even of the inner dialectics of the divine life. It is the principle of negativity. I warned you about seeing Hegel chiefly in terms of the triadic dialectic: thesis, antithesis, synthesis. This can be a caricature of Hegel, but it happens to be a caricature for which he is largely responsible in his later writings, especially in his encyclopedia where it becomes often intolerable. Behind this there is Hegel's idea of the negative element in every life process. The negation drives the positive out of itself and reveals its inner potentialities. This, of course, is another idea taken up by existentialism. The problem of nonbeing in existentialism and in Heidegger is already in Hegel. The difference is that in Hegel the negative is not the continuous threat against the positive, but is overcome in the fulfilled synthesis. Here again Hegel is sitting on the throne of providence, always knowing the outcome. This is the *hybris* which brought Hegel's synthesis, despite its greatness, to its final dissolution. According to Hegel no life is possible without negativity, otherwise the positive would remain within itself in dead identity. Without alteration there is no life. The continuous process of life which goes out of itself and tries to return to itself has in itself the principle of negativity. Here is the deepest point in his theodicy, the necessity of the negative as an implication of life. It is also necessary to know this to understand the rise of existentialism later, and its opposition to essentialism.

6. *The Christ as Reality and Symbol*

Hegel tried to combine all the elements of his period with the basic Christian affirmation that Jesus is the Christ. The universal synthesis between Christianity and the modern mind stands and falls with the christological problem. For Hegel and all essentialists the problem is particularly difficult because Jesus, who is called the Christ, is first of all an individual. But at the same time he is supposed to be the universal individual. So the question arose: Can an individual be at the same time universal? This is the fight that has been going on since Hegel, and in some way also before him in the Enlightenment and mysticism. The problem has not been fully solved even today.

But Hegel tried to solve this problem. For him the essential identity of God and man in spite of actual separation and hostility is embodied in this one man Jesus who is for that reason called the *Logos*. He developed a christology in line with that principle formulated by Nicholas of Cusa of the mutual inherence of the finite and the infinite. In Jesus as the Christ the infinite is completely actualized in the finite; its very center is present in the center of this one finite man Jesus. Jesus therefore gave expression to that which is universal and which is potentially and essentially true of every human being, and in some way of every being. He is the self-manifestation of the absolute mind. Later revivalist or pietistic theology in Europe was to fight against this because for it the unique individuality and the personal relation to this individuality stand in the very center.

Several days ago I had a very interesting christological discussion with a colleague over the question: Is Jesus important for us as *Mitmensch*, that is, as a fellow human being with whom we can have a common relationship as human beings? Or is he important for us as the bearer of the Spirit? Now, it is my personal opinion that on this question Hegel is nearer to the understanding of Paul and the early church than the pietists with their jesuological way of being related to him. In any case, the problem brought up by Hegel is still a living problem and probably will remain so as long as there is a Christian Church.

7. Eternity against Immortality

General piety very aggressively attacked Hegel's mystical and philosophical understanding of immortality. This attack is psychologically understandable. For it is obvious that individual immortality could not be affirmed within the system; it could not agree with the consistency of the system. We participate in the divine life as individuals through the historical process, and to the degree in which we participate in it, we participate in the divine life. This participation was called eternal life by Hegel, as well as by Schelling and the classical German philosophers. They understood this concept of eternal life in opposition to individual immortality. They certainly could claim biblical support for this notion that immortality belongs to God alone, that man has no immortality in himself, not even before the fall according to biblical mythological symbolism. In paradise he could gain immortality only by eating from the tree of life, even as the gods themselves in the myths which underlie the biblical version.

So Hegel here expresses an idea which is in conflict with the feelings and desires of every individual, however profound it might be and however much it might be stressed in mysticism and philosophy. For this reason the philosophical criticism of Hegel found a great deal of popular support.

CHAPTER IV

The Breakdown of the Universal Synthesis

I have shown you the parts which were brought into Hegel's great synthesis. I did not go into the several philosophical elements, how much of Kantianism, how much of Spinozism, how much of the Goethe-Schelling dynamic transformation of Spinoza, how much of Romanticism, etc., are to be found in Hegel. They are all there. But for the purposes of this course I dealt predominantly with the synthesis so far as it had a bearing on the Christian tradition. I have tried to stress how important it was for him to try to create this synthesis. It is a question which is still with us. Can we be schizophrenic forever, living with a split consciousness? Can we be split between the Christian tradition, on the one hand, and the creative concepts and symbols of the modern mind, on the other hand? If that is impossible, how is a genuine synthesis possible? After the breakdown of Hegel's synthesis numerous new attempts were made to reconstruct a synthesis, all of them dependent on Hegel, but none possessing the universality and historical power of Hegel's system.

A. The Split in the Hegelian School

How did the split in Hegel's school take place? Hegel's interpretation of Christ took for granted the historical reality of the biblical image of the Christ. He did not doubt it. His interpretation also stressed the symbolic meaning of the universal essential unity between God and man. So his interpretation included both reality and symbol. Something happened, however, which seemed to undercut the historical side of that interpretation. The question arose: Can we rely on the historical reports concerning the Christ? Such historical criticism was much older than the period in which Hegel lived. Historical criticism existed since the deistic movement in England, and since the eighteenth-century conflict between rationalism and supernaturalism. But now a new element was introduced by Hegel.

1. The Historical Problem: Strauss and Baur

In the eighteenth century the question was whether the reports about the life of Jesus were true or false. The Christian theologians were bent on showing that much of the historical material could be vindicated in face of historical criticism. Some of the critics tried to show that almost nothing remains as historically reliable. Others argued on the basis of Hegel's point of view that even though the reports are not historically reliable, they do not for that reason lose their religious value. It does not matter if there is so much uncertainty regarding the biblical records of the life of Jesus, they may nevertheless have symbolic value. The concept of symbol came from Schelling and Hegel, and was not intended to prejudice the historical question. It was simply a different kind of language from ordinary empirical language.

David Friedrich Strauss (1808–1874) drew out all the consequences from previous historical criticism when he wrote his *Life of Jesus* (1835).[1] It came like lightning and thunder striking the great synthesis and all those who felt safe in it. Strauss showed that the authors of the Gospels were not those traditionally thought to be the authors. But more, he tried to show that the stories of the birth and the resurrection of Jesus are symbols expressing the eternal identity of what is essential in Jesus and God. This was felt as a tremendous shock. For decades later scholars tried to refute Strauss's *Life of Jesus,* and, of course, there were many points in it that proved to be invalid in the light of more research.

[1] *The Life of Jesus, Critically Examined,* translated from the 4th German edition by George Eliot (London: Chapman Brothers, 1846).

But the problem which Strauss raised to the fore in the life of the church could never be removed.

A footnote on Strauss's later development: It contains something tragic. Later he wrote another *Life of Jesus*,[2] this one for the German people, as he said. Here he developed the typical world view of the victorious bourgeoisie, not of the great aggressive bourgeoisie of the eighteenth century, but of the positivistic materialistic bourgeoisie which had become victorious in the nineteenth century, and which he represented. This is characterized by a calculating attitude toward the world, a basic materialistic interpretation of reality, and moral rules derived from the bourgeois conventions. I mention this because of the tremendous attack which Friedrich Nietzsche made against Strauss in the name of the forces of creative life. He attacked this bourgeoisie resting undisturbed in its own finitude.

This has a lot to do with Gospel criticism, for from his bourgeois point of view Strauss eliminated the in-breaking of the divine into the human, of the infinite into the finite. The infinite was adapted to the finite. The image of Christ which Strauss and many later biographers produced was that of a domesticated divinity, domesticated for the sake of the untroubled life of the bourgeois society in calculating and controlling the finite reality. Here Nietzsche was the prophetic victor over Strauss, even more than any theologian.

But this was not the end of the story. The development was furthered by a pupil of Hegel, Ferdinand Christian Baur (1792–1860), who founded the Tübingen school which dealt especially with New Testament research. He tried to apply the Hegelian concepts of thesis, antithesis, and synthesis to the early development of Christianity. The thesis was the early Jewish-Christian communities; the antithesis the pagan, Christian, Pauline line of thought (he emphasized very much the struggle between Peter and Paul over the necessity of circumcision, in which Paul prevailed, opening the way for Christianity to conquer the pagan world); the synthesis of the Petrine and the Pauline types of Christianity was the Johannine. In this point Baur was very much in

[2] *Das Leben Jesu für das deutsche Volk bearbeitet* (Leipzig: 1864). The English translation is *The Life of Jesus for the People* (London: Williams and Norgate, 1879).

the tradition of classical German philosophy. All of these philosophers, Kant, Fichte, Schelling, and Hegel, were great lovers of the fourth Gospel, because of the gnostic terminology in this Gospel, especially the *logos* term. Baur's interpretation of Christianity was very important and influential, however justifiable or unjustifiable his theory may be from a historical point of view. In the face of the orthodox view of a literally inspired Bible, Baur showed how these biblical writings were created in an historical way. The idea of a creative development which was going on in the church and which produced the Scriptures has changed our whole relation to the Bible. The whole development of historical criticism was later to maintain some form of Baur's sense of the historical emergence of the biblical writings over against the view of a mechanically dictated and inspired Word of God, as if God were dictating to a stenographer at a typewriter.

2. *The Anthropological Problem: Ludwig Feuerbach (1804–1872)*

It was Feuerbach who launched an anthropological criticism against Hegel's philosophy of religion. He himself was very much influenced by Hegel before turning against him. Hegel had said that man is that being in whom God recognizes himself. In man's knowledge of God, God comes to know himself. There is thus no knowledge of God apart from that knowledge of him which is in man. Now Feuerbach, under the influence of Western naturalism, materialism, and psychologism, said that Hegel must be turned around. God is nothing else than a projection of man's awareness of his own infinity. You see that this is simply turning Hegel upside down. For Hegel God comes to himself in man; for Feuerbach man creates God in himself. These are two quite different views. Here we have Feuerbach's theory of projection. The word "projection" is widely used today. All education deals with methods of projection; Freudian thought interprets God as a human projection, as a father image, etc. But Feuerbach was much profounder. I recommend to all of you who have just discovered Freud's theory of projection to go back to Feuerbach; he had a real theory of projection.

What does projection mean in a technical sense? It means putting an image on a screen. In order to do this, you need a screen. But I always miss the screen in modern thinking about projection. Granted, God is the projection of the father experience in us; he is the image of it. But why is this image itself God? Who is the screen onto which this image is projected? To this Feuerbach has an answer. He says that man's experience of his infinity, the infinite will to live, the infinite intensity of love, etc., makes it possible for him to have a screen upon which to project images. This, of course, makes sense, and from the point of view of the philosophy of religion one can agree with all projection theories which are as old as Xenophanes, almost six hundred years before Christ. This means that the concrete image, the concrete symbolism applied to the infinite, is determined by our situation and by our relation to our own infinity. This is meaningful. Of course, it is not sufficient, but in any case Feuerbach saw much better than so many seemingly educated people of today that if you have a theory of projection, you must explain why the images are projected on just this screen, and why the result is something infinite, that is, the divine, the unconditional, the absolute. Where does that come from? The father is not absolute. Nothing that we have in ourselves, in our finite structure, is absolute. Only if there is an awareness of something unconditional or infinite within us can we understand why the projected images have to be divine figures or symbols. So in the terms of the greatest theoreticians of projection, I criticize the modern theories of projection which circulate in popular unreflective thought. Here you have a weapon with which to face this popular talk about projection.

Feuerbach did something here which Marx acknowledged as the final and definitive criticism of religion. We cannot understand Karl Marx without understanding his relation to Feuerbach. He said that Feuerbach solved the problem of religion once for all. Religion is a projection. It is something subjective in us which we put into the sky of the absolute. But then he went one step beyond Feuerbach. He said that Feuerbach did a great job, but he did not go far enough. He did not explain why projection was done at all, and this, Marx said, cannot be explained in terms of the individual man. This can only be explained in terms of the social existence of men, and more particularly in the class situation of men. Religion is the escape of those who are oppressed by the upper classes into an imaginary fulfillment in the realm of the absolute. Marx's negation of religion is a result of his understanding of the social condition of man.

Here you see the great influence these ideas have had. The anti-religious attitude of almost half of present-day mankind is rooted in this seemingly professorial struggle between Hegel, Feuerbach, and Marx, with both of the latter coming from Hegel. Feuerbach turned Hegel upside down, and then Marx introduced the sociological element. The projection of the transcendent world is the projection of the disinherited in this world. This was such a powerful argument that it convinced the masses of people. It took more than one hundred years before the labor movements in Europe were able to overcome this Feuerbach-Marxian argument against Hegel's attempt to unite Christianity and the modern mind.

These people whom I have mentioned are called the Hegelian left wing. Against them stood theologians who belonged to the Hegelian right wing: Marheineke, Biedermann, Pfleiderer. They tried to show that it is possible under Hegelian presuppositions to have a tenable and justifiable Christian theology.

B. Schelling's Criticism of Hegel

We have been discussing some of Hegel's critics, people like Feuerbach and Marx. I come now to that critic whom I consider to be the most fundamental philosophically and theologically, and perhaps most important for our intellectual life today. The first great existentialist critic of essentialist thinking since Blaise Pascal (1623–1662), who was in a way the predecessor of all existentialists, was Friedrich Schelling (1775–1854). We have to remember that he was prior to Kierkegaard. In fact Kierkegaard attended Schelling's Berlin lectures in the middle of the nineteenth century, and used many of Schelling's categories in his fight against Hegel.

I know that the name of this man Schelling is almost unknown in this country. There are several reasons for this. One of the reasons is that Schelling, together with Fichte, is a bridge between Kant and Hegel. After you have reached the other side of the bridge, you tend often to forget the bridge itself. Kant is the one who began German classical philosophy, and Hegel is the end. All this happened in no more than half a century. But during this half century Fichte and Schelling were working, first continuing Kant, and then giving basic thoughts to Hegel. Of course, they were not mere bridges between Kant and Hegel. They were independent philosophers having an influence reaching beyond Hegel up to our time. I recall the unforgettable moment when by chance I came into possession of the very rare first edition of the collected works of Schelling in a bookstore on my way to the University of Berlin. I had no money, but I bought it anyway, and this spending of nonexistent money was probably more important than all the other nonexistent or sometimes existing money that I have spent. For what I learned from Schelling became determinative of my own philosophical and theological development.

I have told you already how Schelling synthesized or combined Kant's critical epistemology and Spinoza's mystical ontology. But Schelling was more than this synthesis. In some way Goethe did that too. But Schelling became the philosopher of Romanticism. He represented not only the beginning of romantic thinking in the philosophy of nature. There were elements of this already in Fichte and even in Kant's third *Critique* where he introduced the *Gestalt* theory of biological understanding of life. But Schelling kept pace with the different changing periods of Romanticism, and the decisive turning point was when Romanticism started to become existentialism. In this sense Schelling is far more than a bridge between Kant and Hegel. Long after Hegel's death, he was the greatest critic of Hegel. In Schelling the second phase of Romanticism became existentialist. He arrived finally at an understanding of reality which radically contradicted his former period. This happened through philosophical experiences, understanding of religion, and profound participation in life within himself and around him. He did not, however, abolish what Hegel and he had done before. He preserved a philosophy of essence. Against this he put the philosophy of existence. Existentialism is not a philosophy which can stand on its own legs. Actually it has no legs. It is always based on a vision of the essential structure of reality. In this sense it is based on essentialism, and cannot live without it. If you say that man is evil, you must have a concept of man in his essential goodness, otherwise the word "evil" would not make any sense. Without the distinction between good and evil the words themselves lose their meaning. And if you say that man's structure is distorted in time and space, or that it is "fallen," then you must have something from which he is fallen. You must have some structure which is distorted in time and space. So mere existentialism does not exist. But it can be the main emphasis of a philosophical work and even of a whole period in philosophy. In Schelling's later years it was the main emphasis, although essentialism was presupposed, but not developed. This is also true of our philosophers and poets. I can best illustrate this in terms of the present-day saint of existentialism, the novelist Kafka. In him you will not find that essentialism is explained, but you will always find that it is implicit and presupposed. For without this he could not even describe the futile search for meaning in the novel, *The Castle,* or the horrible experience of a guilt of which he is not conscious in his other novel, *The Trial.* The essentialist understanding of the human situation is behind it, behind the existentialist description. You find this everywhere. If in T. S. Eliot you have the age of anxiety described, this presupposes the possibility of not having anxiety in the radical sense in which he describes it. Thus all existentialism presupposes that from which it breaks away, namely, essentialism. You have it wonderfully expressed in Pascal who relates the God of Abraham, Isaac, and Jacob to both man's greatness and his misery.

Now in his earlier periods, Schelling developed to the extreme the Spinozistic principle, the principle of the ontological unity of everything in the eternal substance. This principle of identity is very hard to understand by people educated in nominalistic thinking, as you all are, whether you know it or not. The nominalistic mind is a mind which sees particulars and relations of particulars, and which uses exclusively logical and scientific methods to get at particulars. The very question of an ultimate identity is very difficult to comprehend. But at least one historical fact should be realized, namely, that by far the greatest part of mankind is not nominalistic, that all Asian religions are based on the principle of identity, and that Greek philosophy from the very beginning started with it when Parmenides said, "Where there is being, there is also the logos of being." This means that the word can grasp being, that the rational structure makes it possible for us to speak about being, and we can use words meaningfully.

Now this fundamental principle underlies the whole history of Christian thought. All the church fathers presupposed this Parmenidean idea, only enriching it by trinitarian symbolism. Where God is, there is his *Logos*, and they are one in the dynamic creativity of the Spirit. It is a necessary idea because it explains something which all thinking presupposes. The presupposition is that there is truth and that truth can be reached by us. In order to have truth, in order to make a true judgment, the subject who makes the judgment and the thing about which the judgment is made must, so to speak, be at one and the same place. They must come together. We use the word "grasp" for this. You must "grasp" the structure of reality. But in order to reach the object, there must be a fundamental belongingness of the subject to the object. This is the one side of the principle of identity, namely, that subject and object are not absolutely separated, that although they are separated in our finite existence, they belong essentially together. There is an eternal unity between them.

The other side of the concept of identity is the problem of the one and the many. This is the great Platonic problem. How is it possible that the many are diverse, but nevertheless form the unity of a cosmos, of a world, of a universe? Even in the word "universe" the word "one" is contained. How is that possible? Again the answer is that there must be an original unity of the one and the many. The principle of identity says that the one substance—Spinoza calls it substance, a very powerful and originally Aristotelian and Scholastic term—makes togetherness possible in the same time and the same space. Without the one substance there could not be causal connections between things, and there couldn't be substantial union and separation of different substances. This latter point is emphasized especially in the Asian religions. I remember a really Spinozistic argument used by a high priest in a Buddhist monastery. In discussing the question of how community is possible between human beings, he said that if every human being has his own substance, then community is impossible. They are eternally separated. I answered that human community is possible only if individuals have their independent substance—substance means, of course, standing upon oneself—otherwise there is no community, but only identity. Where there is no separation, there is no community either. It was with this argument that I left Japan, in the last important discussion I had there.

The philosophers of identity argued that there must be an underlying identity. I would never deny this, for if we were absolute strangers to each other, if there were no element of identity in the common substance of our being human, we could not speak to each other. We would not be able to have any form of community. It is the emphasis on diversity which separates the Western from the Eastern world. It was of the greatest importance that Christianity came from Judaism. In Judaism the individual personality has personal responsibility before the eternal God, and is not dissolved into the identity of everything as in Asia.

These problems in the history of religion are also the problems which preoccupied a philosopher like Schelling. Under the influence of Spinoza he was grasped by the one substance, by that which is beyond subject and object, beyond spirit and matter. His whole philosophy of nature was an attempt to show the indwelling of the potential spirit in all natural objects and how it comes to its fulfillment in man. The romantic philosophy of nature is nothing else than a carrying out of the program of Nicholas of Cusa, the presence of the infinite in the finite, and the program of Spinoza, the one substance in all its modifications, and Schelling's own program, the presence of the spiritual in the material. Thus the philosophy of nature becomes in Schelling a system of intuitions, in a half-philosophical, half-aesthetic way, of the power of being in nature, a power which is beyond the separation of the spiritual and the material.

Now a modern scientist might say that this is all imagination or aesthetic fancy and has nothing to do with his work. But not all modern scientists would say this. I know scientists in biology and psychology of the *Gestalt* school who follow in the line of Schelling, although they have to reject his concrete results. In any case Schelling is the initiator of this romantic philosophy of nature, and because of it he became famous in his mid-twenties. At that time he was the most famous of the German philosophers, with the exception of Fichte, and was better known than Hegel who started much later and developed quite slowly.

In Schelling's philosophy nature is construed dynamically and thus also anti-Spinozistically. In Spinoza nature is presented geometrically whereas in Schelling it is presented partly biologically and partly psychologically. In this construction the process of nature proceeds from the lowest to the highest forms of nature, and finally to man in terms of a contrast of two principles. He called the one principle the unconscious and the other the conscious. He tried to show how slowly in all different forms of nature consciousness develops until it comes to man where it becomes self-consciousness. Then a new development starts, the development of culture and history. Schelling's discovery of the unconscious was, however, a rediscovery, because the philosophers of nature in the Renaissance, Paracelsus and Boehme, around A.D. 1600 already knew about the unconscious element in man and even applied it to both God and nature.

Many of you probably believe that the unconscious is the discovery of Freud. Freud's merit is not the discovery of this concept, but the application of it in terms of a scientific method derived from medical psychology. The concept itself goes back to Schelling, not directly, but by way of Schopenhauer, the voluntaristic philosopher and critic of Hegel, and by way of Eduard von Hartmann who wrote a whole book on the philosophy of the unconscious. And it is possible to show that this book was known to Freud. This is then one element in Schelling's philosophy of nature which has survived and is still valid. In Kant and Fichte you find the predominance of practical reason, of the moral imperative. Religion is only an appendix to the moral imperative. It is at best a tool to express the unconditional character of the moral imperative. The philosophy of Fichte is concerned with the morally deciding self, the ego, the "ich" as he called it, which is completely separate from nature. Nature is only the material which man must use in himself, in his body which is nature, and outside of himself in his surroundings, in order to actualize the moral imperative. Nature has no meaning in itself. So here with a kind of holy wrath Schelling turned against Fichte and said, "It is a blasphemy of the Creator to think that nature is only there in order to be the material for our moral glory; nature has the divine glory in itself." In this way he was brought to the philosophy of nature.

But there is an even deeper consequence of this term. This is the turn toward the concept of grace over against the concept of law. If nature, which makes no conscious decision and has no moral imperative, has within itself the divine presence, then the divine presence is not only dependent on our moral action. It is prior in the development of reality, and it is also subsequent to our moral action. It is below and above the moral imperative. Schelling's philosophy or theology was very much a doctrine of grace, stressing the given divine reality before our merits and before our moral acts. So natural philosophy was a way of rediscovering grace over against the moralism of the Enlightenment. This was one of the great achievements of Romanticism for theology. Here I would say that because American Protestantism has never had a romantic period, aside from a few individuals, it has preserved up to today a religion in which the enlightened moralistic attitude is predominant, and the concept of grace is quite strange. The teachings of Jesus are moral or doctrinal laws. You will not hear very much in sermons in this country about the presence of the divine preceding all that we do. Another consequence of this is the disappearance of sacramental feeling. Sacramental thinking is meaningful only if the infinite is present in the finite, if the finite is not only subject to the commands of the infinite but has in itself saving powers, powers of the presence of the divine. This is a rediscovery of Romanticism. Of course, it was present in the whole sacramental experience of the early church, but to a great extent it was lost in the Reformation criticism, and then finally lost in the Enlightenment which based itself only on the imperative.

So now we have a whole new vision based on the principle of identity. Later Schelling went beyond the philosophy of nature to a philosophical understanding of reality through the arts. The aesthetic element broke through in full power. During his period of aesthetic idealism he made the arts the substitute for religion. Artistic intuition is the way in which we see God. The divine comes to us through the arts. Neither the biblical miracles nor any other are the manifestation of God, but every work of art is the great miracle of the full revelation of the divine substance.

After Schelling had become famous for his philosophy of nature, then developed his philosophy of aesthetic intuition, he finished this period by something which he called the philosophy of identity. Here the principle which was underlying all his periods was expressed, not in a geometrical but in a logical way, and in a way which was the extreme fulfillment of what Spinoza intended. This represented the end of essentialism in Schelling's development. For Schelling 1809 was an important year because of the death of Caroline Schlegel, the wife of his friend Schlegel, the famous translator of Shakespeare. Schelling married her. She was one of the great women of Romanticism. Her letters are a classical document of that period. Her premature death was a tremendous catastrophe for Schelling. Shortly after this two things came out. One was the dialogue *Clara* in which he used the Platonic form of the dialogue to develop the idea that eternal life means the essentialization of what we are in our essential being as seen by God. It is not a continuation of existence in time and space but participation in eternity with what we are essentially. But more important for the history of man's spiritual life was his writing on human freedom.[3] This is probably his most important work because here the concept of freedom breaks into the concept of identity. Freedom, of course, presupposes the possibility of choice. Identity as such is eternally fulfilled. So David Friedrich Strauss could say of Schelling that the principle of freedom drove him out of the restfulness of the principle of identity, which was spelled out in his *System of Philosophy*, as he called it. Here he had spoken like Spinoza of the eternal restfulness, not running for a purpose, but receiving the power of being directly by contemplation.

But then something happened. If you read the two books, *The System of Philosophy*, which is his philosophy of identity, and then *Of Human Freedom*, you feel that you have entered a new world. What had happened was his personal experience of the death of Caroline. But the logic of thought also played a part, the necessity of explaining manifoldness and diversity, and life itself which goes out of identity into alteration and wants to return to itself. How could this be explained? How can we explain that we are living here in time and space in continuous action, as we do, if there is an eternal ground in which the substance which is in all of us lies in eternal rest. The explanation was given in terms of freedom. Freedom breaks out of identity. Here he used

[3] Friedrich W. J. Schelling, *Of Human Freedom*, translated by James Gutman (Chicago: The Open Court Publishing Co., 1936).

the imagery of his philosophy of nature. He construed two or three principles in the ground of the divine, the unconscious or dark principle, the principle of will which is able to contradict itself, on the one hand, and the principle of logos, or the principle of light, on the other hand. There is here the possibility that the unconscious will, the drive in the depths of the divine life, might break away from the identity. But it cannot do so in the divine life itself. The spiritual unity of the two principles keeps them always together. But in man, in the creature, it can break away. In the creature freedom can turn against its own divine substance, its own divine ground. So the myth of the fall is interpreted by him, following the line of Plato, through Origen and Boehme, as the transcendent fall. The fall is not something which happened once upon a time, but something which happens all the time, in all creatures. This fall is the breaking away from the creative ground from which we come in the power of freedom.

This was expressed by Schelling in terms of the problem of good and evil. He showed that the possibility of good and evil is given in God. Evil is possible because the will in the divine ground is able to contradict itself. But in God it never comes to a disruption. Only the free decision of the creature to turn against its created ground accounts for evil. The principles are eternally in union in God, the abysmal depth in the divine life, the prerational development of the will, the principle of the logos or light or reason or structure or meaning, and their unity which he calls the spirit. These three principles are in the divine life, but in the divine life the finite which is present is unable to break away. The unity of the principles can be disrupted only in creatures. This is something which you can find in empirical terminology in Freud and in every modern psychotherapeutic book of profound formulations. You can find it most openly expressed in Jung's writings, and more hiddenly in Freud when he speaks of *eros* and *thanatos*, love and death. In Schelling it appeared in the highest abstraction in the fundamental vision of the nature of the will in relation to the nature of the structure. If you run ahead into the nineteenth century, you will discover the influence of these ideas everywhere. The whole of French voluntarism up to Bergson was dependent on these ideas; in Germany Schopenhauer and Nietzsche were equally dependent on them, and they have had a great effect on the philosophy of Whitehead up to the present time, especially in Charles Hartshorne, the main representative of the Whiteheadian school. So these ideas have had a great influence on history-making personalities.

The influence on theology was not less decisive. Some of the great theologians in the nineteenth century worked in the line of Schelling. But Schelling never rested. After this breakthrough he became silent for many years. In his old age he was called to Berlin in order to fight against the left-wing Hegelians. Many important people attended these lectures in the middle of the nineteenth century. The most important was Søren Kierkegaard, a transcription of whose notes on Schelling's Berlin lectures is to be found in the Copenhagen library in Denmark. This latest period reflected in Schelling's Berlin lectures is a tragic period. These lectures were prematurely published by an enemy of his and, of course, poorly published, which made him many critics, some of them even contemptuous of his work. But what he did is nevertheless worthy of careful study because there is hardly one category in twentieth-century existentialist poetry, literature, philosophy, and indirectly the visual arts, which you cannot find in these lectures. They are to be found in the last four volumes of his collected works. And when people like Friedrich Trendelenburg (1802–1872) and Kierkegaard criticized Hegel's logic, and his confusion of dialectics and history, they were doing what Schelling had done more fully in his latest works.

In these latest writings you will find a distinction between two types of philosophy, negative and positive philosophy. Negative philosophy is philosophy of identity or essentialism. He called it negative because it abstracts from the concrete situation as all science has to do. It does not imply a negative evaluation of this philosophy, but refers to the method of abstraction. You abstract from the concrete situation until you come to the essential structures of reality, the essence of man, the essence of animals, the essence of mind, of body, etc. Negative philosophy deals with the realm of ideas, as Plato called it. But negative philosophy does not say anything about what is positively given. The essence of man does not say anything about the fact that man does exist in time and space. The term "positive philosophy" expresses the same thing that we call existentialism today. It deals with the positive, the actual situation in time and space. This is not possible without the negative side, the essential structure of reality. There could not be a tree if there were not the structure of treehood eternally even before trees existed, and even after trees go out of existence on earth altogether. The same is true of man. The essence of man is eternally given before any man appeared on earth. It is potentially or essentially given, but it is not actually or existentially given. So here we are at a great turning point of philosophical thinking. Now Schelling as a philosopher described man's existential situation. We are then in the second period of Romanticism. The unconscious has pushed toward the surface. The demonic elements in the underground of life and of human existence have become manifest. This can even be called a kind of empiricism. Schelling sometimes called it higher empiricism, higher because it takes things not simply in terms of their scientific laboratory appearances, but in correlation with their essential nature. Thus he arrives at all these categories now current in existentialist literature. We have the problem of anxiety dealt with, the problem of the relation between the unconscious and the conscious, the problem of guilt, the problem of the demonic, etc. Here the observation of things, and not the development of their rational structure, becomes decisive.

What is said against much of twentieth-century existentialism can be said of his philosophy. It is pessimistic. But the term "pessimism" should be avoided because that refers to an emotional reaction. Philosophy cannot be pessimistic. Only a person can be pessimistic in his psychological attitude. This philosophy describes the situation, the conflict between essence and existence, and this conflict is expressed in the concepts of existentialist literature.

But Schelling not only asks the existentialist questions; he also tries to give religious answers to them. This he does in terms of the classical Christian tradition. He is much nearer to Orthodoxy, whereas Kierkegaard is nearer to Pietism and the theology of revivalism, if we can use that term. In any case, for Schelling it is Lutheran Orthodoxy which offers the answers to the existentialist questions. This answer is given in a powerful vision of the history of religion. Here he has given a key, to me and many others, to the meaning of the history of religion. The history of religion cannot simply be explained in psychological terms. It has to do with powers of reality which grasp the unconscious, or which come out of the unconscious and grasp the consciousness of men and produce the symbolism in the history of religion. Of course, he had to use the limited knowledge available to him at that time about the history of religion. He knew much more of this than Hegel, and was himself responsible for the later intensive development in the religious-historical studies of Friedrich Müller (1823–1900). But what Schelling did know was interpreted by him not in terms of meaningless imagination or in terms of subjective psychological projection, but in terms of powers of being which grasp the human mind itself. These go through man's psyche, his soul, through his conscious and unconscious mind, but they do not derive from it. They come from the roots men have in the depths of reality itself.

So the different types of religions express the different powers of being by which men are grasped. The terrible sacrifices in religion, the tremendous seriousness in the history of religions, the fact that religion is the most glorious and the most cruel part of man's history, all this is understandable only if religion is not a matter of wishful thinking, but is a matter of powers of being which men encounter. In this light he explains the inner struggle, the terrible struggles in the history of religion.

This brings my consideration of Schelling to an end. You see that he can be considered the main and the most powerful critic of Hegel, not a critic who breaks out into a merely naturalistic or secularistic opposition to the great synthesis, but one who offers motives for a new synthesis on the basis of his criticism.

C. The Religious Revival and Its Theological Consequences

Most of the theological movements in the nineteenth century began as critical theology, critical of the great synthesis. Theologies and philosophies do not fall like hailstones from heaven, but are prepared in the movement of history, and in all the realms of this movement, sociological, political, as well as religious. Now I come to the religious background of the conservative criticism of Hegel.

1. The Nature of the European Revival

There was around 1830 a movement called the "awakening movement"[4] which swept throughout Europe like a storm. It was not confined to Europe, for at about the same time there was the revivalist movement in America. It touched France, Germany, and Switzerland. In England it was somehow connected with the revival of the Catholic element in the Church of England. Everywhere individuals and small groups were grasped by a new understanding of the problem of human existence and the meaning of the Christian message for them. Usually they would gather around the Bible in small groups. This movement was not restricted to any special sociological groups, although by this time the labor movement was heading in a different direction. It was very strongly represented among the landed aristocracy in East Germany and in Europe generally, among the small peasants in southwestern Germany, and among bourgeois people in other European countries; it was often connected with romantic reactions against the Enlightenment; it was rooted in what I would call the law of nature, valid in both physical and spiritual dimensions, the law, namely, that there can be no vacuum, no void. Where there is an empty space, it will be filled. The Enlightenment with its consequences, especially its materialistic trends in France and later in Germany, created a feeling of a vacuum in the spiritual life. The preaching of the Enlightenment was a kind of lecturing on all possible subjects, agricultural, technical, political, or psychological, but the dimension of the ultimate was lacking. So into this empty space an intense pietistic movement stressing conversion entered and filled it with a warm spirit of vital piety. When I began my studies in the University of Halle in 1904, now in the East Zone of Germany, I was a pupil of the greatest personality of this faculty, Martin Kähler. He was an unusual personality, standing within the classic-romantic tradition. He told us that when he was a young man he knew his Goethe by heart. He was filled with the traditions of German classical poetry, literature, and philosophy. Then this movement of revivalism grasped him, and he was converted in the literal sense of "being turned

4 In German, die Erweckungsbewegung.

around." He became a biblical theologian with the highest spiritual power over us. There in Halle one could see the influence of this movement. In the student corporations at the University—what are called fraternities here—the leading activities centered around dueling and drinking. Revivalism changed all this. Some fraternities were set up on definitely Christian principles, forbidding excessive drinking and dueling between students. This was the great side in the revivalist movement. This was still visible in the fraternity of which I became a member in 1904. The Christian principles were taken in utter seriousness. One of the most common topics of discussion was: Can you be a member of such a group if you are in doubt? In one of the meetings of all the Christian fraternities all over Germany and Switzerland I formulated the statement that the foundation is not dependent on us, but on the Christian principle. The individual person doubts, or he does not doubt, and his doubt might even be very radical, but if he takes very seriously the problem of his doubt and his faith, and struggles with the problem of the loss of faith in him, then he is a member of our fraternity. Ever since as a professor of theology I have told my students that faith embraces itself and the doubt about itself. Younger and older ministers have had to be told the same thing. When Martin Kähler was in his seventies and lecturing on the principle of justification by grace through faith, he told us: Do not think that at my age one becomes a fully serene, mature, believing, and regenerated human being. The inner struggle is going on to the last day no matter how old one becomes. This means that his pietism was not a perfectionist pietism, as it often became on Calvinist soil. Rather it was a typically Lutheran type of pietism in which the paradox of justification by grace through faith, God's acceptance of the unacceptable ones, is a fundamental principle.

So here is a motive for theology which looks a bit different from others we have discussed. Out of this some interesting things came. In this second wave of pietism, as in the first one (cf. Zinzendorf and the Moravians, the Wesley brothers and the Methodists) the missionary interest became important. It is interesting that in both the original pietist reaction against Orthodoxy and the second pietist reaction against the Enlightenment there arose a renewed missionary zeal. In the power of their experience those grasped by the revivalist movements wanted to communicate that power to paganism all over the world. So in the thirties a new theology of missions arose. It was a limited one. The main idea was still as in early pietism to save souls out of all nations. Just as the conversion experience was an individual one, so the missionary activity was individualistic in character. It had the idea of converting as many pagans as possible to rescue them from eternal damnation. There was, however, one new element in the nineteenth-century missionary zeal. It was directed not only to the pagans outside of Christendom, to non-Christians and Jews, but also to those at home. This was home missions or "inner missions," as it was called in Germany. This was particularly interesting because it was connected with a strong feeling of social responsibility for the disinherited people.

The way in which this idea of social responsibility developed was interesting. On Lutheran soil it was impossible to have revolutionary movements as could happen on Calvinist or radical-evangelical soil. Yet, this Lutheran pietism was very much interested in the social conditions of the masses in the beginning of the industrial revolution. But it did not have the revolutionary idea of changing the structure of society. It only worked to help the victims of the social conditions. The revolutionary idea was taken over by the socialists, and later in the twentieth century, by the communists. We find the germ of this revolutionary idea already in Thomas Münzer, the leader of the peasant revolt in the Reformation period. Thomas Münzer is a very interesting phenomenon. He did not say that we must change society as such, but that we must give the poor people who are enslaved in work, day and night without interruption, the possibility of reading the Bible, and of having spiritual experiences, experiences of the Spirit. He had observed in the small towns of Saxony where some early capitalist forms of production were used in the factories that these people had no Sunday, insufficient hours of rest and sleep, no chance for an education, no schools, no reading or writing. His socialist ideas came out of this observation of the spiritual situation of the urban working classes, and of the peasant classes.

The reasoning of the nineteenth-century revivalist movement was the same. The healthy part of society should give help to the sick part. The sick part is composed of the laboring people who were exploited in those victorious days of a ruthless capitalism. But home mission was still basically conceived of as conversion of those who were estranged from the church. Indeed the laboring masses were completely estranged from the churches. There was no call for revolution. Revolution was out of the question on Lutheran soil. But there was the call to assume the responsibility of helping the other classes to understand spiritual values of which they were being deprived by their life situation. I cannot develop here all the sociological background—the conditions of the agricultural workers, out of which all the city workers originally came, because there was no industry, and when the industry started, they came from the villages, but in the villages the lowest classes were already estranged from the churches, because the churches were always on the side of the upper classes.

This sense of social responsibility was certainly important, but it was not enough. The members of the church were given the feeling that it was enough to exercise personal charity toward unfortunate individuals. This in itself, however, served to estrange church people from a real understanding of the new sociological situation created by the industrial revolution. Therefore, in spite of the feeling of revivalism and social responsibility for the disinherited people, the rise of socialism and communism could not be prevented in Europe, because it was not seen that individual help was entirely fruitless in relation to the masses of industrial workers who soon numbered in the millions. No individual help could possibly cope with this situation.

To anticipate what happened much later, I would like to say a few words about the religious socialist movement of the twentieth century. This movement tried to combine two elements: on the one hand, a sense of social responsibility for the laboring, disinherited masses, which characterized the theology and piety of the awakening movement, and on the other hand, taking seriously the transformed sociological situation, by not thinking only in terms of individual relations, but accepting the analyses of the social situation of the French and German socialists, especially the profoundest of them made by Karl Marx. So the religious socialist movement combined the heritage of nineteenth-century revivalism and the rise of socialism. When we founded this movement in

Germany after the first World War, we were deeply aware that the social attitudes of the revivalist people and of the Ritschlians, who thought on an individualistic basis, were inadequate to the new situation described by the socialist writers as a complete dehumanization, a *Verdinglichung*, a thingification, an objectification of the masses of people. They were transformed from being persons into being objects of working power which could be bought. They had to sell themselves in order to survive. The quarters in which they lived were not slums in the modern sense, but they were bare of anything human. I remember my horror when I went into the living quarters of the working people in cities like Berlin or in the Ruhr country where the largest industry is concentrated, and saw the kind of dehumanized existence these people endured. Our response to this situation came in the form of combining the revivalist tradition of social responsibility and the sociological analysis of the socialist writers, especially Marx and Engels.

2. *The Theology of Repristination*

There were still other consequences of the awakening movement, especially a revival of traditional theology. The pupils of Schleiermacher, Hegel, and Schelling had produced a theology of mediation, which combined the rediscovered biblical reality with the concerns of the modern mind. But alongside of this theology of mediation there arose a theology of restoration or of repristination, or as we would call it today, a conservative theology as over against a liberal theology. This repristination theology was a radical return to and rediscovery of the orthodox tradition. The theologians in this movement did not produce many new theological thoughts, but they did one valuable thing for us. They opened up the treasures of classical Orthodoxy. I say this even though I am completely opposed to a theology of repristination, for I wish that every student would learn in Latin the classical formulations of Protestant Orthodox theology. Then he would be as educated as the Roman Catholic theologians who know their Thomas Aquinas or their Suarez or some other classical theologian. Then, of course, one can go beyond that. But to go beyond without having been within Orthodoxy is not a wholesome attitude. But this is what has happened more and more. So I say now that the one good thing that the theology of re-pristination did for us was to show forth the treasures of the past as matters which still concern us. It still concerns me what Johann Gerhard or other great Protestant scholastics said about a given doctrine. They knew many of our problems and offered solutions which we should not simply forget. Besides, they were not unlearned as our present-day fundamentalists who are direct products of revivalism, but without theological education. It is a fundamentalism based simply on piety and on biblical interpretation which is ignorant of the way in which the Bible was written and came into existence. So you cannot compare classical Orthodoxy with fundamentalism. But in any case, a repristination theology could not last, because history does not run backward but forward.

This restoration theology was an expression of the dissolution of the great synthesis. These forms of Orthodoxy despised what had happened since the Enlightenment. They went back to classical Orthodoxy. They did not accept the historical criticism of the biblical literature. They took the Bible literally. They even believed that the Pentateuch was written by Moses, even though one of the books tells about his death. Such absurdities are always the consequence of the doctrine of literal inspiration. This view could not and did not last. The real bearers of the development in theology were the theologians of mediation, people like Martin Kähler and the theologians of the Ritschlian school.

3. *Natural Science and the Fight over Darwinism*

Another attack against the great synthesis came from the direction of modern science. Schelling's philosophy of nature and Hegel's mechani-cal application of the categories of man's spirit to nature produced the great reaction of empirical science. Empirical science followed the method of analysis and synthesis, as we have it in the physical sciences, the mathematical structure of nature as a presupposition, the mechani-cal movement as the metaphysical background, the Newtonian ideas about natural laws, in short, a mechanical naturalism in all realms, especially in physics and medicine. This movement came to its direct expression in Darwinism, which is worth considering from the point of view of Christian theology.

This mechanical or mechanistic naturalism threatened Christian theology and so Christian theology had to do the work of defense.—There are other kinds of naturalism, the vitalistic naturalism of Nietzsche, the dynamic naturalism of Bergson and Whitehead. This mechanistic naturalism we sometimes call materialistic, but the term "materialism" itself has three different meanings, so I do not use it here.—In any case, Christian theology became a theology of retreat and defense in the face of this mechanistic naturalism. This was true of the Ritschlian theology, the theology of mediation or apologetic theology, and of most of the theological books that were written in the second half of the nineteenth century. Christian theology was like an army retreating in face of an advancing army. With every new breakthrough of the advancing army, in this case modern science, Christian theology would attempt to protect the Christian tradition which still remained intact. Then a new breakthrough would make the previous defense untenable, and so another retreat and setting up a new defense would be necessary. This went on and on.

This whole spectacle, this fight between science and religion, has brought contempt upon the term "apologetic." It was a poor form of apologetic. The first great shock which had to be accepted was the Copernican world view. Galileo, the greatest representative of this idea, was forced by the Inquisition to recant, but his recanting did not help the church at all. Soon the theologians had to accept the Copernican world view. Then there was Newton's mechanics of bodies moving according to eternal natural laws; the concept of natural law was established and philosophically formulated by Kant. This prevented thinking about interferences of a divine being; God was placed alongside the world, and not permitted to interfere with it. Then theology came to the defense of miracles, the idea of the possibility of divine interferences, which of course presupposes a miserable concept of God who would have to destroy his creation in order to do his work of salvation. But this was the apologetic situation. Then another retreat was required because the defense of miracles in this way was untenable. A further shock came with the idea of evolution. Then a six-day creation was defended, then abandoned. Evolution said that life has developed out of the inorganic realm. Then where is God? According to the traditional idea of creation God has created the organic forms; they have not developed out of the inorganic forms. Therefore, a particular work of God's creation must be postulated and on this thin thread the whole apologetic position was suspended. There was the lacuna in scientific knowledge, for science was not able to show how the organic developed out of the inorganic. Theologians enjoyed this lacuna, for they could place God in this gap left by science. Where science could not work any more, God was put to work, so to speak. God filled the gaps left by science.

That was an unworthy idea of God. The position was indefensible so theologians had to withdraw again. But one last point was kept. That is the creation of man. Here the Roman Church still sticks to the idea that even if the evolutionary process is as presupposed by biology today, there is still one point that cannot be explained biologically, namely, the immortal soul which God has given man, the higher animal, at some moment in the process of evolution. This was and still is a last defense against science, but this last defense is not tenable either, for it presupposes a substance, the soul, which is a separate form from the form of the body. But in the Aristotelian sense, the soul is the form of the body and you cannot separate them. Moreover, the concept of eternal life has nothing to do with such a dualistic construction of an immortal soul put at one moment into man's body. When this last defense is given up, science has conquered all apologetic positions. And this is a good thing. Then the situation must be seen in an absolutely new way. Science lives and works in another dimension and therefore cannot interfere with the religious symbols of creation, fulfillment, forgiveness, and incarnation, nor can religion interfere with scientific statements. No scientific statement about the way in which living beings have come into existence or how the first cell developed out of large molecules can have direct bearing on theology. Indirectly, of course, everything is a concern of theology. For when science describes the way in which life is construed and is developed, then indirectly it says something about God, the creative ground of life, but not in terms of an interference of a highest being in the processes of nature.

This whole struggle between science and religion is no doubt in the past for you. But it was not so when I began the study of theology. At that time apologetic theology was full of confidence that science would never find a way of showing the development from, let us say, the original mud to the first cell. But science can show this to a great extent, perhaps not fully, but this is a matter of experiment. Theology does not need to put God to work to fill an empty space in our scientific knowledge.

The struggle over Darwin dealt not only with this general evolutionary idea, but more concretely with the genesis of man. The "monkey trial" was a last remnant of this struggle which was so prominent in the nineteenth century. It was a great shock which the church had to absorb after the initial shocks of the Copernican revolution and the Newtonian idea of natural law. I may be wrong, but I believe that aside from some literalists in the South or in the Bible belt no one in the younger generation or among theologians is involved in this conflict any longer. People presuppose that science has to go its way, and that the religious dimension is different from the scientific. But in the nineteenth century this affair disrupted the faith of millions of people. The laborers who read the socialist literature decided negatively against religion; they looked at religion as always interfering in the arena of scientific discussions. And when religion did this, it was a lost cause. It has taken over a half a century to overcome the antireligious attitude among the scientists and the antiscientific attitude among the religious people. If we are out of this situation now, I hope we never return to it. And we should avoid remnants of this kind of apologetics today. For instance, we should not try to base our doctrine of freedom on Heisenberg's principle of indeterminacy, as if to say that since there is some element of indeterminacy in nature, we can speak of freedom. Perhaps tomorrow this principle will be replaced by another, and then your whole wonderful apologetic collapses, and you join the retreating army of apologists. The theologians of the twentieth century should learn this lesson from the nineteenth century. You cannot apologetically establish symbols which belong to the dimension of the ultimate upon a description of finite relations.

You can speak of the structure of nature, as I have done in the third volume of *Systematic Theology,* through all the realms of the natural. But this is not done for apologetic purposes, but is in line with Thomas Aquinas' statement that he who knows anything, knows something about God. Whatever we know in any realm bears witness to the creative ground of it. In this sense we must deal with statements of science. But we must do so also in another sense. For the work of the scientists is of the highest theological interest insofar as it reveals the logos of being, the inner structure of reality, which is not in opposition to the Logos which has appeared in the Christ, but is the same Logos. Therefore, in this sense the witness of science is the witness to God. This is the right relationship and is not one of fighting against each other in terms of unjustified interferences.

D. KIERKEGAARD'S EXISTENTIAL THEOLOGY

Søren Kierkegaard must also be dealt with as a contributor to the breakdown of the universal synthesis, although his greatest influence has been exercised in our time rather than in his own. He made a new start based on a combination of an existentialist philosophy and a pietistic, revivalistic theological criticism of the great synthesis. More specifically, he combined Lutheran pietism of the revivalist type, including the orthodox content of revivalism, with the categories of Schelling's existentialism. Although he denied Schelling's solution, he took over the categories. His criticism, together with that of Marx and Nietzsche, is historically most important. But none of these three became influential in world-historical terms in the nineteenth century. Kierkegaard was largely a forgotten individual in his century. I recall with pride how as students of theology in Halle we came into contact with Kierkegaard's thought through translations made by an isolated individual in Württemberg. In the years 1905–1907 we were grasped by Kierkegaard. It was a very great experience. We could not accept the theological orthodoxy of repristination. We could not accept especially those "positive"—in the special sense of "conservative"—theologians who disregarded the historical-critical school. For this was valid science which was carried on by this school. It cannot be denied if honest research is conducted into the historical foundations of the New Testament.

But on the other hand we had a feeling of moralistic distortion and amystical emptiness, an emptiness in which the warmth of the mystical presence of the divine was missing, as in the whole Ritschlian school. We were not grasped by this moralism. We did not find in it the depths of the consciousness of guilt as classical theology had always had. So we were extremely happy when we encountered Kierkegaard. It was this combination of intense piety which went into the depths of human existence and the philosophical greatness which he had received from Hegel that made him so important for us. The real critical point would be the denial that Hegel's idea of reconciliation is a genuine reconciliation. Man is not reconciled by the reconciliation in the philosopher's head. We will hear the same thing from Marx later on.

We could discuss Kierkegaard in connection with the existentialist movement of the twentieth century, because he became effective only in our own century. Nevertheless, in the structure of this course I prefer to place him in his own historical place where he represents one of the decisive criticisms of Hegel's great synthesis. We will discuss him fairly thoroughly, and you can take this discussion not only as a treatment of nineteenth-century theological thought, but also of twentieth-century theology, for while he wrote in the nineteenth century, his real influence has been significant in the twentieth century. Later we will see similar situations with regard to two other thinkers who were not inner-ecclesiastical representatives of theology, but anti-ecclesiastical representatives. They are Marx, especially in his earlier existentialist protest against Hegel, and then Friedrich Nietzsche, who followed Schopenhauer.

You may be a little surprised that I do not deal more with the theological movements within the church of this period. The reason I do not is that they are not as important as the great critics of Hegel for our own situation. These critics are more fundamental for our theological situation today than are the theologians of mediation. There are some rare exceptions, as for example my own teacher Martin Kähler in Halle. The real impact came from people outside. Of course, Kierkegaard was religiously inside, but as a critic of the church he was perhaps even more radical than Marx and Nietzsche put together.

Kierkegaard has become the fashion in three respects: (a) Religiously, which is most justified, because his religious writings are as valid today as they were when they were written. (b) As the inspiration for the dialectical theology, called neo-orthodoxy in this country. In Europe it is usually called dialectical, which shows its relation to Hegel, for this term is the main principle of Hegel's thinking. (c) As the inspiration for Heidegger, the philosopher who has given the name existentialism to the whole movement which derives from Kierkegaard.

1. Kierkegaard's Criticism of Hegel

As in the case of most of the anti-Hegelians, Kierkegaard's criticism is based on the concept of reconciliation. For Hegel the world is reconciled in the mind of the philosopher of religion who has gone through the different forms of man's spiritual life: the subjective spirit (which is the psychological side), the objective spirit (the social-ethical and political side), and the absolute spirit (art, religion, and philosophy). The philosopher lives in all of them. He is deeply in the religious realm; he lives in the aesthetic realm; and on the basis of the religious realm he conceptualizes what is myth and symbol in religion. Out of all this he develops his philosophy of religion. In this way he mirrors in his mind the final synthesis after the whole world process has gone through thesis, antithesis, and synthesis. The divine mind, the absolute mind, comes to its rest on the basis of religion within the mind of the philosopher who achieves his highest power when he becomes a philosopher of religion, conceptualizing the symbols of the religious life. This is for Hegel reconciliation. This reconciliation in the mind of the philosopher was the point attacked by all those whom I have mentioned—Schelling, Feuerbach, pietists, and natural scientists. They all said the world is unreconciled. The theologians went back to Immanuel Kant and said the prison of finitude is not pierced, not even by Hegel's great attempt. The reconciliation of the finite and the infinite has not yet happened.

Kierkegaard did the same thing in a particular way. In the system of essences reconciliation might be possible, he argued, but the system of essences is not the reality in which we are living. We are living in the realm of existence, and in the realm of existence reconciliation has not yet happened. Existence is the place of decision between good and evil.

Man is in the tragic situation, in the tragic unavoidability of evil. This contradiction in existence means that Hegel is seen as confusing essentialist fulfillment with existential unfulfillment or estrangement. I told you that estrangement or alienation is one of the terms which Hegel created, but which is then turned against him. Nature is estranged spirit for Hegel; the material reality is self-estranged spirit. Now Kierkegaard said that mankind is in this state of estrangement, and Hegel's construction of a continuous series of syntheses in which the negativity of antithesis is overcome in the world process is true only with respect to the essential realm. Symbolically we could perhaps say that it goes on only in the inner life of God. But Kierkegaard emphasized that estrangement is our situation. Only in the inner divine life is there reconciliation, but not in our situation.

Hegel had described the inner divine life in his great logic. The logic is the science of essences in their highest abstraction and their inner dialectical relationship. Then the logicians came along. The man who is very important for the criticism of all essentialism is Trendelenburg. Kierkegaard was dependent on him for his logical criticism of Hegel. His criticism was that the logical process is not a real process; it is not a process in time; it is only a description of logical relations. What Hegel did was to confuse the dialectical process of logic with the actual movement in history. While reconciliation is always a reality in the dialectical process of divine life, it is not a reality in the external process of human existence. So from the logical point of view Hegel was criticized for his fundamental confusion of essence and existence.

Hegel was not able to understand the human situation in terms of anxiety and despair. Kierkegaard could not follow Hegel; all his life he possessed a melancholic disposition. This melancholy of which he often spoke was associated with a curse which his father made against God, and he felt that the reaction to this blasphemy of his father was upon him and never left him free. The point is that such a personality was able to discover things which were not so deeply felt by a character as Hegel, who existed in a bourgeois situation, who felt psychologically more safe and was able to conquer the negative and tragic elements of life which he saw.

2. Ethical Existence and the Human Situation (Anxiety, Despair)

One of the main points connected with Kierkegaard's melancholic personal condition and his feeling of unreconciled reality was his experience of the lonely individual. Here again we have an anticipation of present-day existentialism. The individual stands in solitude before God and the process of the world cannot liberate him from the tremendous responsibility by which he lives in the situation. Again and again he said that the last reality is the deciding individual, the individual who in freedom must decide for good or evil. We find nothing of this in Hegel. It is very interesting that Hegel who was so universal in his thinking and all-embracing never developed personal ethics. His ethics are objectivist; he subsumed ethics under philosophy of history and philosophy of law. Ethics of family, ethics of state, of community, of culture, all that is in Hegel, but not ethics which has to do with the personal decision of the individual. This was already an element in Schelling's attack against Hegel, but it was stressed more by Kierkegaard than by anybody else.

What is the reason for this experience of solitude? It is due to human finitude in estrangement. It is not the finitude which is identical with the infinite, but it is separated finitude, finitude standing upon itself in the individual person. As long as the identity principle was decisive, it was possible to overcome the anxiety of finitude, of having to die, by the experience of being united with the infinite. But this answer was not possible for Kierkegaard. So he tried to show why we are in anxiety because of being finite and in despair because of being in separated finitude. The first is his description of anxiety and the second is his description of despair. There are two writings which every theologian must read. Both are comparatively short: *The Concept of Dread* and *The Sickness Unto Death*.[5] I have always criticized the title of the English translation of *The Concept of Dread*, because dread is different from anxiety. Dread has in it the connotation of something sudden,

[5] Søren Kierkegaard, *The Concept of Dread*, translated by Walter Lowrie (Princeton: Princeton University Press, 1944); and *The Sickness Unto Death*, translated by Walter Lowrie (Princeton: Princeton University Press, 1941).

whereas what Kierkegaard describes is an ontological state of man. But now in English the term "anxiety" has generally replaced "dread" to describe this state which Kierkegaard has in mind. *The Concept of Dread,* in any case, is a fundamental book on the theory of anxiety. It has been more fully developed by others, so that now there is a vast literature on the subject, including the works of people like Freud, Rollo May, *et al.*

Kierkegaard wrote about two kinds of anxiety. The first is connected with his theory of the fall. He symbolized this with the biblical myth of Adam and Eve, and found profound psychological insight there. This is the anxiety of actualizing one's own freedom, which is a double anxiety: the anxiety of not actualizing it, of being restricted and of not coming into real existence, and the anxiety of actualizing it, with the knowledge of the possibility of losing one's identity. This is not a description of an original historical Adam, but of the Adam in every one of us, as the word "Adam" means. In this double anxiety of actualizing oneself and of being afraid to actualize oneself, every adolescent finds himself with respect to sex, his relation to his parents, to the political tradition in which he lives, etc. It is always the question of actualizing or not actualizing one's potentialities.

Finally the decision is made for actualizing oneself, and this is simultaneously the fall. But after the fall there is another anxiety, because the fall, like every trespassing of limits, produces guilt. The anxiety of guilt at its extreme point is despair. This despair is described in *The Sickness Unto Death.* This sickness unto death is present in all human beings. This condition is described with the help of many Hegelian categories, as the conflict between spirit and matter in man, man having finite spirit, man experiencing the conflict in himself, having the desire to get rid of himself, and of being unable to commit suicide because the guilt consciousness makes it clear that suicide cannot help you to escape the situation in which you are. One thing ought to be kept in mind, and that is that the term "guilt" means both the objective state of *being* guilty for something that is wrong, and the subjective state of *feeling* guilty. To confuse these two states can be very bad, for example, when many psychoanalysts say that we must abolish guilt. That is very ambiguous, for what they really have to overcome is misplaced guilt feeling, which is one of the worst mental diseases. But this can be done only if they manage to bring the patient to the point where he faces up to his real state of being guilty, his true guilt in the objective sense. We must make a clear distinction between guilt and guilt feeling. Guilt feelings may be very misleading. In neurotic and psychotic conditions they are always misplaced. One of the defenses of the neurotic is to insist on misplaced guilt feeling because he cannot face reality and his own real guilt. This real guilt is his estrangement from the ultimate that expresses itself in actual acts directed against his own true being.

3. *The Nature of Faith (the Leap and Existential Truth)*

There is no escape from the sickness unto death; therefore, something must happen which cannot be mediated in logical terms. You cannot derive it from anything in you; it must come to you; it must be given to you. Here the doctrine of the "leap" appears in Kierkegaard. It has already appeared, in fact, in his description of the fall. Anxiety brings man before a decision, for or against actualizing himself. This decision is a leap; it cannot be logically derived. Sin cannot be derived in any way. If it is derived, then it is not sin any more but necessity. Here we can recall what I said about Schleiermacher for whom sin is the necessary result of the inadequacies of our spiritual life in relation to our physical life. That makes sin a necessity, and thus takes the sharpness of guilt away from sin. Kierkegaard repudiates this notion of sin. For him the fall of man is a leap of an irrational kind, of a kind which cannot be derived in terms of logical necessity.

But there is the opposite leap, the leap of faith. You cannot derive this either from your situation. You cannot overcome the sickness unto death, the anxiety of estrangement. This can only be done by faith. Faith therefore has the character of a nonrational jump in Kierkegaard. He speaks of the leap from the point of view of the individual. He is so well nourished on Hegelian dialectics that he builds up a dialectic of spheres. Between these spheres there is a leap. That is non-Hegelian. But the spheres themselves follow each other hierarchically, and that is truly Hegelian. There are three steps or spheres. You can also call them stages, but they are not so much stages following each other in time as levels lying above each other in space, and coexisting all the time in ordinary human beings. These levels or stages are the aesthetic, the ethical, and the religious. Man lives within all of them, but the decisive thing is how they are related to each other and which one is predominant for him.

Kierkegaard's description of the aesthetic stage was perhaps the most brilliant thing he did. His *Diary of the Seducer*, often abused for other purposes, is the most complete description of the aesthetic stage in its complete actualization. Also his analysis of Mozart's *Don Juan* is a great work of literary criticism, philosophy, and theology all in one. The characteristic of the aesthetic stage is the lack of involvement, detachment from existence. It has nothing to do with aesthetics as such or with the arts. Of course, this attitude of mere detachment and of noninvolvement in the situation can take place in relation to music, literature, and the visual arts; but it can also be found in the theoretical or in the cognitive relation to reality. Cognition can have the merely aesthetic attitude of noninvolved detachment. I am afraid this is seen as the ideal even in many humanities courses in the universities. To be sure, there are elements of mere detachment in every scholarly inquiry; detachment will be necessary when dealing with dates, places, and connections, etc., but as soon as you come to interpretation, detachment will be reduced by existential participation. Otherwise you cannot understand reality; you do not "stand under" the reality.

Hegel was regarded somehow as a symbol of the aesthetic attitude, and so were the romantics. Because of their aesthetic detachment they took all the cultural contents on the basis of a nonexistential attitude, a lack of involvement. When I came to this country and first used the word aestheticism in a lecture, a colleague of mine at Columbia University told me not to use that word in describing Americans. That is a typical European phenomenon. Americans are activists and not aestheticists. Now I do not believe this is true. I think there is quite a lot of this aesthetic detachment even in popular culture. It is present in the buying and selling of cultural goods—I spoke about this on the occasion of *Time* Magazine's fortieth anniversary—in which you often see a nonparticipating, nonexistential attitude. Here Kierkegaard's criticism would be valid. Perhaps on the whole this is not a very great danger among the American intelligentsia. My observation has been that they jump very quickly out of the detached aesthetic attitude—in all lectures and discussions, in philosophy and the arts—to the question, "What shall we do?" This attitude was described by Kierkegaard as the attitude of the ethical stage.

In the ethical stage the attitude of detachment is impossible. Kierkegaard had a concept of the demonic which means self-seclusion. This belongs to the aesthetic stage, not going out of oneself, but using everyone and everything for one's own aesthetic satisfaction. Opposed to this demonic self-seclusion is love. Love opens up and brings one out of self-seclusion, and in doing so conquers the demonic. This character of love leads to the relations of love. Here Kierkegaard accepted Hegel's objective ethics—the ethics of family, of vocation, of state, etc. In the aesthetic stage sex produces isolation; in the ethical stage love overcomes isolation and generates responsibility. The seducer is the symbol of irresponsibility with respect to the other one, for the other one is manipulated only aesthetically. Only through responsibility can the ethical stage be reached.

It is interesting as a biographical fact that Kierkegaard never reached two of the decisive things that he attributed to this stage, that is, family and vocation. He lived from some income as a writer, but he never had an official vocation, either in the church or outside of it. And he had this tragic experience with his fiancée, Regina Olson, whom he loved dearly. But because of the inablity to transcend his self-seclusion, his melancholic state, he finally dissolved the relationship, and never really overcame the guilt connected with it.

Then Kierkegaard dealt with the religious stage. The religious stage is beyond both the aesthetic and the ethical and is expressed in relation to that which interests us infinitely or which produces infinite passion. You recall that I told you about Hegel's two concepts: interest and passion. Hegel's critics took these terms from him and then used them in their criticism of him. Hegel said that without interest and passion nothing great has ever happened in history. This notion was now taken over by Kierkegaard into the religious situation and by Marx into the quasi-religion of the nineteenth-century revolutionary movement.

Religion has within itself two possibilities, identity and contrast. The principle of identity is based on mysticism, the identity of the infinite and the finite; and the principle of distance is based on estrangement, the finitude and the guilt of the human situation. We have discussed this often in these lectures. We saw this especially in the contrast between Spinoza and Kant, Spinoza the representative of the principle of identity and Kant the representative of critical detachment. This duality which permeates all human existence and thought is also present in Kierkegaard's description of the two types of religion. He calls these two types "religiousness A" and "religiousness B," but a more powerful way of expressing the same thing is to use the names of "Socrates" and "Jesus." Both of them have something in common. Both of them are existentialists in their approach to God. Neither is simply a teacher who communicates ideas or contents of knowledge. They are the greatest teachers in human history because they were existential. This means they did not communicate contents, but did something to persons. They did not write anything, but they have produced more disciples than anybody else who has ever written anything. All four Greek schools of philosophy were pupils of Socrates who never wrote a thing, and Christianity is the result of Jesus who never wrote anything.

That alone shows the person-to-person situation, the complete existential involvement of these two types of religiousness. But then there arises the great difference. Religiousness A or the religion of Socrates presupposes that truth is present within every human being. The fundamental truths are in man himself. The dialectical or existential teacher has only to evoke them from man. Socrates does this in two ways. The one is irony. This concept is in the best tradition of Romanticism of which I spoke. This means that every special content of which a person is sure is subjected to radical questioning until its insecurity is revealed. Nothing remains as self-evident. In Plato's dialogues Socrates is the leader of the discussions, and he applies irony to the Sophists who know everything, who are the scholars of their time. The Socratic questioning undercut their scholarly self-consciousness, their belief in their infallibility. Socrates did the same thing with the craftsmen, the businessmen, and the aristocratic people who were his followers. The other way is midwifery. This means that the existential teacher brings to birth what is already inside a person, helps him to find the truth in himself, and does not simply tell him the truth. This presupposes the Platonic idea that man's soul has an eternal relation to all the essences of things. So knowledge is a matter of memory. The famous example given in Plato's dialogue *Meno* is of the slave who is asked about the Pythagorean proposition of the three angles of a triangle, and although he is completely uneducated, he is able to understand it because of the mathematical evidences within him. This is not produced in him by external teaching. This is indeed true of geometry and algebra. Everyone can experience in himself the evidence of such things, but this is not true of certain other things. This then led to the resistance of the empirical school against Socrates and Plato, on the one hand, and leads to the other religious type represented by Jesus, on the other hand.

Both Socrates and Jesus communicate indirectly, as Kierkegaard says, but they do not have textbook knowledge of any kind. By indirect communication Socrates brings to consciousness what is in man. Therefore, he is called a religious teacher. I am in full agreement with that. I think it is ridiculous to say that Socrates is a philosopher and Jesus is religious, or perhaps a religionist, a really blasphemous term. Both of them deal with man in his existential situation from the point of view of the meaning of life and of ultimate concern. They do it existentially. In this sense we can call Socrates the founder of liberal humanism, as one of the quasi-religions. Now, if the difference between Socrates and Jesus is not that of the difference between philosophy and religion— which is absolute nonsense here—then what is the difference? The difference is that the indirect ironical teacher, Socrates, does not transform the totality of the being of the other person. This is done only in religiousness B, by the teacher who is at the same time the Savior, who helps the person whom he teaches in terms of healing and liberating. Here another type of consciousness comes into existence. According to this idea, God is not in man. Man is separated from God by estrangement. Therefore God must come to man from outside, and address him. God comes to man in the Christ.

God is not the paradoxical presence in the individual, but he is present outside of man in the Christ. Nobody can derive the coming of the Christ from the human situation. This is another leap, the leap of

God into time through the sending of his Son. This cannot be derived from man, but is given to him. This makes Jesus the teacher into the Savior of men. While Socrates is the great existential teacher, Jesus is both the teacher and the Savior who transforms man.

In this way the religious stage has within itself a tension. Hegel's interpretation of the Christ was in the line of Platonism. In Hegel the eternal essential unity of God and man is represented in a complete way in the Christ, but it is also present in every individual. For Kierkegaard God comes from the outside or from above. Here you see immediately the starting point of Karl Barth. According to him, you cannot start with man, not even in terms of questioning. You must start with God who comes to man. The human situation is not such that you can find in man's predicament the question which may lead to the religious answer. In terms of this conviction Barth criticizes my own systematic theology, which in this sense is un-Kierkegaardian. This idea of God coming to man totally from the outside had great religious power, but I would say that its religious power is disproportional to its philosophical power, to the power of thought. It cannot be carried out in such a way. But that is not the point here. The point is that you see the bridge from Kierkegaard to Barth and neo-orthodoxy in the idea of God coming to man from above and from outside him, with no point of contact in man. When Emil Brunner wanted to say that there must be some point of contact, Barth answered with his passionate "No"—this famous essay in which he defends his idea of the absolute otherness of God outside of man. Now, I do not believe this idea can be maintained, but, in any case, negatively speaking, it had great religious power.

This is connected with a concept of truth that has to do with the metaphor of leap. This truth is quite different from the objective truth in the scientific sense. So Kierkegaard makes the following statement, which gives the gist of all his philosophical and theological authorship: "Truth is the objective uncertainty held fast in the most personal passionate experience. This is the truth, the highest truth attainable for the existing individual." Here he defines faith as well as truth, for this is just the leap of faith. A very important element is what he calls the objective uncertainty. This means that theology is not based on objective certainty. A merely objective certainty, as Hegel wanted to reach, is not adequate to the situation between God and man. This would be possible only if the individual had already entered the system of essences, the essential structure of reality. But he has not; he is outside of it, as God is outside of him. Therefore, objective certainty in religion is impossible; faith remains objectively uncertain. Truth in the realm of the objective scientific approach is not existential truth. Kierkegaard would not deny the possibility of scientific truth, but this is the truth of detachment. It is not the truth of involvement; it is not existential truth. Existential truth is objective uncertainty and personal, passionate experience or subjective certainty, but a certainty which can never be objectified. It is the certainty of the leap.

This subjective certainty of the leap of faith is always under criticism and attack, and therefore Kierkegaard speaks of holding fast to it in a passionate way. In personal existence there is passionate inner movement, and in the power of this passion we have the only truth which is existentially important for us. This is the most significant thing in the world, the question of "to be or not to be." It is the ultimate concern about man's eternal destiny, the question of the meaning of life. This is, of course, different from the truth we approach in terms of approximative scientific objectivity. If we use the term "subjectivity" in connection with Kierkegaard's idea of existential truth, then please avoid the mistake of equating it with willfulness. This is the connotation the word has today. Therefore, it is so difficult to understand a man like Kierkegaard and practically all classical philosophers. Subject means what it says, something standing upon itself, *sub-jectum*, that which underlies. Man is a *sub-jectum*, one who stands upon himself, and not an *objectum*, an object which is in opposition to a subject looking at it. If man is this, then he becomes a thing. This is the sickness of our time. The protest of subjectivity does not mean the protest of willfulness. It means the protest of freedom, of the creative individual, of personality, of man who is in the tragic situation of having to decide in a state of estrangement, in the human predicament. In these ideas we have almost the whole summary of Kierkegaard's theology.

But then Kierkegaard goes beyond this to the question: What can be done to give content to this situation? With respect to the content we must say that not much can be found of it in Kierkegaard. He was not a constructive theologian, and he could not be, because one can be a constructive theologian only if he is not only existentially interested and passionate, but also has an essentialist vision of the structure of reality. Without this, systematic theology is impossible. So we find very little content in the theological or religious writings of Kierkegaard. We have only a continuous repetition of the term "paradox"—leap is simply another word for paradox, that which cannot be derived, that which is irrational and surprising.

There is, however, one content to which he refers all the time, and this is the appearance of the Christ. Thus the leap which is necessary to overcome the situation of doubt and despair is the leap into the reality of the Christ. He states this in a very unusual, paradoxical, and theologically questionable form. He says that only one thing matters: In the year A.D. 30 God sent the Christ for my salvation. I do not need any more theology; I do not need to know the results of historical criticism. It is enough to know that one thing. Into this I have to leap. Then we must ask: Can we solve the problem which historical criticism has opened up by a theology of the leap? I do not believe it is possible. Philosophically the question is this: In which direction am I to leap? You can leap in all directions, but if you have a direction in mind, you already have some knowledge, so it is not a pure leap anymore. If you are in complete darkness and jump without knowing in what direction you are jumping, then you can land anywhere, maybe even on the place from which you jumped. The danger in this concept is asking someone to jump without showing him the direction. Then we have more than subjectivity and paradox; we have willfulness and arbitrariness; we have complete contingency. But if you already know in which direction to jump, in the direction of Christ, for example, then you must have a reason for this. This reason may be some experience with him, some historical knowledge, some image of him from church tradition, etc., but in any case, you have some content. The mere name alone does not say anything. And if you have these things, you are already in the tradition of theology and the church, and it is not a sheer leap any more. This is a problem which we have to say Kierkegaard left completely unsolved. His statement that you have to leap over two thousand years to the year A.D. 30 is simply unrealistic, because nobody can do that. The intellectual leap, or the emotional-intellectual leap, which you are supposed to make with your whole self, is conditioned by two thousand years of church and cultural history. You cannot do that without using contemporary language, and you use language even though you are silent, for internally you speak whenever you are thinking. When you make such a leap, you are using the language of the 1960's, and so you are dependent on the two preceding millennia. It is an illusion to think we can become contemporary with Christ insofar as the historical Jesus is the Christ. We can be contemporary with the Christ only in the way described by the apostle Paul, that is, insofar as the Christ is the Spirit, for the Spirit is present within and beyond the intervening centuries. But this is something else. Kierkegaard wanted to solve the problem of historical criticism by this concept of contemporaneity. You can do this if you take contemporaneity in the Pauline sense of the divine Spirit present to us, and showing the face of Jesus as the Christ. But you cannot escape historical criticism by becoming contemporaneous with Jesus himself. This is the fundamental criticism which we must make from a theological point of view.

4. Criticism of Theology and Church

We have still to discuss Kierkegaard's critical attitudes toward theology and the church.[6] One can almost say that when Kierkegaard deals with the church or theology, the image which he presents is more a caricature than a fair description. In particular the ecclesiastical office was an object of criticism. He attacked the fact that the minister becomes an employee like all other employees, with special duties and economic securities. This position of the minister, especially its bourgeois elements, of having a career, getting married, raising children, while at the same time proclaiming the impossible possibility of the Christ is for Kierkegaard involved in a self-contradiction. But Kierkegaard does not indicate how this conflict might be solved. Certainly it is a reality, and for Kierkegaard a reality which contradicts the absoluteness of the essence of Christianity. One cannot take this as an objectively valid criticism,

[6] Cf. Kierkegaard's *Attack upon 'Christendom,'* translated by Walter Lowrie (Princeton: Princeton University Press, 1944).

because if one did, then one would have to abolish every church office. If the office is not abolished, it is inevitable that the laws of sociology will make themselves felt and influence the form of the office and those who hold it.

The same thing is true of his attacks on theology. He attacks theology because it is an objectifying attempt to construct a well-formulated system out of the existential paradox. Here again the inadequacy of the situation of the theologian is marvelously expressed, but in terms of a caricature. On the other hand, the question is whether theology is a necessary service of the church. If it is—and it has always been that as long as Christianity has existed; there is theology in Paul and John—then the question arises: Can the theological task be united with the paradox of the Christian message in a different way? When Kierkegaard speaks about the theologian in his attack on theology, he sarcastically suggests: Since Christ was born, let us establish a chair in theology dealing with the birth of Christ; Christ was crucified, so let us make a full professorship for the crucifixion of Christ; Christ has risen, so let us make an associate professorship, etc. This kind of comical attack on theology makes a great impact on anyone who reads it, whether he is a theologian or not. But if it is taken as more than a reminder, if it is taken as a prescription, it means the abolition of theology.

The truth which we can gain from this kind of criticism of theology is the truth of the inadequacy of the objectifying attitude in existential matters. This refers both to the ministry and to theology. In the ministry there is the objectifying factor, the factor of a sociological structure in analogy with all sociological structures. In theology there is a structure of thought in analogy with all structures of thought. This reminder is, of course, of great importance. The minister and the theologian should be forever reminded of the inadequacy, and not only that but also of the necessity of what they are doing. The impossible possibility, as Reinhold Niebuhr, I believe, following Kierkegaard has expressed it, is incarnated in the position of the minister and the theologian. For something which is a matter of paradox, contrary to all expectation, is brought into a form of existence comparable to any other object in time and space. But this is the whole paradoxical situation of the church in the world. You can also express it by saying that the Christian religion is one of the

178 PERSPECTIVES ON PROTESTANT THEOLOGY

many sections of human culture, but at the same time stands vertically in relation to everything which is culture. From this you can draw the conclusion that Christianity should be removed from every cultural relationship, but if you try to do that, you will find it impossible. The very words you use in order to do it are dependent on the culture from which you will try to detach Christianity. On the other hand, if you do not see the vertical aspect, if Christianity is merely for a class of human beings who are blasphemously called religionists and becomes merely a part of the whole culture, this may be very useful for undergirding patriotism, but the paradox is lost.

Here we face a conflict which is as real, permanent, and insoluble for us as it was for Kierkegaard. Since in Denmark at Kierkegaard's time there was a sophisticated theology of mediation, the prophetic voice could hardly be heard any more. Kierkegaard became the prophetic voice. The prophet always speaks from the vertical dimension and does not care about what happens in the horizontal dimension. But then Kierkegaard became a part of the horizontal; he became the father of existentialist philosophy, of neo-orthodox theology, and of much depth psychology. Thus he was taken into culture just as the prophets of Israel who, after they had spoken their paradoxical, prophetic word out of the vertical, became religious reformers, and were responsible, for example, for the concentration of the cult in Jerusalem because of the cultic abuses in other places. So out of the vertical there comes a new horizontal line, that is, a new cultural actualization of the prophetic word. This cannot be avoided. Therefore, there is need for the prophetic word again and again which makes us aware that the situation of every servant of religion is a paradoxical one and is in a sense impossible. Kierkegaard's word was not accepted widely in his time, but when people in the beginning of the twentieth century realized the coming earthquake of this century, Kierkegaard's voice could be heard again.

* * * * * * * * * *

Question: You summarized Kierkegaard's understanding of Socrates. Do you consider this a correct interpretation of Socrates, or does it contain features peculiar to Kierkegaard?

Answer: First, I would say that it contains features peculiar to Plato.

THE BREAKDOWN OF THE UNIVERSAL SYNTHESIS

We do not know how much it has to do with the historical Socrates. It is parallel to the relation between the Synoptic Gospels and the fourth Gospel. The fourth Gospel has its analogy in Plato, and the Synoptic Gospels in Xenophon. Perhaps neither is right from a strictly historical point of view. But this is the way that a great historical figure appears to us. What is historically decisive is the impact a figure has on those who are with him. So here is a strict analogy between Socrates and Jesus, neither of whom wrote anything.

We know them only through their impact on their disciples, and this impact makes them not only historically significant, but also symbolic figures, figures in whom a symbol or archetype is embodied. Through this elevation to the status of a symbol the figure continues to influence history.

Now the Socrates of Plato certainly does what Kierkegaard says in connection with the Socratic irony and the Socratic maieutic or midwifery. The irony destroys that which one believes he knows, and the maieutic method is a way of bringing thoughts out of someone which are implicit in the depths of his soul. These two parts are certainly there in the Socrates whom Plato presents. How high the probability is of the historical accuracy of Plato's picture of Socrates is something that has been discussed for two thousand years. It cannot be said with certainty how much of Plato's image of Socrates is based on the actual Socrates himself. Scholars try to determine that, and with our modern methods of historical research we can perhaps come very near to the historical truth. We find that it is likely that the historical Socrates was not as banal as Xenophon makes him, but neither was he a pupil of Plato; it was the other way around.

But Kierkegaard is right in making another fundamental distinction. We spoke about religiousness A and religiousness B. Religiousness A is a religion in which the divine is present in every human being immediately and can be found in the depths of his being. This is basically a mystical form of religious experience, with God in us, the infinite within the finite. We showed how the whole modern development is dependent on this principle which was most sharply expressed by Nicholas of Cusa, the principle of the coincidence of the infinite and the finite in every finite thing. On the other hand, in religiousness B the basic point is the separation, the estrangement. This means that there is a gap between the divine and the human, so that man needs more than a midwife like Socrates who brings out of us what we already have within us; something new must come from the outside. The Savior or the Christ must come. This is the difference between Jesus and Socrates. Jesus is not only the existential teacher as Socrates; he is also the Savior who overcomes the gap between God and man. I think you have realized that the dialectic between these two principles is important in my own theological lectures, the dialectic between the principle of identity or the coincidence of the infinite and the finite in every person and the principle of a revelatory communication from outside, which is both revelatory and saving or transforming. Revelation in Kierkegaard's sense is not the communication of doctrines or knowledge *about* God. That is a badly distorted concept of revelation. But revelation is the self-manifestation of the divine to a human being which has transforming power. Both the symbolic and the doctrinal statements which arise out of the revelatory experience are secondary.

* * * * * * * * * * *

E. POLITICAL RADICALISM AND ITS THEOLOGICAL SIGNIFICANCE

What I will do now is perhaps surprising to you. I want to give you here the theology of the most successful of all theologians since the Reformation, namely, Karl Marx. I will consider him as a theologian. And I will show you that without doing this, it is impossible to understand the history of the twentieth century and large sections of the late nineteenth century. If you consider him only as a political leader or as a great economist, which he also was, or as a great sociologist, which he was even more, then you cannot understand from what sources the power came which transformed the whole world and conquered nearly half of it in the twentieth century. How can Marx have been a theologian in view of the fact that every word he said is connected with the split in humanity which he is largely responsible for having produced? Yet, there is a deep gap between the original Karl Marx and what is going on now in Russia or China, although the historical effects of his work are manifest in these countries.

1. The Bourgeois Radicals

There was in the time that Marx was starting his work a group of people whom we can call liberal radicals. On the basis of the principle of autonomy in bourgeois society a liberal radicalism developed. A man whose name you should at least know is Max Stirner (1806–1856) who wrote a book entitled *The Individual and His Right.*[7] In this very radical book he tried to remove all the overarching norms which traditional society, including the Enlightenment, had imposed on people. Very similarly to Kierkegaard he placed the individual in the center, but unlike Kierkegaard it was the individual without any relationship to God, but only to himself, and therefore without any norm. This was one of the things which produced the resistance of Marx. For this reason I must mention Max Stirner here. He was a neurotic personality and an extremist. Of course, as a mere individual he could not survive for one day without being dependent on others who provided for him. But this is not important for him; he forgets it. The absolute autonomy of the individual is described by him in almost ecstatic words.

Now you can imagine that Marx with his analytic knowledge of society would be full of aggressive irony against such an idea. He knew of the economically productive society, about the peasant and the grocery store, etc., and could not abstract from them as the neurotic bohemian could do so easily. And the beatniks of today who attack society forget the fact that it is the basis of their whole existence every minute. The same is true of Kierkegaard. The church which he attacked so radically, with its tradition within culture, was the basis of his statement that in the years A.D. 1–30 God came to man. Without the tradition of the church which produced both the Bible and the church nothing would have come to Kierkegaard, and his whole relationship to God would not have been possible. This is an idea that you should remember when someone attacks "organized religion"—a bad term—and says, I am very religious, but I am against organized religion. That is nonsense. It is nonsense because in his personal religiousness—excuse this terrible word—he is dependent on the tradition of the church for

[7] Max Stirner is the pseudonym of Johann Kasper Schmidt, author of *Der Einzige und sein Eigentum* (Leipzig: O. Wigand, 1901).

every word, every symbol that he might use in prayer, in contemplation or mystical experience. Without the community of speaking, there is no speaking whatsoever, and without an inner speaking, there is no spiritual life whatsoever. In this way it is easy to refute these attacks against organized religion. You can and should attack the forms and the ways in which it may be organized, but to use the term "organized religion" as name-calling is totally senseless. It simply shows lack of thought, and is usually rooted in bad experiences in childhood or more likely in Sunday School, which is one of the great laboratories in which Christian faith is expelled from children.

2. Marx's Relation to Hegel and Feuerbach

Now we must start with Marx's relation to Hegel and Feuerbach. He was a pupil of Hegel. Feuerbach, another pupil of Hegel, had put Hegel on his feet after he had been standing on his head, as Marx said. Hegel believed that reality is identical with the head of the philosopher. Feuerbach showed that the philosopher like everybody else is dependent on the material conditions of life. So Feuerbach developed a materialistic or naturalistic doctrine of man—man's dependence on his senses, etc. Marx said that Feuerbach had done the main thing; he had criticized Hegel's explanation of religion. Marx felt that he did not have to do that any more. But he had to criticize Feuerbach's materialistic ontology, and Feuerbach's idea that being is individual being, that the individual as such is the one who is decisive for the whole situation. Marx's criticism of Feuerbach held that materialism is not much better than idealism. It is a little bit better because idealism is merely ideology without any basis in reality. Materialism is closer to reality. But if only the individual is considered in the materialistic philosophy, then it is as bad as idealism. For its universal concept of man is abstracted from the individual and overleaps the social conditions in which man finds himself.

So Marx attacked both the materialists and the idealists. In regard to the term "Marxist materialism" it would be much better to leave that to the propagandists who use and confuse three different meanings of materialism in order to carry on their propaganda. But that has nothing to do with historical truth and an academic education. So it is better for you to understand that there are three meanings of materialism.

a. The one is the ontological or metaphysical materialism. You find this in Feuerbach who derives everything in nature from the movements of atoms in terms of calculable mechanical causality. It is a theory which has not often been represented in history. Present-day naturalism in America is certainly not materialism. Metaphysical materialism is also called reductionist naturalism, whereby reductionism means reducing everything to the mechanical movement of atoms and molecules. This is an obsolete philosophy. It existed in Europe at the end of the nineteenth century; also it existed in France at the end of the eighteenth century in the French encyclopedists of the pre-Revolution period; and it has existed only very rarely in this country. But on the whole it is a philosophy which has been overcome, and is very remote from Marxism.

b. Then there is ethical materialism, which means being interested only in material goods, in money, etc. When someone is called a materialist in propaganda, no clear distinction is made between ethical and metaphysical materialism. If Marxism is called materialistic, for example, the trick of propaganda is to leave the impression of an ethical materialism. In reality, however, the original socialist movement and also the kind of communism you find in the original Marx attacked the materialism of the bourgeois society, where everything was dependent on buying and selling, on profit, etc. So Marxism was just the opposite. Now the critics of the materialism of the bourgeois society are called materialists, usually with the connotation of ethical materialism, of being interested only in material goods.

c. Historical materialism is the third type. This means that the whole historical process is ultimately dependent on the ways of economic production. This is Marxist materialism. It should be called historical or economic materialism. It is quite different from the other two meanings.

Marx deals with the question of the individual and society. This was not so new in France, England, and Holland, but it was very new in Germany. In Germany the social structure was always taken for granted as something ordained by God. This was in accordance with Lutheran doctrine. Sociological analysis was avoided. Sociology had been fully developed in France in the nineteenth century before German scholars even started to think sociologically. Marx received his sociological view partly from France and partly from his insight into the miserable social conditions of large sections of people in Europe. Man is not man as an individual. The idea of the individual existing by himself is an illusion. This sounds quite different from Kierkegaard and Stirner. But Marx saw that we are really members of a social group. It is impossible to abstract ourselves from sociological reality. So he criticized Hegel and Feuerbach because they did not see individual men as members of a social structure. What is needed is an analysis of the social structure and the individual's place within it.

3. *Marx's View of the Human Situation (Alienation)*

Like Kierkegaard, Marx speaks of the estranged situation of man in the social structure of the bourgeois society. He uses the word "alienation" (*Entfremdung*) not from the point of view of the individual but of society. In Hegel estrangement means the absolute Spirit goes over into nature, becoming estranged from itself. In Kierkegaard it means the fall of man, the transition by a leap from innocence into knowledge and tragedy. In Marx it means the structure of the capitalist society.

Marx's description of modern society is of great importance. If we as theologians speak of original sin, for example, and are not aware of the problems of estrangement in the social situation, then we cannot really address people in their actual situation in everyday life. For Marx estrangement means that the social situation results in dehumanization. When he speaks of mankind in the future, he speaks of true humanism. He looks forward to a situation in which true humanism is not a pleasure merely for the cultured few; humanism is not the possession of cultural goods either. He looks for the re-establishment of a true humanity to replace the dehumanization in an estranged society. The main thing in the idea of dehumanization is that man has become a cog within the great process of production and consumption. In the process of production the individual worker has become a thing, a tool, or a commodity which is bought and sold on the market. The individual must sell himself in order to live.

These descriptions imply that man is essentially not an object, not a thing, but a person. Man is not the tool but the highest end or aim. He is not a commodity but the inner *telos* for everything that is done. Man is the inner meaning and aim. Marx's description of dehumanization or the particular form of estrangement that existed in capitalist society completely contradicts what he had inherited from classical humanism. He saw no reconciliation. In historical reality there is only dehumanization and estrangement. Out of this came the power to change the situation. When Marx in the *Communist Manifesto* spoke about the liberation of the masses from their chains, these chains were the powers of dehumanization produced by the working conditions of capitalist society. Consequently, the essential character of man is lost. Man on both sides of the class conflict is distorted by the conditions of existence. Only if these conditions are removed can we know what man truly is. Christian theology says that we can know what man essentially is because essential man has appeared in the conditions of existence in the Christ.

Estrangement refers not only to human relations, characterized by the cleavage between classes, but also to the relation of man to nature. The eros element has been taken away. Nature is only the stuff out of which tools are made, and by means of the tools consumer goods are manufactured. Nature itself has ceased to be a subject with which we as subjects can be united in terms of eros, the love which sees in nature the inner power of being, the ground of being which is creatively active through nature. In the industrial society we make nature only the material out of which to make things for buying and selling.

4. *Marx's Doctrine of Ideology and His Attack on Religion*

Ideology is another extremely important concept for theology. What is ideology? The word itself is older than Marx. It was used, for instance, by Napoleon when he criticized professors for being ideologists instead of being practical statesmen and generals. The word has a history which remains ambiguous even today. Ideology can be a neutral word, meaning simply the system of ideas which one can develop. Every group or class has such a system of ideas. But ideology can also mean—becoming then the most dangerous weapon in the class struggle—the unconscious production of ideas which justify the will-to-power of a ruling group. This is mostly an unconscious production, but it can be used in a conscious way.

Marx used this word "ideology" as a weapon. It was probably his sharpest weapon against the ideas of the ruling classes with which the churches were allied. All the great European churches, the Orthodox, the Lutheran, and the Episcopalian, were on the side of the ruling classes. The Roman Catholic Church was better in this respect for it had preserved a tradition of social feeling and social analysis from its classical medieval period.

A term which we used in our daily language that is very close to the meaning of ideology is rationalization. We speak of the rationalization of individuals who use ideas to justify the power they hold over other persons or to justify their indulgence in certain kinds of pleasures. Applied to social groups rationalization becomes ideology. This is a very important theological concept. Every Christian and every church should always be suspicious of their own ideologies which they use to justify their own traditional self-satisfactions. Every church should be suspicious of itself lest it formulate truths only as an expression of its will-to-power.

This notion of ideology is used by Marx to supplement Feuerbach's criticism of religion. He says that in principle Feuerbach succeeded in removing religion, but his criticism was not founded on sociological analysis. Marx says that the religious symbolism of a transcendent fulfillment (of heaven or immortality) is not merely the hope of every human being, but is the invention of the ruling classes to prevent the masses from seeking fulfillment in this life. Their attention is diverted to a so-called life hereafter. This is formulated in the famous phrase that religion is the opiate of the people. He simply means that if you have the assurance of an eternal fulfillment, you will not fight in a revolutionary way for the temporal fulfillment of man on earth.

Now I do not think that this is true. It is very similar to the way that Kierkegaard criticized the church of his time. It is the radicalism of the prophetic word. But then, of course, this same idea has to be applied to Marx himself and to all the movement which followed him. Then we must ask: What about the ideological character of the ideologies of the victorious revolutionary movements? Are they not also expressions of a new will-to-power? When we see what has happened to the Marxist ideas in Soviet Russia, we must immediately answer in the affirmative. The ruling classes in Russia maintain ideologies derived from Marx to keep themselves in power, although their ideas have only an indirect connection with Marx. There is the ideological element in the will to maintain themselves in power. The reason for this is that Marx lacked a vertical criticism against himself. This is the same situation that we have in all Communist countries, the lack of a vertical criticism. On the horizontal they have a lot of truth, but they cannot put this under the criticism of the vertical, because they have cut it off. Nobody can do that completely, but they have done it to a great extent. The danger in our culture is that we do the same thing with less radical and revolutionary methods, but with the more refined and sophisticated methods of mass culture.

A great gap between the churches and the labor movements in Europe developed. The churches were the representatives of the ideologies which kept the ruling classes in power over against the working masses. This was the tragic situation. It is a great thing that in America this tragedy has happened on a much smaller scale. But in Europe it has led to the radical antireligious and anti-Christian attitudes of all labor movements, not only of the Communists but also of the social democrats. It was not the "bad atheists"—as propagandists call them—who were responsible for this; it was the fact that the European churches, Orthodox, Lutheran, and Episcopalian, were without social sensitivity and direction. They were directed toward their own actualization; they were directed toward liturgical or dogmatic efforts and refinements, but the social problem was left to divine providence. The Czarist ruling classes, the German imperial ruling classes, and the British ruling classes were not in contact with what was going on in the working classes either. In Great Britain the situation was much milder, and therefore Great Britain never had a Marxist revolution. Nevertheless, the situation was very similar.

This situation can be seen the world over. On the one side there is a theology of mere horizontal fulfillment, with the kingdom of God being identified with the classless society or with a continuous transformation of society as in the British Labor party and in German social democracy. On the other side are the churches with their theology which has a vertical dimension. But a few things have happened which attempt to bridge the gap. In England there was a religious socialist movement very early; whether it called itself by that name or not, its ideas were the same. Then in Germany there was a religious socialist movement which came from some prophetic personalities in Switzerland. But nothing of this existed in Germany before the first World War.

I remember the great churches in the workers' quarters in Berlin. Workers did not enter the church except for baptism, marriage, and the funeral. The churches provided some glorification of these events. But any inner relation to the churches did not exist. To a typical Lutheran minister of that time I said: The workers cannot hear the Christian message. You must do it differently. You cannot expect that they will come into the churches. His answer was: They hear the church bells ringing every Sunday morning, and if they do not come to the church services, they will feel guilty. But they did not hear anything, and they did not know anything. They had no relation to the religious symbols of the tradition. The Lutheran attitude was that the people can come to hear the Christian message in the church. At least the people hear the bell ringing, and that is enough. If they do not come, they will be rejected by God. Fortunately, this attitude has ceased to exist. But it was this kind of attitude which produced the tremendous gap between the church and the laboring classes. Religious socialism tried to close that gap.

5. Marx's Political Existentialism

The existentialist element in Marx is very great. His concept of truth has a similarity to Kierkegaard's. Truth is truth for human existence, truth which concerns our life-situation. We said that Kierkegaard defined truth as an objective uncertainty passionately held. Marx defines truth in terms of the gap between theory and practice. That is to say, truth must be related to the social situation. A philosophical theory which is not involved in the social situation is not true. We have something of this in pragmatism and in John Dewey. There are in fact great similarities between existentialism and pragmatism. One of the things which has made John Dewey the great educator in this country is his insistence that all knowledge must be united with practical activities in the educational process. This was even more basic for Marx. We cannot know the truth about the human situation without existential participation in the social structure in which we are living. We cannot have truth outside the actuality of the human situation. Therefore, in our period of history one must participate in the proletarian situation in order to understand the depths of estrangement. Here we must cautiously avoid a mistaken idea. In Marx there is no glorification of the proletariat. The revolutionary movements made the proletariat the messiah, the savior, so to speak, not because the proletarians are such wonderful people—Marx never believed that; he knew them—but because they stood at a particular point in history which involved them in a class struggle, and through this struggle a new reality might come into existence. Marx knew that the class split distorted both sides in the situation. Men were made into objects. The leading bourgeois and the working masses are in the same boat with respect to dehumanization. But the proletariat had one advantage. They experienced the estrangement in such a way that they would be forced to revolt. The proletarians are the blessed, in the sense of the Beatitudes, for they exist on the extreme negative edge of the class situation. So in the Marxist criticism of society a biblical truth has been applied to an analysis of the social situation. When one speaks about the saving power of the proletariat, this does not mean that the proletariat is good and the others are bad. Marx's friend Engels was a big businessman, a capitalist. But the structure of the situation puts the proletariat on the lowest level where the need for revolution is felt. Through its revolutionary role it is thought to be the saving power.

6. The Prophetic Element in Marx

We cannot miss the messianic note in Marx's writings. Especially in the earlier writings we hear the voice of a modern secular prophet. He speaks like the old prophets of Israel. Marx as a Jew was in the tradition of Jewish criticism which had lasted through the millennia. His wrath against the reality as he saw it had something of the old prophetic wrath in it, although it was distorted by propagandistic elements as happens in every political leader. Nevertheless we cannot overlook the prophetic element in his whole work. When the prophets spoke to Israel, even when they spoke about the other nations, the whole weight of their attack was directed also against their own nation. They saw that their word did not transform their own nation. So, they said, the wrath of God would strike Israel. Especially Jeremiah was aware of this. But there is also the promise of God. It could not come to naught; it would come to fulfillment. So the prophets had the idea of the remnant, the small group which would be the bearer of the divine promise.

The idea of a remnant is not the idea of only the prophets. Everybody who speaks prophetically to a large group or to a nation has such an idea. Without such an idea you would be driven to despair and forced to give up. But you do not need to give up, because there is the remnant. The word "remnant" means those who are left over, those who do not adore the idols, who do not do injustices, etc. In the larger sense this word means those few within the group who are conscious of the situation and who therefore become the bearers of the future development. This idea of the remnant restricts to a certain extent the messianism of the proletariat. In the last analysis it is not the whole proletariat, but the leading groups in it, the vanguards, who are decisive. So a simple identification of the proletariat with messianism is limited by the fact that it is those who are the vanguards who have a messianic role. These vanguards are not always even members of the proletariat. They are people like Marx and Engels who come from the intelligentsia or the upper classes and have broken through their own ideological self-seclusion. They have learned what is going on in history and can join the vanguards.

The difference between Marx's secularized prophetism and that of the Jewish prophets is that the latter always kept in mind the vertical line and did not rely either on human groups or on logical or economic necessities of development, as Marx did. They ultimately relied on God, and this was lacking in the modern secularized movement. Certainly, this movement is quasi-religious. It is not pseudo-religious, for pseudo-religious means "deceptive" or "lying." But it is quasi-religious because it has in itself the structure of prophetism, but with one difference—the transcendent, the vertical line, has been lost.

The tragic thing is that the revolutionary movements in Europe, Asia, and Africa originally came from a prophetic message, but when they became victorious, they did not apply their own criticism against themselves. They could not do it, because they had nothing above themselves. The Communists in Russia answer all the problems in the East-West discussion without showing the element of ultimate self-criticism. Of course, there is much self-criticism in individual groups in Communist countries. There are individuals who confess they have sinned. But they have always sinned against the party; there is nothing higher than the party; the party cannot err; the party is infallible. The lack of the transcendent line is the reason for the tragic situation that the revolutionary movement which set out to liberate a whole social class has resulted in a new slavery, the totalitarian slavery as we have it today in the Communist systems. This is a world-historical tragedy. Similar things have happened before in history. Consider, for example, how the movement of Jesus Christ resulted in the church of the Inquisition in the later Middle Ages. All these tragic transformations come about because of the lack of the self-criticism derived from the vertical line. When the church did not judge itself any longer in terms of the vertical line, something like the Inquisition could happen. The Marxist movement was not able to judge itself because of its whole actual structure, and so it could become the social group which we now identify as Stalinism. In this form everything for which the original groups were struggling became suppressed and distorted. It is in our century that we can best see the tragic reality of man's estrangement in the social realm.

F. Voluntarism and the Philosophy of Life

Now I come to the last of the movements which contributed to the collapse of the great syntheses of Schleiermacher and Hegel. This movement is voluntarism, a term derived from *voluntas*, the Latin word for "will." Voluntarism is a philosophy in which the element of will is decisive. It began in the nineteenth century with Schelling who in his earlier years was a philosopher of the will before he became the philosopher of nature. For him will is original being. It is being itself. We can describe being most adequately in terms of will. Being is not a thing; it is not a person; it is will. This idea of will refers to what is often called today "unconscious instinct." But the word "instinct" should be dropped if you are translating Freud. The word "drive" should be used instead. Man has no death instinct. That is a misuse of the word "instinct." But man does have the death drive in himself.

Voluntarism is one of the great lines of thought in the history of philosophy and theology, which has been in continual tension with the other great line of thought which goes back to Aristotle and includes among others Thomas Aquinas, the nominalists, the British empiricists, Kant, to a great extent Schelling and Hegel, and modern language analysis. These two lines of thought have made the Western philosophical movements full of life and tension. In naming Thomas Aquinas we should also mention immediately Duns Scotus and William of Ockham as his voluntaristic opponents.

1. Schopenhauer's Idea of the Will

From Schelling we come to Schopenhauer. What impressed him was not Hegel's great synthesis nor Schelling's philosophy of identity, but rather Schelling's doctrine of will. Usually he is considered as the first representative of voluntarism in nineteenth-century thought. He combined with his voluntarism a deep pessimism. He is always quoted if one speaks of philosophical pessimism. But voluntarism is not necessarily pessimism, as we shall see in Nietzsche, his great pupil and critic.

Not only Schopenhauer's temperament but also his personal destiny must be kept in view. He lived in the overwhelming shadow of Hegel and never really came into his own during his lifetime. His famous book, The World as Will and Idea,[8] became known only very late. It had a tremendous influence in the second half of the nineteenth century and through Freud in our own century. The most important pupil of Schopenhauer was Nietzsche. The line then runs from Nietzsche to Bergson, the French voluntarist, Heidegger and Sartre, and to White-

[8] Translated by R. B. Haldane and J. Kemp (London: Trübner and Co., 1883–86).

head, the great metaphysician of our century. All this came from the powerful voluntaristic element in Schelling, but became generally influential only later through Schopenhauer and Nietzsche.

To understand this nineteenth-century movement it is helpful to go far back for a moment. Where does voluntarism come from? Its first clear appearance is in Augustine, who embodies the element of will in his own personal character in a much more dynamic way than it appears in most of the Greek philosophers and writers. Augustine is the philosopher of will, and especially of that will which is love. The substance of all reality for him is will. He could have written Schelling's statement that original being is will, but since it deals with the creation of God he calls it love. Love is original being; the power of love is the substance in everything that is. This love (*amor*) loves itself (*amor amoris*), the self-affirmation of the will which is divine love.

In the Middle Ages Augustine's ideas were represented by the great Franciscan theologians, while the Dominican theologians represented Aristotle's ideas. The tensions between these two in the thirteenth century represent the high point in medieval thought. In the Franciscan school will precedes intellect. In the Aristotelian-Thomistic school, or Dominican school, intellect precedes will. This is not a vague statement about man's psychology; it is always meant ontologically. That means that in God himself, in the creative ground of being, either will or intellect is the primary power. In this course we have dealt mainly with people who represent the primacy of the intellect. This is very much the case in German classical philosophy. It is also predominant in the eighteenth century, with some exceptions. The priority which Kant gave to practical reason represents a breakthrough of the element of will. In Schelling we have a complete breakthrough, and also in Fichte. But throughout that period the emphasis on intellect was predominant. Now in the thirteenth century Bonaventura was one of the great Franciscans in whom will was the decisive thing, that is, will as love. He was a great mystic and also an early general of the Franciscan order. This mysticism of love goes back also to Saint Francis. Standing in radical opposition to Thomas Aquinas was Duns Scotus, himself a Franciscan, and the greatest critical mind of the whole Middle Ages and one of the most important philosophical minds of the Western world. Both Thomas and

Scotus lived in the thirteenth century. Scotus defined God as will and nothing other than will. In another Franciscan, William Ockham, this became an irrational will. Ockham is the father of nominalistic philosophy of the later Middle Ages. There was an earlier nominalistic movement about which Abelard and Anselm of Canterbury were fighting.

If God is sheer will, he can do what he wants. He has within himself no intellectual limits. There is no logos structure which would prevent him from doing what he wants. The world is in every moment dependent on something absolutely unknown. Ultimately nothing in the world can be calculated. Only insofar as it is ordered by God can it be calculated, but God can withdraw both the natural and the moral orders. If he wanted, he could make murder good, and love bad. The theology of Martin Luther was influenced by nominalism, although not really dependent on it. Luther himself was a voluntarist and had in himself much of the Dionysian awareness of the underground of life in man. He was a great depth psychologist before our present-day depth psychologists. He had insight into the demonic forces in the world and in man. As the legends tell us, he had to fight continuously against the demonic forces in himself, during the attacks which he called *Anfechtungen*. When he described these demonic attacks—perhaps the best translation of *Anfechtungen*—he said that one moment in this situation of absolute despair, which is an element of the demonic attack, is worse than hell itself.

I must mention several other bridges to nineteenth-century voluntarism. There was the philosopher and shoemaker, Jacob Boehme, who saw in his visions the full demonic power, the will element, in God himself. He called it the nature of God and saw that element in God which contradicts the light in God, the logos in God, the wisdom and truth in God. He understood the conflict in the divine life, the tension between these two elements. This tension makes the divine life not simply a sheer actuality (*actus purus*) as in Aristotle, but a dynamic process with the potentiality for conflict. In God this inner conflict is always victoriously overcome, but in creatures it breaks out destructively as well as creatively.

Boehme had a great influence on Schelling's ideas concerning the inner life of God. If all this sounds very mythological, then read the books of Charles Hartshorne, A. N. Whitehead, and Henri Bergson. They were all influenced by Boehme (who himself was dependent on Luther's voluntarism) and Schelling. Even Hegel was to some extent dependent on Boehme.

One of the ways in which you can envisage the Western world in its philosophical and theological developments is in terms of this tension between the merely Apollonian—this means putting intellect over against will as the decisive thing in man—and the combination of the Apollonian and the Dionysian—which puts the will in the center and the intellect as a secondary force over against will. If this is said about man, it is also said about God, both in the Middle Ages and in modern theology. So we have here a very dynamic picture of Western philosophical development. It is important for us to know about this, because we are still in the midst of it. This struggle is still going on, for example, between the Whiteheadian school and the philosophy of logical analysis.

That gives you the historical perspective. But let us go into a few other considerations here. First the term "will." It is very important that in all these men you understand what the idea of will means. If you examine a text on psychology, you will find that usually will is derived from other elements, the vital drive, on the one hand, and the intellect, on the other hand. It is presented as a secondary phenomenon and primarily as a conscious phenomenon. If will is taken in this way, it is impossible to understand how will can be identified with being itself. How can there be will in stones and crystals and plants and animals? They have no consciousness; they have no purpose which is directed by an intellect expressing itself in language, using universals, etc. But this is not what will means if it is understood in an ontological sense. Will is the dynamics in all forms of life. Only in man does it become conscious will. If I decide to go to my office after this lecture, that is a conscious act of my will. In voluntaristic philosophy will is not restricted to a conscious psychological act. You cannot derive the meaning of will from man's psychological experience of himself as a consciously willing being. Nevertheless, the word must be used. Will for these ontologists appears in man as conscious will, in animals as instinct or drives—these appear also in man—in plants as urges, and in material reality as trends such as gravitation, etc. If you understand will as the dynamic element in all reality, then it makes sense.

The term "intellect" is also subject to misunderstanding. The idea as the ontologists have used it does not refer to the I.Q. of the college boy. Intellect comes from the Latin *"inter-legere,"* to read between. To read between means to be in something, to be in the reality and reading it, being aware of it. That means participating in the form of things. Readable things have a form. The substance, the dynamics, you cannot read; they are dark; they are the drives. Reading, which is here meant metaphorically, is only possible where there is form. The word "understanding" has a similar metaphorical meaning. Standing under or reading between have the same meaning. They refer to a position in which we are in the reality itself and are able to become aware of its particular form. This awareness we call cognition.

Schopenhauer's idea is that will, unconscious will, drives toward the actualization of that which it is willing, and since it can never reach it, it reacts with the desire for death. This is a concept which we also find in Freud's death tendency or death drive which is derived from the always unsatisfactory fulfillment of our will. The will never gets what it wills. Out of this the dissatisfaction with life arises. According to Schopenhauer this drives the will to ever new attempts to fulfill its desire and ever new impossibilities of doing it. Life is a restless driving toward fulfillment which can never be attained. The result is the disgust of life, a deep dissatisfaction with every fulfillment. In all the voluntarists the sexual drive plays a great role—from unfulfillment to fulfillment, then to ever new fulfillment. The restlessness of these drives leads finally to a desire to come to rest by not willing any more.

With this idea something very important for the history of Western civilization occurred. Schopenhauer discovered Buddhism and in it the idea of the will to self-negation, the will to bring one's will to rest by not willing any longer. Of course, Schopenhauer was not a historian but a philosopher and as such identified his own philosophy with the fundamental Indian idea that blessedness is the resignation of the individual will, the overcoming of the self in a formless self, as the Zen-Buddhists call it, or the return into the Brahman principles, the eternal ones, as the Hindus call it. From this the ascetic tendency in life is derived. Schopenhauer did not follow along in this point, but anyway he introduced these ideas into the Western world where they have had an influence up to now.

Schopenhauer made one exception to his general view, and this placed him in line with the romantic philosophy of his time. He said that when we hear music we are able to come to rest in time and space. Music was for him the anticipatory salvation of the restless will. In music the will comes to rest, but since one cannot always be listening to music, one must finally tend toward the ultimate salvation which happens only in the moment of death. Schopenhauer is to be considered as the man who overcame in many people the progressivistic optimism of Hegel and prepared the way for the existentialist pessimism of the twentieth century.

2. Nietzsche's Idea of Will-To-Power

Even more important than Schopenhauer for the twentieth century and the theological situation is Friedrich Nietzsche. He was a pupil of Schopenhauer. He used the word "life" rather than "will." Life is essentially will, but a special kind of will. It goes in quite the opposite direction from Schopenhauer's will. It is not the will which brings itself to rest and ceases to will, but it is the will which Nietzsche calls will-to-power.

First we must say something about this word "power." I have already had to rescue the word "will" from the misunderstanding that it is merely a psychological phenomenon; rather, it is the universal driving dynamics of all life processes. Now I must rescue the word "power" in Nietzsche from a similar misunderstanding. For him power is the self-affirmation of being. Will-to-power means will to affirm one's power of living, the will to affirm one's own individual existence. In man this will-to-power becomes will to personal and social power. That is not the primary concept, but it is a part of the whole concept. This power has nothing to do with Nazism, with its irrational power. It is the power of the best; only the power over oneself can give one social power. If one is not able to exercise the aristocratic self-restriction, then one's power will decay. So the abuse of it by the vulgar Nazi movement has nothing to do with Nietzsche's vision of will-to-power. It is one of the tragedies that this great symbol created by Nietzsche should become something devilish in the mouths of vulgar people.

Nietzsche's style is oracular in contrast to Hegel's dialectical philosophy. He is one of the great fragmentists in the history of literature. Fragments can be very powerful. In the pre-Socratics we have almost only fragments. In part this is an accident of history, for much of the early pagan literature was destroyed by Christian fanaticism and later by Islamic fanaticism. But in any case these fragments are in themselves complete, understandable, and full of mystery. The same is true of the fragments of Nietzsche. He tells us that he wrote them at a time of an inspired state of mind. He also wrote great poetry.

Nietzsche knew of the ambiguity in all life. He knew of the creative and destructive elements which are always present in every life process. If you want to find out about his idea of God, do not look first to his statement that "God is dead." Read instead the last fragments of The Will To Power,[9] which is a collection of fragments. It is not a book in itself. The last fragment describes the divine demonic character of life in formulations which show the ambiguity, the greatness, and the destructiveness of life. He asks us to affirm this life in its great ambiguity. Out of this he then has another kind of God, a God in which the demonic underground, the Dionysian underground, is clearly visible. The victory of the element of rationality or of meaning is not as clear as in other philosophers like Kant or Hegel, Hume or Locke, but there is an opening up of vitality, and its half-creative, half-destructive power.

3. Nietzsche's Doctrine of Resentment

Now where do the norms of life come from? Nietzsche has a theory very similar to that of Feuerbach and Marx. This is his theory of resentment. The Jewish-Christian idea of justice, the Greek-Christian idea of logos, and the Christian idea of love are all ideas which result from the resentment of the masses against the aristocratic rulers. It is the revolution of resentment. This is the same type of thing that Marx

[9] Translated by Anthony M. Ludovici (London: T. N. Foulis, 1913–14).

called ideology when he derived the Christian and generally religious ideas and values from the state of negativity of the masses of people to whom the upper classes promised a fulfillment in a transcendent heaven. Marx used this word as a powerful weapon in the revolution. And psychoanalysis shows how individuals use rationalization to justify drives in themselves which they want to maintain or fulfill. So Nietzsche added a third concept, that of resentment. These three concepts have had tremendous power because they are really revealing of the human situation. The concept of *rationalization* shows how the individual man tries to give reasons in a system of values for his natural drives of eros and will-to-power. Freud with his empirical methodology discovered how little our conscious life represents what we actually are. This was a revolution in our climate of thought in the twentieth century; it undercut the bourgeois and puritan moralistic conventions in all Western countries, and in particular the Protestant-dominated countries. Most of you belong to the third generation of this revolution, but I belonged to the first generation; I tried to show what it means for Protestant theology that not the surface consciousness but the underground of human existence is decisive in human experience and relations. The concept of *ideology* revealed the interest of the ruling classes in preserving their power by producing a transcendent system to divert the masses from their immediate situation of disinheritance. We see the same thing today going on in the underdeveloped countries where there are revolutionary tendencies. They often look at our democratic ideas, which are rooted partly in Stoicism and partly in the Old Testament, as an ideology of the Western world to maintain its predominance and to introduce its values.

In Nietzsche's psychology of resentment all the ideas of justice, equality, democracy, liberalism, etc., are born out of the resentment of the masses, and the most powerful bearers of this resentment are the religions of Judaism and Christianity. Therefore, this resentment functions in the exact opposite way from Marx's notion of ideology. The ideas produced by resentment are an attack against the ruling classes, while in Marx the ideological system is a weapon of the ruling classes to keep the others down.

One especially interesting idea in Nietzsche is his attack on the

Christian idea of love. The idea of love is indeed a great problem. First of all, in the modern languages we do not have the distinctions we have in Greek. *Epithumia* is the vital drive (in Latin this is *libido*, the word used by Freud); *philia* is the friendship type of love, the person-to-person relationship; *eros* is the creative, cultural love toward the good, the true, and the beautiful; *agape* is the word used in the New Testament meaning the acceptance of the other one as a person, which includes the principle of justice. It is the power of reuniting with the other person as one standing on the same ultimate ground, and therefore he is the object of acceptance, forgiveness, and transformation. That is the Christian idea of *agape*.

Now this *agape* was sentimentalized long before our time. It was sentimentalized in Romanticism. The concept of Christian love could hardly be distinguished from sentimental desire or from pity. Especially pity was identified with the Christian idea of love. So charity replaced love in the sense in which I have just defined it. Against all this Nietzsche fought with the will to the self-affirmation of life. He is the greatest critic, not of the Christian idea of love, although he thinks it is the Christian idea of love, but of the sentimentalized idea of love, where love is reduced to compassion. In the name of power, the will-to-power, self-affirmation of life, he fights against this idea which undercuts the strong life.

Nietzsche made a good point which we ought to remember in our preaching of love. He said, you speak of selfless love and want to sacrifice yourself to the other one, but this is only a way for the weak person to creep under the protection of somebody else. Erich Fromm, the psychoanalyst, has called this wrong kind of love which Nietzsche attacked "symbiotic love"—from *syn* and *bios*, meaning "living together." This is a love of the weak man for the other one who once lived from his strength, and it is a form of love which exploits the other one. This kind of self-surrender has the unconscious desire for exploitation. This is what Nietzsche was actually fighting against. We should not forget this when speaking of love in Christianity. Love can mean any of these four things which are distinguished in Greek, and therefore it does not mean anything unless we explain in what sense we are using the word. Usually it is connected with a sentimentalized type of love.

Nietzsche was also interested very much in music. He was a great friend of Richard Wagner, the great composer and bridge to modern music. But one of the most interesting events was the break between Nietzsche and Wagner. They were friends, but gradually Nietzsche noticed in Wagner the restoration of a religion of sentimentality. As far as I remember the final break happened in connection with Wagner's *Parsifal,* the romantic sentimentalization of the myth of the representative suffering. Here Nietzsche with his will-to-power, the will of self-affirmation of life, reacted with radicalism and intensity. If you keep in mind that Hitler was a great lover of Wagner's music, you have a clue to how far away Nazism is from Nietzsche's philosophy, although words like "will-to-power" and "superman" sound as if they were a preparation for Nazism. Somehow they actually were, but not in the mind of Nietzsche, just as Marx was a preparation for Stalin, but not in the intention of Marx. These are tragedies in history.

4. The "Death of God" and the New Ideal of Man

The concept of the "death of God" is a half-poetic, half-prophetic symbol. What does it mean? Ordinarily one would think that it means simply the spread of atheism, whatever that word means. But this is not the point in interpreting Nietzsche. Nietzsche did not repeat the atheistic or naturalistic criticism of the theistic idea of God. He accepted just as Marx did Feuerbach's criticism of religion. But Nietzsche meant that when the traditional idea of God falls, something else must fall along with it. The system of ethical values on which society is based fell, and this is the important consequence of this symbol of the death of God. Of course, this is a symbol, for it can only mean that God is dead as far as man's consciousness of him is concerned. The idea that God in himself is dead would be absurd. The idea is rather that in man the consciousness of an ultimate in the traditional sense has died. The result is—and this confirms this interpretation—that somebody else must replace God as the bearer of the system of traditional values. This is man. In the past man had to hear the "thou shalt" and the "thou shalt not" as that which is derived from God or an objective system of values. But now this is gone. So in place of this Nietzsche put man who says "I will." Man no longer says "I shall" because of God, but he says "I will" because I will. I act because I will and I decide what is good or evil.

This idea has many implications. One of them is Nietzsche's famous phrase, "the transvaluation of all values." All the traditional values must be replaced by other ones. Not any transcendent authority does this, but man does it. Who is this man? Does this not imply a tremendous over-estimation of man's greatness? Certainly Nietzsche did not think very highly of man. The mass man who appeared with the industrialization of the European countries was full of resentment; he was weak; he surrendered to the powerful; he produced ideologies which promise him happiness in heaven because he cannot have it on earth. That is man as Nietzsche knew him. So it is not this man, this mass man, who can say "I will." It is the superior man. Nietzsche speaks of the *Übermensch,* which could be translated as superman, except that this has become a character in the funny papers. Other suggestions have been made: higher man or superior man, or simply using the foreign word *Übermensch.* Perhaps superior man is the best.

Where does this superior man come from? He comes from the development of mankind in a Darwinian sense. When you study Nietzsche you should not forget that this was the time in which Darwinism reached its high point. He simply accepted Darwin's idea of the selective process of life in which the weaker species are annihilated and the stronger ones survive to produce still stronger ones. This evolutionary idea of Darwin is the background to Nietzsche's idea of the superior man. Of course, in all evolutionary thinking there is an image of a higher man, of mankind being on a higher level. But Nietzsche did not think merely of an educational, spiritual development of mankind from lower to higher levels of moral education and ethical life, as has usually been thought of in the Western world. Nietzsche would accept this idea too, but he took Darwin in a much more literal and naturalistic way. The superior man is also stronger physically. He is a man straight in body and soul, as he said. In some of his metaphors, this man is even the wild beast, but the wild beast on the human level, not irrational, but powerful, representing a new type of existence in which man is not like the mass man of the present day.

The question has often been asked whether if there is evolution, does the evolution cease with man? Why should it cease with man, and not go beyond him? There are two possible answers. The one answer is that in man the biological possibilities on earth are exhausted; no higher developments can follow. If there is to be any further development, then it must happen in the realm of the mind or soul or spirit of man. But in any case, it is an inner development of man, and not of a bodily kind. Of course, logically this cannot be proved. It presupposes that there is no possibility of a higher bodily development on earth. If this presupposition is not accepted, Nietzsche would be justified. The superior men are the strong ones, full of unbroken vitality, shaped by strict self-discipline, indeed the very ideal of the aristocratic personality. In contrast to them there is the one symbolized in his expression "the last man." His description of the last man is the antitype to the superior man. He is the man who knows everything, but does not care for anything—half-sleepy, half-indifferent, completely conformist, and full of abandoned creativity. He is like the caricature of the "organization man" described in current sociological literature. The mass man avoids at all costs being controversial; therefore he accepts subjection to conformism in all respects. He is disinterested, without any ultimate concern, bored, cynical, empty. All of these descriptions are given in a poetic way by Nietzsche. This is what he calls the nihilism toward which our culture is running.

These ideas have had world-historical consequences. Not only Nazism, but also Fascism used the symbol of the powerful man with the strong self-affirmation of life in himself and in his group. When Fascism and Nazism and early Communism used Nietzsche's categories, they did it with the feeling that the coming nihilism of which Nietzsche spoke would make mankind into a herd of higher animals without creativity, satisfied merely with food and clothes, etc. So this ideology was welcomed by the Fascists and the Nazis. They often used Nietzsche, but they left out one thing. They left out the spiritual aspect. Nietzsche's idea of the superior man includes the bodily and the spiritual or the mental. One of the Nazi leaders said that when he hears the word "spirit" he takes out his pistol, because he felt that this implied the diminution of vitality and creativity. Such ideas were behind the Nazi movement. But do not imagine that we can derive Nazism from

Nietzsche, or from Luther or Hegel for that matter, although some of Nietzsche's formulations have a similarity to the Nazi ideology. But this was only a vulgarization and distortion of ideas which these great men had.

For Nietzsche the idea of the higher race is the aristocratic idea which you can find in all races and nations. It is the vertical idea of racial superiority. It comes from the medieval ideal of the aristocratic personality shaped by strict self-discipline. But in Nazism there was the horizontal idea of race, the idea that a particular biological race is superior to others. Then a particular nation or a particular race, like the Nordic race, becomes the group of superior men. Everything becomes vulgar. In this light you can understand better the quasi-religious demonry of Nazism. It was in opposition to the danger of the industrial society symbolized in the idea of the last man who only looks at things with cynicism and without eros.

Nietzsche's affirmation of life goes beyond all this to a classical metaphysical idea, or mythological idea, expressed by the Stoics, the idea of the eternal return. This is the idea that history does not run ahead but returns to its beginning. This is the classical Greek idea of eternal return. It means that everything that happens now happens an infinite number of times. In *Thus Spake Zarathustra* he described the moment as a door which opens in both directions. In every moment there is a repetition of infinite moments. Everything that happens happens an infinite number of times. This again is symbolic and mythological. If we ask about its meaning, it means the eternalization of the moment. The moment is eternal, not by the presence of eternal life in it, however, as in Schleiermacher and in my own thinking, following the fourth Gospel's idea of eternal life, but for Nietzsche it is a circle. The eternalization of transitory moments means that everything has happened before and will happen again an infinite number of times. It is one of the attempts to understand eternity on the basis of a non-mechanical dynamic naturalism. Religiously it is an affirmation of the eternal meaning of every moment and of everything in every moment. It is eternity not in terms of a hereafter, not in terms of the unique moment into which the eternal breaks, but in terms of any point in a circle from which the circle may start and to which it may return. This is the famous idea of the eternal return. What is decisive in it is the affirmation of life. Nietzsche expresses this by having Zarathustra teach his disciples to say that in the experience of death they will affirm every moment of it. This is Nietzsche's eschatology; this is his hope. Although his life was full of misery, in opposition to this he affirmed it infinitely.

All these ideas have had a great influence on the thinking of our time insofar as it deals with problems of ultimate concern. They have influenced many theologians, at least insofar as they try to answer this form of eschatology by some other form, and to show the difference. They have had infinite importance for all preaching which contains apologetic elements. For here was a man who was not holding to a mechanistic, materialistic form of naturalism. It was an ecstatic naturalism. When we use the word "naturalism" we should be clear about what type we have in mind. Today we call the mechanistic or materialistic type of naturalism a reductive naturalism in which everything is reduced to the movement of atoms. It denies that mind and life have any independent reality. They are supposed to be epiphenomenal; *phenomenal* because they exist and you cannot deny that there is life and spirit; and *epi* because they are secondary and superficial, and not a part of any substantial reality. That is not a profound philosophy at all. But it is only one form of naturalism. Nietzsche represented quite another one which was great, although presented in a half-demonic form.

* * * * * * * * * *

Question: You have given a description of Nietzsche, but not a criticism of him. Would you please do so?

Answer: I would like to do so, although this would be a long story if my criticism would take in all the elements of his thought. But let me start with his concept of the will-to-power. I told you that Nietzsche's idea of the will-to-power does not use the terms "will" and "power" in the ordinary sense. Rather, it is the urge toward life in everything that is, even beyond the organic life. It is a metaphysical concept. For the nonhuman dimension the word "urge" would even be more adequate. And "power" is not social, political, or economic power, but rather the self-affirmation of life, not only in the sense of preserving life, but of the further development of life. In this respect, Nietzsche's idea is an adequate description of life processes as we can observe them in ourselves and in nature, so no criticism is needed. But insofar as the world of norms in relation to the will-to-power is lost in Nietzsche, criticism proves to be necessary. It is precisely this lack of normative principles which has made it possible for the Nazis to misuse Nietzsche. Nietzsche himself had the aristocratic norms. His ideal was the republic of Venice in the sixteenth and seventeenth centuries. The strict self-discipline which was characteristic of all members of the aristocratic class was his ideal. So there was not only arbitrariness but also discipline. But this discipline had no norms which could be applied to men as a whole. Therefore, people like Heidegger could simply replace the older norms which, according to Nietzsche himself, have disappeared with the death of God. I spoke about this last time. Heidegger replaced them by the resolve, the decision to do something without any norm, as Nietzsche also did. Since there is no norm, there is only my will, and this is the highest norm. This "I will" of Nietzsche, his highest norm, is not able to provide criteria for good and evil, so Nietzsche could write his little book, *Beyond Good and Evil*. This is the one criticism, the lack of norms. The result of this lack is apparent, for it provided the possibility of misusing Nietzsche's idea for the sake of an irrational will-to-power as in a phenomenon like Nazism.

I would also have to criticize his doctrine of the eternal return. His idea is a return to the classical circular notion of repetitious time. There is a lack of novelty, of the really new. True, Nietzsche did have a strong emphasis on the new in history. He could speak of the renewal of all values, the transvaluation of values, and the coming of the superior man. There the concept of the new is present. But this happens only within a particular segment of the circle. Nothing absolutely new is created. A symbol such as the kingdom of God as the aim of history is very remote from Nietzsche. Nietzsche denied Augustine's idea that time is running toward something and not toward a point from which it has started. That is, time is going in circles. This was a relapse in Nietzsche, and an inconsistent relapse because he also had the Darwinian notion of movement from lower to higher forms of life in history.

A third criticism would have to focus on the idea of the superior man. The biological increase of perfection in man would not increase the heights of man's spirit. The biological development of man has come to a point from which a new development has started, namely, the development of man's spiritual self-realization in terms of culture, religion, and ethics. This new series of developments cannot be enhanced by any further improvement of bodily existence. One could say that with respect to nature, man is an end, just as with respect to history, the kingdom of God is an end. Nietzsche was driven by naturalism to a misunderstanding of the new beginning which was inaugurated in life when the first man used the first word to describe the universal.

Then we can also say that his idea of the death of God is only relatively true. For the God of the tradition is still alive and Nietzsche himself introduced another God, this divine-demonic being which he called life. I referred you to the last collection of fragments in his *Will to Power*. It gives an ecstatic vision of the irrationality and paradoxical character of life as a whole, and calls for obedience to this life by affirming it as it is. He certainly is not atheistic in the popular nonsensical term. But he has a different God than the God of the religious tradition, especially of the Christian tradition. This holds true as well of the Asian tradition. He denied the Asian tradition when he denied Schopenhauer who introduced the Asian tradition into the Western world. He denied both traditions. Yet, I would say that the presupposition of his negation is an awareness of eternity, and this awareness of eternity was as much alive in him as in every human being.

I could also go into his theory of resentment and theory of morality, which is self-contradictory, because the aristocratic groups which imposed their ethics upon the masses had their own ethical norms independent of individual willfulness. Nietzsche is an irrational prophet, a naturalistic prophet. But Christian theologians can learn very much from him. I regretted nothing so much as the fact that he could be so misused by Nazism. For this reason he lost much of his significance in Germany, and probably also in other countries.

CHAPTER V

New Ways of Mediation

Wsynthesis, the attempt to overcome the cleavages in the modern
mind. There is an interesting fact that at the end of the nineteenth
century people who sensed very deeply what was happening through
the destruction of the great synthesis, the distortion of its elements, the
approaching nihilism, etc., all seemed to live on the boundary line of
insanity. Nietzsche himself was on this boundary line and was finally
completely encompassed by it. So was a man like Baudelaire, the French
poet, and Rimbaud and Strindberg. They could not deal with the *fin
de siècle* (the situation at the end of the nineteenth century). And
painters like Van Gogh and Munch were afflicted in the same way.
They are all expressions of the disturbing and destructive consequences
of the breakdown of the great synthesis. Their inability to find a roof
for themselves drove them into this situation. Or one can say that people
who because of their makeup were in danger of falling into insanity
could become the prophets of the coming catastrophe—because of their
intense sensitivity—and at the same time the representatives of the new
situation. These men were lonely geniuses who anticipated the catastrophes of our century and also contributed to the catastrophes by
destroying the unifying traditions of the Western world and the syntheses of Hegel and Schleiermacher.

Now we must deal with a large group of highly intelligent, scholarly,
and pious theologians who are usually classified in general as theolo-

gians of mediation. The term "theology of mediation" (*Vermittlungs-theologie*) can be understood in two ways. It can be understood as something merely negative, by identifying mediation with compromise. It is very easy to accuse a theologian of compromising the message with the modern mind. This places him before the alternative of simply repeating the given tradition or of mediating the tradition to the modern mind. If he simply repeats he is superfluous, because the tradition is there and everyone has access to it, whether or not he understands it at all. But if he is not to be superfluous, he becomes a theologian of mediation, mediating the tradition. And this is the second sense, and something positive. We could say that theology by definition is mediation. The term "theology of mediation" is almost a tautology, for a theology that does not mediate the tradition is no theology. In this sense I would defend every theologian who is accused of being a theologian of mediation, and I myself would cease being a theologian altogether if I had to abandon the work of mediation. For the alternative to it is repetition, and that is not theology at all.

The critical undertone in the term "theology of mediation"—for the term has taken on a negative connotation—is directed against those who tried to rescue as much as possible in Schleiermacher's theology and in Hegel's philosophy (and vice versa)—for both were philosophers and theologians—and to make them more adequate to the religious tradition. The theology of mediation did not represent a new breakthrough, a new beginning, but more an attempt to save what could be saved, and to combine parts of the tradition of Hegel and Schleiermacher with the Christian tradition.

Most of these theologians of mediation are not known even by name in this country, and since they do not have any direct influence here, we will for the most part bypass them. This is not true, however, of the famous attempt to go back to Kant as a help in the situation. This battle cry, this signal of return or retreat, as I like to call it, was sounded by Ritschl and his group. This had great influence in this country. When I came to this country Ritschlianism was dead in Germany, but here to my great surprise it was very much alive.

Let us look at some of the types of theology of mediation. The problem they all had was to gain certainty about the contents of the

Christian message, after the critical movements of the eighteenth and nineteenth centuries had arisen. Everything fell under criticism. Everything was in doubt. The traditional forms had no power of resisting historical criticism or philosophical criticism, even if they would be repeated again and again by the theologians of restoration. So it was necessary to answer this fundamental question: Is there a way of re-establishing certainty in the religious realm?

A. EXPERIENCE AND THE BIBLICAL MESSAGE

One of the answers to the fundamental questions of certainty was given through a return to Schleiermacher's concept of religious consciousness. The word "experience" was used rather than "consciousness." But it was obviously dependent on Schleiermacher's idea of religion. We can see many theologians in whom the problem of religious experience was in the center of their thinking. In this country there was a theology of experience, the so-called empirical theology. For the moment I want to speak of some of these important theological schools of mediation.

1. The Erlangen School

There was the Erlangen school in Germany which preserved a strong attachment to the Lutheran tradition. In this school Schleiermacher's idea of the religious consciousness was enlarged in significance under the heading of the concept of experience. The religious experience meant everything. Let us look at this word. Experience can mean many things. During my first years in America, in the thirties and forties, the atmosphere around Columbia University was influenced by Dewey's pragmatism to such an extent that the word "experience" was used for almost everything. Then I realized that it was simply another word for "reality." For the objective reality was questioned and experience expressed the going beyond of subjects and objects. This word was used so much that I finally had the feeling that the word had become useless. Probably this is still the situation. For this reason I have tried to introduce the word "encounter" which is taken from Buber's concept of the I-Thou encounter.

In any case, the theologians following Schleiermacher asked the question: How can we attain to certainty about God, about revelation, about Christ, about the divine Spirit, etc.? Kant had criticized every way of reaching God by arguments. These theologians of experience accepted Kant's criticism. Nor could they go along with the speculative theology which followed Hegel, using much more refined arguments. Then there was the way of historical research. But this way was closed because historical research, so far from giving contents, actually removed them or made them doubtful, and questioned the whole historical foundation of Christianity. How can we reach a history which happened two thousand years ago when we know so little about it in terms of sound historical research? If this is the case, there is only one possible answer left. There must be a point of immediate participation, and for this the word "experience" was used. The experience of the divine reality must be the presence of the divine reality in us, and this must be the only possible assuring element. Then, however, the question arose: How can the inner experience which we have in our century guarantee anything which has happened hundreds of years ago? The answer to this question was: The reality of the past event is guaranteed by the effect it has on me.

A man named F. H. R. Frank (1827–1894), professor in Erlangen, produced a whole system of theology in which he tried to show how my status here and now as a Christian is dependent on the witness of the Old and New Testaments to what has happened. All the biblical stories, including creation, ultimate fulfillment, the coming of Christ, even the miracles, are guaranteed by my personal experience here and now. It is a kind of projection of my experience into the divine-human reality of the biblical peiod. Such a method was very impressive and was at that time the only way out. But, of course, it was not difficult for the critics to reply that everything that you project out of your own experience has been given to you originally by the Bible and the tradition, and that therefore you cannot escape being dependent on them. So you cannot guarantee the contents by your own experience. But if not, then in what way is it possible? This brings us to the fundamental problem with which modern theology is still wrestling. We cannot accept as the Roman Catholics do the authority of councils and popes. Of course, ultimately they cannot do that either, that is, without having within themselves the experience of the spiritual power of the Roman Church. As long as they do not ask questions, there is no problem, but if they ask questions, then their answer is also experiential. It is based on the experience of the glory, the truth, and the power of the Roman Church and that to which it witnesses. In other words, even the authoritarian Roman Catholic Christians are not able to escape that element of subjectivity which we call experience. But this experience does not give them any contents. All the contents come from the church, its tradition, and the Bible. The fact that they accept *these* contents is due to their participation in the spirit of the church.

The same thing can be true with Protestants. As I mentioned before, Kierkegaard had the idea of becoming contemporaneous with Jesus by leaping over two thousand years. How is that possible? It is a matter of question what Kierkegaard really meant, but perhaps he meant what Paul said when he said that we do not know the Christ any longer according to the flesh but according to the Spirit. We are in Christ (*en Christo*) insofar as he is the Spirit. This is immediate participation. Here you see a theological problem which arose out of the dissolution of the great synthesis. How much can experience guarantee? Can it guarantee any of the contents in space and time? I do not believe that this is a settled question. We are still in the midst of this situation. When today we ask, What guarantees the Christ-character of Jesus of Nazareth? we cannot give a merely historical answer, because the historical scientific answer leaves us in a state of doubt, of degrees of probability or improbability, and does not carry us beyond this. But if we say that something has happened to me, we speak in terms of experience. This thing which has happened to me is related to an event which must have happened in history, because it has had an impact on my own historical existence. This is something which certainly can be said and must be said. Then there remains the question as to how much can actually be guaranteed by religious experience? I leave you with this question, the question with which all the theologians of mediation struggled in trying to overcome the gap between subject and object which was opened up during the Enlightenment, which was seemingly closed in the great synthesis, but then opened up again. And so it stands wide open today, with some new attempts to close it being made at the same time.

2. Martin Kähler

At this time another theologian appeared who dealt with the same problem, but tried to answer it in a different way. He was Martin Kähler, also a theologian of mediation. He found an answer which became very important and which will be discussed for a long time to come, but mainly, no doubt, in the form which Bultmann has given to it. The impact of Kähler was very great in many directions. In his time his impact was limited by the Kant-Ritschlian school which dominated the European universities. Today the situation has changed and the lifework of this theologian has become visible again.

What Martin Kähler did for us—now I speak half-historically and half-autobiographically—was of twofold significance. First, he understood the problem of doubt; he understood the question: How can the subject in religion come to the object? How can they be reunited after having been separated by the criticism of the Enlightenment and the subsequent events? And he answered: This doubt is an element in the continuous human situation which we cannot simply overcome by putting everything into the subjectivity of experience. We must combine the subjectivity of experience, which he also had to accept like everyone else, with the objectivity of the biblical witness. So he pointed to the reality which is described in this witness, not only its central manifestation, namely, the Christ and all that is connected with him, but also the reality of the divine in nature and history, and beyond nature and history, in creation and fulfillment. But how can these two things come together, the subjective and the objective? His answer was that they cannot in an absolute way. They can come together only in a way which accepts the limits of our finitude. This means that we cannot reach absolute certainty. He placed this in analogy to the Protestant message of justification by grace through faith, namely, the acceptance of man in spite of his disrupted inner life and estrangement, which can never be fully overcome. This is the Lutheran idea of the impossibility of being a saint without being at the same time a sinner (*simul iustus et peccator*).

Now Kähler applied this message of justification not only to the inner moral acts of man, but also to his inner intellectual acts. Not only he who has sinned in the moral sense of the word, but also he who has doubted—the intellectual form of sin—is accepted by God. The doctrine of justification is applied to thoughts and not only to morality. This means that doubt does not necessarily separate us from God. This is what I learned from Kähler at that time and developed further in my own theology. But the first impact came from the theology of mediation rooted in the fundamental principle of the Reformation, and then applied to the situation of the split between subject and object since the beginning of the modern period. That is the one thing which came out of this theology of mediation. Similar ideas have become increasingly common in both Europe and America because of the enduring split between the objectivity of the Bible and tradition, and the subjectivity of experience. They come together, but never fully. The split remains, and so doubt remains.

The other point in Kähler's impact on us had to do with historical criticism. Historical criticism is a way of approaching the objective side, namely, those events which we say have had a transforming impact on us. How can we become certain of those events? They are the events that are responsible for our inner experience of being saved in spite of being sinners and doubters. Kähler's answer to the problem of the historical treatment of the Bible was given in terms of a sharp distinction between the historical Jesus and the Christ of faith. His famous book, *The So-called Historical Jesus and the Historic, Biblical Christ,* is coming out in English translation, with an introduction to Kähler and his theology by a former student of mine, because it is so relevant to our own situation.[1]

What is the relationship between the historical Jesus and the Christ of faith? Can we separate them? Must we accept the idea that Christ can never be reached by us apart from faith? Is there anything that can

[1] Translated, edited, and with an Introduction by Carl E. Braaten (Philadelphia: Fortress Press, 1964).

be done about the doubts produced by historical research into the biblical writings? Kähler himself did not believe that the two must be separated. For Kähler the Jesus of history is at the same time the Christ of faith, and the certainty of the Christ of faith is independent of the historical results of the critical approach to the New Testament. Faith guarantees what historical research can never reach. How can faith do this? What can faith guarantee? There lies the problem today, a problem which has been sharpened in the meantime by people like Bultmann and his whole school. The first real view of this situation in its radical aspects, however, we owe to Kähler, who came from the great synthesis, lived in it during a certain period of his life, then was transformed by the awakening movement and became one of the leading theologians of this period. But, as I told you, this position of Kähler was not decisive for the situation in the nineteenth century. He was a prophetic forerunner of what developed more fully only in the twentieth century. The heritage of Martin Kähler has been rediscovered only in the present-day discussion in view of the radical criticism, and not only in Europe but also in this country.

B. The "Back To Kant" Movement

Now I want to deal with the Kant-Ritschl-Harnack line of thought which led to Troeltsch in Germany and to Rauschenbusch and the so-called liberal theology in this country.

Why did a certain theological group suddenly raise the cry "back to Kant" after the great synthesis crumbled and they were surrounded by its many pieces? Why Kant and nobody else? None of these people said "back to orthodoxy" or "back to pietism." There were philosophers as well as theologians in the neo-Kantian school which was dominant at the time that I was a student. It was the Ritschlian school which introduced Kantianism into theology. You recall what we said about Kant's prison of finitude. Kant's critical epistemology determined that we cannot apply the categories of finitude to the divine. But, there was one point of breakthrough in the sphere of practical reason, namely, the experience of the moral imperative and its unconditional character. Here alone can we transcend the limits of finitude. But we cannot do it theoretically. We cannot prove God or speak of God directly, but only in terms of "as if." We call this a regulative way of speaking, not a constitutive way which can affirm something directly of God.

This retreat to Kant goes in the opposite direction of that other slogan which I used before: "Understanding Kant means transcending Kant." This was the idea of Fichte, Schelling, Hegel, and Schleiermacher. The Ritschlians argued that the result of this transcending Kant was the ruins of the great synthesis which now lay before them, like the broken pieces of the Tower of Babel. But the Ritschlians did not believe that these pieces could be put back together in the way that the other theologians of mediation tried to do. Nor was a return to Orthodoxy or Pietism or biblicism possible as the theologians of restoration tried to do. So another way had to be found. This way was a withdrawal to the acceptance of our finitude as we have it in Kant's critical philosophy. The Ritschlians said that Kant is the philosopher of Protestantism. Protestantism does not aspire to climb up to the divine, but keeps itself within the limits of finitude. The attempt of the great synthesis is ultimately a product of mysticism, of the principle of identity between the divine and the human. Therefore, this "back to Kant" movement was extremely hostile to all forms of mysticism, including the theologies of experience, because there is a mystical element present in Schleiermacher's idea of religious consciousness and the other forms of experiential theology. Experience means having the divine within ourselves, not necessarily by nature, but yet given and felt within our own being. But this was not admitted by the neo-Kantian school. They protested not only against genuine mysticism, but also against every theology of experience. What then was left? Only two things. The one is historical research. This is the greatness and at the same time the shortcoming of liberal theology. It is the greatness insofar as it dares to apply the historical method to the biblical literature; it is the shortcoming insofar as it tries to base faith on the results of historical research. That was what they tried to do. There is thus a positive and a negative side in this school.

But there must be a second factor, for how can there be religious certainty? According to the Ritschlians, Kant has left but one window out of our finitude, and this is the moral imperative. The real basis of certainty is the moral point of view. We are certain of ourselves as moral personalities. This is not the experience of something mystical outside of ourselves; this is the immediate personal experience, or more exactly, the experience of being a person as such. Religion is then that which makes us able to actualize ourselves as moral persons. Religion is a supporting power of the ethical. These defenders of Christianity tried to save Christianity with the help of the moral principle, but in doing so they aroused the wrath of all those for whom the mystical element in religion is decisive. So here we have a religion argued for on the basis of the ethical experience of the personality. Religion is the help toward moral self-realization. So the two sides of the Ritschlian theology are: objective, scientific research and the moral principle or experience of the ethical personality.

The great synthesis about which we have been speaking dealt seriously with the question of truth. Christianity's claim was that it mediated truth, truth about God, the world, and man. That means there is ontological, cosmological, and anthropological truth. Both Schleiermacher and Hegel wanted to affirm the truth in connection with the whole of reality. The critics of Hegel and the Hegelians denied that a satisfactory synthesis had been achieved between Christianity and philosophical knowledge about man, nature, the universe as a whole, and the divine source and ground of the universe. So the neo-Kantians and the Ritschlians gave up the claim to truth in this sense. They withdrew to Kant's critique of practical reason and said: The divine appears through the moral imperative and nowhere else. The problem of truth was replaced by the moral answer. The function of Christianity is then to make morality possible. From this point of view all ontological questions were dropped so far as possible. Of course, it is never fully possible for anyone to do that. In the neo-Kantian school itself there arose people at the beginning of this century who showed that there are always ontological presuppositions in every epistemology. It is self-deception to believe that you can answer the famous question, "How do you know?" before you know something, before you answer questions, and then put them under criticism. Epistemology cannot stand on its own feet because knowing and the reality which is known are both ontological concepts. You cannot escape definite presuppositions if you deal with knowledge. The same is true of modern analytic philosophy. It analyzes man's logical and linguistic structures, but it always has a hidden presupposition about the relation of logic and language to reality, even if it does not acknowledge it. Sometimes this relation is completely negative when it is said that we do not know anything about reality, and that our logical and linguistic structures have nothing to do with reality. But this must then be proven, and if somebody tries to prove it, he is an ontologist. Or if there is a positive relation, they have to do what philosophers have always done: they have to show how language and logic are related to reality.

So Ritschlianism was a withdrawal from the ontological to the moral. The whole religious message, the message of Jesus which had to be described in historical terms, is a message which liberates the personality from the pressures of nature both outside of and within man. The function of salvation is the victory of spirit or mind over nature. The way this happens is through the forgiveness of sins. This is the inner meaning of the Ritschlian theology of retreat. It was a theology which could fortify the strong development of the bourgeois personality in the middle and the end of the nineteenth century. In an article in the book, *The Christian Answer*,[2] edited by Van Dusen, formerly president of Union Theological Seminary, New York, I have given a long description of this development of the personality ideal from the Renaissance to the end of the nineteenth century, by showing some works of the visual arts. There you can see what a bourgeois personality is. The Ritschlian theology provided the theological foundation for this development of the strong, active, morally disciplined individual person. It was connected with liberal elements in the social and political structure, with autonomous thinking in the sciences and with the rejection of all authority. It was compatible with the mood of the time, the liberal personalistic mood, but this was not to last long into the twentieth century.

The Ritschlian negation of ontology was joined with another concept which is still being discussed in modern American philosophy, although not as much now as thirty years ago when I came to this country. This is the concept of value judgments. Instead of making ontological statements, it was alleged that Christianity makes value judgments. This means that everything is related to the subject who makes value

2 "The World Situation," *The Christian Answer*, edited by Henry P. Van Dusen (New York: Charles Scribner's Sons, 1948).

judgments. This was a typical device of escape. It was taken from Rudolf Lotze, (1817–1881), an important figure in the history of philosophy in the middle of the nineteenth century. How could man's spiritual life, man's personality, be saved in the face of the increasing naturalism which dissolves everything into a constellation of atoms? The answer was that although we are unable to make ontological judgments, we can make value judgments. On the basis of value judgments, we can evaluate Christianity as that religion which can overcome the forces of the natural and secure us as personalities of disciplined moral character.

You can see an analogy to this in the secularized puritanism—not the original puritanism—of this country. This was the reason for Ritschl's influence in this country long after it had died out in Germany. It was mediated through pupils of Ritschl himself or of Wilhelm Herrmann (1846–1922) in Marburg under whom many Americans studied. He was a man in whom liberalism was connected with a profound piety and a strong desire to liberate Christianity from all authoritarian ties.

Out of the Ritschlian antiontological feeling came a doctrine of God in which the element of power in God was denied or reduced almost to nothing. It tried to overcome the polarity of power and love in God, and to reduce the idea of God to love. The message of salvation was reduced to forgiveness. The symbol of divine wrath and judgment was removed from practical piety. This was in line with the Enlightenment, with Kantianism and the whole humanistic tradition. It was also very successful. But a criticism is necessary. When we pray, we usually start our prayers with "Almighty God." In doing so we immediately attribute might and power to God. The divinity of God lies in his being the ultimate power of being. This was one of the weakest points in the Ritschlian theology, and at this point the criticism set in.

C. ADOLF VON HARNACK

The greatest figure in the Ritschlian school was Adolf von Harnack ('1851–1930). He was a very impressive figure, basically a church historian. His greatest achievement was the *History of Dogma*,[3] still a classical work in this area of research. Any student of the history of

[3] Seven vols., translated by Neil Buchanan (New York: Dover Publications, 1900).

Christian thought must reckon with it. Those of you who come from very conservative traditions may have the feeling, without admitting it, that the dogmas sort of fell down from heaven. If you read Harnack's *History of Dogma*, you will see how the great creeds—the Apostles', the Nicene, and the Chalcedonian—came into existence, how much historical drama, how much of human passions, and also how much divine providential guidance were involved in this development. You will see that the ecumenical councils of Nicaea and Chalcedon used a lot of terms from Greek philosophy in formulating the trinitarian and christological dogmas. Harnack saw in this development a second wave of Hellenization. The first wave was gnosticism, and the second wave was the formulation of the ancient dogma. The first was rejected by the church; the second was accepted and used by the church.

Harnack's research into the history of dogma raised a lot of problems which are still being discussed in theology today. The relation of Christianity to gnosticism is still a live issue. Perhaps the most important book on gnosticism is the one written by Hans Jonas, entitled *Gnosis und spätantiker Geist*.[4] His interpretation of gnosticism is based on existentialist categories as used by Heidegger and other existentialists. It shows you that the speculations of the gnostics were not all nonsense, but were based on the human situation in the late ancient world, which—like our own situation—was one of complete disruption and meaninglessness. There was the longing for salvation, the continual looking for saving powers in a deteriorated world at the end of the Roman Empire. Gnosticism was an attempt to express the saving forces and describe the human situation in categories very like those of the present-day existentialist philosophers.

But Christianity rejected gnosticism for one reason. These gnostics were anti-Old Testament. That means they were against the idea of creation, that the world is created good, that there is no matter from which one must be liberated, etc. Liberation according to Christianity is liberation from finitude and sin, and not from matter in which we are involved. In other words, the dualistic form of gnosticism was rejected, the dualism between a highest God and a counter God. The church

[4] Göttingen: Vandenhoek & Ruprecht, 1934. Cf. Hans Jonas, *The Gnostic Religion* (Boston: Beacon Press, 1958).

succeeded in rejecting this gnostic dualism. But the church nevertheless used the concepts of the hellenistic world. You should not call them Greek pure and simple, for classical Greek did not last far beyond the second century before Christ. Hellenism followed this, and Hellenism is a mixture of Greek, Persian, Egyptian, Jewish, and even Indian elements, and mystical groups of all kinds. It is a mixed religiosity in which the Greek concepts were used, but in a religiously transformed sense.

In order to be received the Christian message had to be proclaimed in categories which could be understood by the people who were to receive it. The Christian Church did this without fear. Harnack's criticism was that in this way Christianity became intellectualized. But Harnack was wrong in this respect. My main criticism of him has been right on this point. The more our knowledge of the gnostics and the whole Hellenistic culture has increased in the last fifty years, the more we see how wrong he was in this respect. He considered Hellenism as identical with intellectualization. This is not at all true. This is not even true of Plato, or Aristotle and the Stoics. Every great philosophy is rooted in an existential emergency, in a situation of questioning out of which saving answers must come. If you read Plato and Aristotle you will find that this is certainly the case with them. But in Hellenism this is manifestly so, because the whole period from B.C. 100 to about A.D. 400 is a period in which the question of salvation from distorted reality stands in the center. The Greek concepts already had a religious tinge when they were used by the Christian dogmas. So Harnack was right in saying that Hellenization had taken place, but wrong in defining this as intellectualization.

According to Harnack a foreign element entered into Christianity when terms like *ousia* and *hypostasis* were used in constructing the official dogma of the church. This process began not only in the fourth- and fifth-century councils, but already in the apostolic fathers, and that means in the generation which is contemporaneous with the latest biblical writings. Then this process received a strong impetus from the apologists who elaborated the logos concept in theology. All this can be called Hellenization, but how else could it have happened? The pagans were not Jews, and so the Jewish concepts could not be used. Besides, the Jewish concepts were not used so much even in the circles in which

Jesus and John the Baptist arose. If you read the Dead Sea Scrolls, you will find that the Old Testament concepts are there, but even more you will find elements from the apocalyptic movements from the intertestamental period. Even Judaism had adapted to the new situation. It could not have been done in any other way if Judaism or Christianity were to survive.

Harnack's greatness is that he showed this process of Hellenization. His shortcoming is that he did not see the necessity of it. Those of us who studied under the influence of Harnack's *History of Dogma* sensed a tremendous liberation. It was the liberation from the necessity of identifying Hellenistic concepts with the Christian message itself. On the other hand, I would not accept the idea which one hears so much that all the Greek elements must be thrown out and only the Old Testament terms should be used. Christianity, it is suggested, is basically a matter of the Old Testament language and a continuation of Old Testament theology and piety. If this were to be done consistently, at least two-thirds of the New Testament would have to be ruled out, for both Paul and John used a lot of Hellenistic concepts. Besides, it would rule out the whole history of doctrine. This idea is a new bondage to a particular development, the Old Testament development. Christianity is not nearer to the Jews than to the Greeks. I believe that the one who expressed that was the great missionary to the Greeks and to the Hellenistic pagan world.

There is another side to Harnack which was much more impressive for the masses of educated people at the turn of the century. He himself once told me that in the year 1900 the main railway station in the city of Leipzig, one of the largest in Central Europe, was blocked by freight cars in which his book *What Is Christianity?* was being sent all over the world. He also told us that this book was being translated into more languages than any other book except the Bible. This means that this book, which was the religious witness of one of the greatest scholars of the century, had great significance to the educated people prior to the first World War. It meant the possibility of affirming the Christian message in a form which was free from its dogmatic captivity and at the same time very much rooted in the biblical image of Jesus. But in order to elaborate this image, he invented the formula which distinguished sharply between the gospel of Jesus and the gospel about Jesus. He stated that the gospel about Jesus does not belong in the gospel preached by Jesus. This is the classical formula of liberal theology: the gospel or message preached by Jesus contains nothing of the later message preached concerning Jesus.

Such a statement presupposes the reduction of the gospel to the first three Gospels, then the elimination from these Gospels of all that shows the influence of Paul. Baur's theory of the conflict between Paul and Jesus is revived here in a more refined, modern way, namely, that Paul interpreted Jesus in a way which is very far removed from the actual historical Jesus. This idea of course has some contemporary followers. Only it is not Paul who is so much at the center of the discussion, but the early community, which existed before Paul. This early community, on the basis of the resurrection experience, produced the doctrines about Jesus, doctrines which cannot be found in the original message of Jesus himself. This original message is the message of the coming kingdom, and the kingdom is the state in which God and the individual member of the kingdom are in a relation of forgiveness, acceptance, and love.

Again someone might say, you have merely presented this, but have not criticized it. So I will anticipate this question and say, I don't believe that this is a possible approach. I believe that the whole New Testament is united, including the first three Gospels, in the statement that Jesus is the Christ, the bringer of the new eon. I think this fundamental statement overcomes the split between Jesus, on the one hand, and the early community, or Paul or John, on the other hand. That the differences are there no one who views the literature historically can deny or conceal, but whether the differences are of absolute significance systematically is quite another question. My criticism of the whole liberal theology, including Harnack, is that it had no real systematic theology; it believed in the results of historical research in a wrong way. Therefore, its systematic utterances were comparatively poor. But at that time they had meaning for many people.

D. Miscellaneous Movements in Theology

Now a few other movements must be dealt with very sketchily.

1. The Luther-Renaissance

The Luther-Renaissance was a movement which happened within the Ritschlian school itself, and gave to this school a greater dimension of depth. When Luther was rediscovered, it became clear that Luther's God was not the moralistically reduced God of liberal theology. Luther's God is the hidden God, the unknown God, the God in whom the darkness of life is rooted as well as the light, the God who is seen in terms of the voluntaristic line of thinking to which we referred in a previous lecture. This was very important for it liberated the figure of Luther from a kind of popular distortion; it showed the tremendous inner forces in the great revolutionary, the first reformer whose breakthrough was the root of all the reformatory movements, including Zwingli's and Calvin's and those of the radical evangelicals. This all happened on the basis of the Ritschlian school, but it resulted in an inner deepening of it.

2. Biblical Realism

There was another school which was in a certain respect a biblicistic reaction against Ritschlianism, but it was not a biblicism bound to the inspiration doctrine and other fundamentalist tenets. The inspiration doctrine had been given up except by a few fundamentalists in Germany. Rather, it was a biblical realism which was much more adequate to human nature, just as Luther was much more relevant to the human nature than the moralistically determined individual personality of the late nineteenth century ever could imagine. One of those responsible for this biblical realism was Martin Kähler, and along with him were his friends Adolf Schlatter, Wilhelm Lütgert, and Hermann Cremer. Their weakness was that in spite of their biblical realism and their understanding of the deeper aspects of human nature in the light of the

Bible, they resisted the historical criticism. It was not possible to justify this resistance, because historical criticism was a matter of scientific honesty. Whether one was more conservative or more radical in the historical investigation of the biblical literature, the methods had to be accepted in the long run. I myself experienced a real crisis in my development after I left Halle where this kind of biblicism was firmly established, and began independently to study the history of biblical criticism. It was especially in studying Albert Schweitzer's history of research into the life of Jesus[5] that I became convinced of the inadequacy of the kind of biblicism in which the historical questions are not taken seriously. This experience prevented me from remaining silent about the historical critical problems in face of the Barthian influence during the years of the church struggle in Germany. Barth silenced these problems almost completely in his own school, and when I came to America theologians here were not worried about them either.

But genuine problems cannot be ignored in the long run. The explosion produced by Bultmann was not so much due to anything new that he did, but to the fact that he brought to the surface problems which had been suppressed by the Barthian school. Of course, Bultmann had his own particular kind of radical criticism, but there was nothing methodologically new in the situation ever since historical criticism arose two hundred years ago. The explosion came when Bultmann wrote his article on demythologizing, "New Testament and Mythology."[6] This shock might have been much less severe if the German theologians— and others too—had realized all along the impossibility of disregarding the historical approach in New Testament interpretation.

3. Radical Criticism

The increase of radicalism in historical criticism undercut the presuppositions of Harnack and the whole liberal theology. The presupposition of Harnack's What Is Christianity? was that one can arrive at a

5 The Quest of the Historical Jesus, translated by W. Montgomery (London: Adam & Charles Black, 1910).
6 Rudolf Bultmann, Kerygma and Myth, Vol. I, edited by H. W. Hartsch, translated by Reginald Fuller (London: S.P.C.K., 1954).

fairly accurate picture of the empirical man, Jesus of Nazareth, guaranteed by the methods of historical science. One can arrive, that is, at a definition of original Christianity by deleting all the additions of the early congregations and of Paul and John. But it turned out that this was not possible.

Radical historical criticism began first with the Old Testament. Previously the Old Testament had been read in the old Luther Bible in which certain passages had been printed in large letters. These were the consoling passages or those specially related to the New Testament fulfillment of prophecy. The confidence in this way of reading the Old Testament was broken by the Wellhausen hypothesis. This was an event of great religious significance. Now the Old Testament could be read not as a collection of edifying words printed in big letters, but as a real development in history, as the history of revelation, in which the divine and the human are both involved.

New Testament criticism proceeded in an even more radical way. If Harnack could speak about Jesus in terms of God and the soul, as he did, then the problem was: What about the inner self-consciousness of Jesus? What was Jesus' understanding of himself? The answer to this is largely dependent on the "Son of Man" concept in the Gospels. What did this mean in Jesus' own mind? Did he apply it to himself, and if so, in what sense? And if not, what did the early Christians mean by it? The two possible ways of answering this question were presented by Albert Schweitzer in the conclusion of his book, *The Quest of the Historical Jesus*. One of the ways is presented and defended by Schweitzer himself. It is the solution of thoroughgoing eschatology. Jesus considered himself as an eschatological, apocalyptic figure, identifying himself with the Son of Man in the sense of Daniel. Here the Son of Man is an emissary of God standing before the divine throne, then leaving it to descend into the evils of this eon and to bring in a new age. Then Schweitzer goes on to describe the catastrophe when Jesus cried out from the cross, feeling that God had abandoned him. Jesus had expected that God in his power would intervene to save him and the world, but to no avail. This is the one version.

There are many other versions. But the other one that Schweitzer contrasted with his own is that of radical historical skepticism, represented by Wilhelm Wrede and later by Bultmann himself. Skepticism here does not mean doubt about God, the world, and man, but doubt about the possibility of reaching the historical Jesus by our historical methods. My own heritage has been this school of historical skepticism. If Schweitzer's apocalyptic interpretation of Jesus is not right, we must admit that we are in a position where we cannot know very much about the historical Jesus. This radical situation is the background for my own attempt to answer the systematic question how we can say that Jesus is the Christ if historical research can never reach a sure image of the historical Jesus. The second volume of my *Systematic Theology* is an attempt to draw out the consequences for systematic theology created by this skeptical attitude to the New Testament generally and to the historical Jesus in particular.

4. Rudolf Bultmann

We can deal with a certain aspect of Bultmann's work while we are on this subject of historical criticism. If you read his *History of the Synoptic Tradition*,[7] you will see the radicalism of his skepticism, and why he is unable to reach conservative results. But for systematic theology the question is not whether the results are more or less conservative or radical. Historians who oppose Bultmann because they are a bit more conservative use the same method he does. The two poles of conservatism or radicalism in criticism do not mean a thing for systematic theology, because a conservative criticism, as much as a radical criticism, can never get beyond probabilities on historical matters. Whether we are offered more positive or more negative probabilities does not make any difference for the fundamental problem of systematic theology.

In this connection we can make some remarks about the so-called new quest of the historical Jesus carried on by some of Bultmann's followers. They are obviously more optimistic with respect to the probabilities, but no change results for the systematic situation. Our knowledge of the historical Jesus never gets beyond probabilities of one kind or another.

Bultmann has combined his radical historical research with a systematic attempt. He calls this systematic attempt "demythologization." He means by this expression that we must liberate the biblical message from

[7] Translated by John Marsh (New York: Harper & Row, 1963).

the mythological language in which it is expressed so that the modern man who does not share the biblical world view can honestly accept the biblical message. This, as I said, amounted to a real explosion in the theological world because the Barthian influence had suppressed the radical critical questions of biblical interpretation. So Bultmann's name became central in the theological debates.

Since you all know what Bultmann is trying to do, let me give you here merely my mild criticism of it. I feel that on most points I am on Bultmann's side. But he does not know the meaning of myth. He does not know that religious language is and always must be mythological. Even when he says that God has acted in Jesus in order to confront us with the possibility of decision for or against authentic existence, this is a symbolic or mythological way of speaking. He resists admitting this; he cannot go beyond it. I have often stated that he should speak not of demythologization but of deliteralization, which means not taking the symbols as literal expressions of events in time and space. This is something indeed that has to be done because the possibility of presenting the Christian message to the pagans of our time depends on it, and all of us are among these pagans by virtue of at least half of our education. We are all on the boundary line between humanism and Christianity. We cannot even speak to ourselves honestly in biblical terms unless we are able to deliteralize them.

While this is the importance of Bultmann, he is not able to bring this into a real systematic structure, not even with the help of Heidegger's existentialism. But this existentialism does help him to show the existential character of the New Testament concepts. The existentialist interpretation of the New Testament deals with the concepts of anxiety, care, guilt, and emptiness, and this is important. I have also applied an existentialist interpretation of biblical texts in all the sermons I have preached. But Bultmann is not able to present all this in a real systematic structure.

5. The History-of-Religions Approach

Hermann Gunkel (1862–1932) was the first great critic from the point of view of the history of religions. He was primarily an Old Testament scholar, but his method and results had implications for New

Testament scholarship. In Germany we call the movement in which he participated the *Religionsgeschichtlicheschule,* one word for the "school of the history of religions." This was not a school in the sense that there was special interest in the living religions like Islam, Buddhism, Hinduism, etc., but it was a method of analyzing the contents of the biblical writings. It tried to discover the extent to which both the Old and New Testaments are dependent on the religious symbolism of the surrounding religions. This, of course, excludes the Asian religions as well as Islam, which came much later, but it includes the religions of Persia, Egypt, and Assyria; it includes the primitive forms of religion and especially the mystery religions which grew up in the Hellenistic world. To what extent are the biblical writings dependent on these pre-Jewish and pre-Christian religious movements?

Gunkel's approach and discoveries had a tremendous influence. I believe that Gunkel's *Commentary on Genesis*[8] is still the classic work which shows the influence of the pagan religions on the Old Testament books. It traces the motifs of the primitive pagan religions which appear in the Genesis stories. It demonstrates how the Jewish spirit, how prophetism and later the priestly writers transformed the pagan myths and purified them under the impact of the prophetic spirit. All this has given us a much better understanding of the Old Testament.

The same thing was done with the New Testament. The surrounding contemporary religions influenced the writers of the New Testament. The influence from the apocalyptic period is obvious. Certain concepts are related to the mystery religions. The term "Lord" (*kyrios*) itself may have some connection with the mystery religions. Nobody can deal with the New Testament today in a scholarly way if he is not aware of this situation. There are always differences of scholarly opinion on these questions, but the approach itself must be taken seriously.

* * * * * * * * * *

Question: It seems that most of the systematic theologians that we have studied this quarter have faltered at the point where they talk about or fail to talk about the problem of sin. Can such a generalization

---

[8] *Genesis übersetzt und erklärt* (Göttingen: Vandenhoek and Ruprecht, 1901). Cf. his *The Legends of Genesis,* translated by W. H. Carruth (Chicago: The Open Court Publishing Co., 1901). This book is a translation of the Introduction to the author's *Commentary on Genesis.*

be made in any true sense, and if so does it have any particular significance for the theological enterprise?

Answer: This is not true of the theologians of mediation. We did discuss Schleiermacher's doctrine of sin and pointed out its shortcomings. He derived sin in an evolutionary way from the inadequacies of man's mental development in contrast to his bodily development. In the Ritschlian school too sin did not receive its full significance because it was described in a similar way as the conflict between man's selfhood and his natural basis. Salvation was then conceived of as the spiritual power of man overcoming his natural basis. For the Ritschlian school salvation was especially forgiveness of sins, but not transformation, for the idea of the Spirit being present in man and transforming him was very remote from Ritschlian thinking. So the generalization is true with respect to the leading theologians whom we discussed. But this is not true of the theologians of mediation, some of whom we touched on very briefly. I left out one theologian who is very important on the doctrine of sin. His name is Julius Müller (1801–1878). He earned for himself the additional name sin-Müller because he wrote a very large and classical work on the doctrine of sin,[9] especially in terms of Schelling's philosophy. And, of course, when we dealt with the existentialist philosophers and theologians, we showed their grasp of the situation of human estrangement. Kierkegaard especially was discussed in this connection; his idea that sin presupposes itself, his concept of the transition from innocence to guilt and the problem of sickness unto death are all profound aspects of the reality of sin. There is a strong tradition of understanding the depth of sin in the theologians of mediation, much profounder than in both Schleiermacher and Ritschl.

* * * * * * * * * *

6. *Ernst Troeltsch*

With only one lecture left, we are going to have to limit ourselves to a few remarks on four subjects. The first is the thought of Ernst

[9] *The Christian Doctrine of Sin,* translated by William Urwick (Edinburgh: T. & T. Clark, 1868).

Troeltsch, who was formerly my colleague in the University of Berlin and whom I consider in a special way as one of my teachers, although I never heard him lecture. Secondly, I want to talk about the foundations of religious socialism in Germany. Thirdly, about Karl Barth, and fourthly about existentialist motifs.

I will speak first of Troeltsch as a philosopher of religion. His main problem dealt with the meaning of religion in the context of the human spirit or man's mental structure. Here Troeltsch followed Kant by accepting his three critiques, but he said that there is not only the theoretical *a priori*, man's categorical structure, as Kant developed it in the *Critique of Pure Reason*, not only the moral, as Kant developed it in the *Critique of Practical Reason*, and not only the aesthetic, as he developed it in the *Critique of Judgment*, but there is also a religious *a priori*. This means that there is something which belongs to the structure of the human mind itself from which religion arises. It is essentially present, although always only potentially as with the other three structures. Whether it becomes actualized in time and space is another question, but if it is actualized it has its own kind of certainty as the others have. It is an *a priori*. To say that it is *a priori* does not mean that it is to be understood temporally, as if all the Kantian categories are clear in the consciousness of a new born baby. This is not what *a priori* means. What it means is that if somebody has the character of man, if he has a human mind and human rational structure, then these categories develop under the impact of experience. This is what Troeltsch tried to show in regard to the religious *a priori*. I would say that on this point he stands in the great tradition of the Franciscan-Augustinian school of the Middle Ages. It is impossible for me to understand how we could ever come to a philosophical understanding of religion without finding a point in the structure of man as man in which the finite and the infinite meet or are within each other.

In his book, *The Absoluteness of Christianity*,[10] Troeltsch criticizes Harnack's famous book, *What Is Christianity?* He asks, What is the essence of Christianity and whence do we derive it? Is it the classical period of Christianity, the period of the apostles? Is it an abstraction

---

[10] *Die Absolutheit des Christentums und die Religionsgeschichte* (Tübingen: J. C. B. Mohr, 1929).

from all the periods, by using the Aristotelian method which abstracts from all the concrete realities in order to reach the essence? In either case we are confronted by impossibilities, because in history there is not such an essence. History is open toward the future. If one wants to speak of an essence, one can do so only by anticipating the entire future, which is impossible. For this reason he denied the possibility of finding an essence.

Troeltsch was not only a philosopher of history; he was also a man with great historical vision. I remember the excitement which was aroused when he published a great essay on the meaning of Protestantism in relation to the modern world.[11] In this particular article he wrote about the medieval character of early Protestantism and challenged the idea that Protestantism had brought an end to the medieval world. He tried to show that early Protestantism had all the medieval characteristics. Instead, the Middle Ages came to an end only with the Enlightenment. This, of course, was a fundamental expression of what one usually calls liberal Protestantism.

Troeltsch's philosophy of history is rooted in a negative attitude toward what he calls "historism," or perhaps in English one might call it "historicism." In any case, it is an attitude of relativism toward history. For historicism, history is mere observation of the past. It is not an attitude of participation in history and of making decisions which are decisive for the course of history. At the end of the nineteenth century under the influence of historicism history was at best an interesting subject to be observed with a detached attitude. I know people who have carried this attitude with them into the twentieth century and have remained historicists in this respect. Now, Troeltsch tried to overcome this by an interesting construction. He asked the question: What is the aim of history? Toward what is history running? That aim would determine the meaning of history. But he denied the possibility of knowing or giving such an aim. He said that we can only speak of the concrete historical structure in which we are living. This was certainly an

---

[11] *Protestantism and Progress: A Historical Study of the Relation of Protestantism to the Modern World*, translated by W. Montgomery (Boston: Beacon Press, 1958); translated from the German edition of 1911, *Die Bedeutung des Protestantismus für die Entstehung der Modernen Welt*.

advance over historicism. He was not only an observer; he also wanted to transform history. But he did this in a limited way. He said that our task is to care for the immediate next stage of history, and he called this Europeanism. It coincides with what we today call the Western world. He included the United States as well, of course. He did not use our expression of the Western world, because at that time the conflict between East and West had not started. Europeanism is a combination of Christian, Jewish, Greek, Roman, and Germanic elements. Christianity is the religion of Europeanism; it belongs to the Western world. Therefore, missions cannot have the intention of converting people in the Eastern world, but instead of fostering the interpenetration of the great religions. He was the president of a special missionary society guided by the liberal theology, and as president of this society, he developed his concept of missions, namely, the interpenetration of cultures and religions. This means that the idea of the absoluteness of Christianity—whatever this questionable concept may mean—would have to be given up. Christianity was relativized by limiting it to the Western culture, by making it the religion of Europeanism. Christianity and Western culture belong to each other, but with respect to the Eastern culture, the best that we could hope for is the interpenetration of the religions.

The next point we wish to discuss is of the highest importance for theology. The history of theology in the past had usually been discussed as the history of dogma or of the doctrinal statements of the church. This was the case in Harnack too. But Troeltsch was influenced by Max Weber (1864–1920), the great sociologist and perhaps the greatest scholar in Germany of the nineteenth century. So Troeltsch now posed the question: What about the social teachings of the Christian churches?[12] That, in fact, is the title of his great work. Should we not look at the dogmatic statements in the light of the social doctrines of the churches? Perhaps we might understand the dogmatic statements better in this light, rather than dealing with them apart from their relation to social reality. This method was influenced by the methodological principles of Marxism, but in a way that was counterbalanced by Max

[12] *The Social Teachings of the Christian Churches,* translated by Olive Wyon (New York: The Macmillan Company, 1931).

Weber's own interpretation of the relation of thought to social reality. For instance, Max Weber tried to show that Calvinism had a tremendous influence on the way in which the capitalistic rulers gained their fortunes and ran their factories by a personal inner-worldly asceticism as called for by the Calvinist ethic.

Troeltsch's method was thus a two-way street. On the one side was the understanding that all doctrines are dependent on social conditions and cannot be understood apart from these social conditions. This was the Marxist side. But on the other side was the equally important insight that the way in which the social conditions are used by people is largely dependent on their ultimate concern, by their religious convictions and their ethical implications. In this way he together with Max Weber tried to give a new key to the interpretation of the history of religion.

These are the main points in dealing with Troeltsch, and, as I told you, I have been deeply influenced by these ideas. But in two respects I already belonged to a new generation. Many of us were not satisfied with the way in which Troeltsch tried to overcome historicism. We felt that he himself was still under its power. The other point at which we departed from Troeltsch had to do with the existentialism that arose in the meantime. Troeltsch was not at all in touch with these existentialist ideas. Ultimately he came from the Ritschlian school, and the Ritschlian school was a rationalistic essentialism. While attempting to overcome these limitations of Troeltsch, we remained always grateful for the often devastating criticism which he leveled at many traditional forms of Christian theology. He taught us a kind of freedom which transcended the often narrow biblicistic attitude of the Ritschlian school and of liberal theology, which despite its liberalism often hangs on to a pietistic biblicistic element.

7. Religious Socialism

Religious socialism can be seen as an attempt to overcome the limitations of Troeltsch's effort to overcome historicism. I would like to have had time to trace the underlying sources of religious socialism. These sources are in the line of development that includes men like Boehme, Schelling, Oetinger, and generally a tradition of biblical realism which was neither orthodox or fundamentalist, on the one hand, nor pietistic, on the other hand, and which transcended the doctrinal Lutheranism by its closeness to social and political realities. The fundamental ideas in this line have become very important in our days again. Accordingly, we emphasize that God is related to the world and not only to the individual and his inner life and not only to the church as a sociological entity. God is related to the universe, and this includes nature, history, and personality. May I add that Martin Kähler and Adolf Schlatter were also in this line of thought. They stressed the freedom of God to act apart from the church in either its orthodox or pietistic form. They were also emancipated from the moralistic transformation of religion in the escapist theology of Ritschlianism.

There are two names we must mention, the Blumhardts, father and son: Johann Christoph Blumhardt (1805–1880) and Christoph Blumhardt (1842–1919). Both of them were ministers, and the son later became a political leader of the socialist movement. The father Blumhardt, as he is called, was a man who felt he had the power to expel demonic forces. He practiced healing in his parish in Bad Boll in Württemberg. He did it in a way that the Synoptic stories say that Jesus did it, not with faith healing, which is mostly a matter of magical concentration, but with the power of the divine Spirit radiating from him. From this experience he came to the realization that God is a healing God, that he has something to do with the world and all the dimensions of reality and not only with the inner conversion of the human soul.

The son Blumhardt applied these ideas to the social realities. His special emphasis was that God loved the world, not only the church and not only Christians. He fought against the egocentricism of the individualistic type of religion which characterized pietistic Lutheranism at that time. For this reason he participated in the socialist movement which was becoming more powerful at the turn of the century. He did this in terms of an inner historical understanding of the kingdom of God, without giving up the transcendent fulfillment of the kingdom of God, as the social gospel theology in this country often tended to do. He could say that the works of those who do not know God are often greater works for God than those which are done in the church by Christians in the name of God.

These are the ideas which we later developed in the religious socialist movement, and I remember that we represented them also at the Oxford Conference in 1937, which was one of the important conferences of the modern ecumenical movement. At that time I was chairman of a small committee which included among others some Eastern Orthodox theologians. Our task was to make a statement about the relation of the church to socialism and communism. We presented a report under rather dramatic conditions to the plenary assembly of the conference, in which we stated that often God speaks to the church more directly from outside the church, through those who are enemies of religion and Christianity, than within the church, through those who are official representatives of the churches. We related this to the revolutionary movements of the nineteenth and twentieth centuries, and especially to the socialist movement. This was accepted almost without any changes by the Oxford Assembly. Although this was a step of great significance, it was too early for it. Today if the National Council of Churches or the World Council of Churches should make such a statement, it would be heard and understood, and perhaps attacked by some. But at that time this type of statement was so far in advance of the actual situation that it was almost forgotten. Thus, out of the experience and insight of people like the Blumhardts a new understanding of the relation of the church to society was opened up in an unheard-of way in most of the European churches. Religious socialism was one of the movements which mediated this new power and vision.

In this connection we might say something about Pope John XXIII. He was able to criticize the church, his own church, and could declare publicly how the church had become irrelevant for many people in our time. He has shown us that the spirit of prophetism which can criticize the religious group in which the prophet lives has not completely died out in the Roman Church. It is still there and surprisingly has been voiced from the top of the hierarchy from where one would least expect it. The other thing that he has done is to make it possible to reach out to those outside the churches, not only to the "separated brethren" outside the Roman Catholic Church, but to the secularists and even to those who are enemies of the church and Christianity. On the basis of my own religious socialist past I feel a kinship with him. He shares the prophetic self-criticism which is open to the truth which has been forgotten in the church and which is now represented against the church by the secular and the anti-religious movements of our time.

The immediate predecessors of the religious socialist movement were in Switzerland, Hermann Kutter (1869-1931) and Leonhard Ragaz, (1868-1945), both of whom you will learn about in every biography of Karl Barth. Both fought for justice and peace in the name of Christianity, Kutter more prophetically and Ragaz more politically. It is important to remember that Karl Barth himself was a part of the religious socialist movement before he made his great break with all such movements. We tried to develop a special type of religious socialism in Germany after the first World War which took into account the particular historical situation in Germany. With the revolution of 1919 in Germany, the country was split into the labor movements and the traditional churches, which were practically all Lutheran, except in the West where there is some Calvinist influence. The problem we faced after the first World War was how to overcome the split between Lutheran transcendentalism and the secular utopianism in the socialist groups. The Lutheran idea was that the world is somehow in the hands of the devil, and that the only counter-power here is the authority of the state. Therefore revolutionary movements were entirely denied and the idea of transforming society in the name of God received no response in the German Lutheran tradition. The secular idea was that the revolution is right around the corner. Its coming is a matter of scientific calculation; it does not even require much political action. This secular idea has nothing transcendent in it, but only believes that if socialism is achieved, all human problems will be solved.

These were the two poles between which we moved as religious socialists at that time. Our answer to the situation was given in terms of some basic concepts. The first was the concept of the *demonic*. Our interpretation dealt with the demonic structures of evil in individuals and social groups. When we first used the concept of the demonic in the early twenties, nobody had heard of it except in history books in connection with the superstitious kinds of belief in demons. We used the word "demonic" to describe the structures of destruction which prevail over the creative elements. The experiential basis of this was the psychological description of the compulsive powers in individuals and the sociological description as given in the Marxist analysis of the bourgeois society. The structures in society are creative and destructive at the same time.

Then we went on to say in terms of the concept of *kairos* that when the demonic power is recognized and fought against, there takes place a breakthrough of the eternal into history. *Kairos* means time, the right time, the qualitative time in contrast to *chronos,* clock time, quantitative time. The idea of the *kairos* is a biblical idea attached in particular to the biblical messages of John the Baptist and Jesus and to Paul's interpretation of history. For us this concept was the main mediating concept between the two extremes. Against the Lutheran transcendentalism *kairos* means that the eternal can break into the temporal and that a new beginning can take place. Against utopianism we knew of the fragmentariness of historical achievements. No perfect end is reached in history free of the demonic. We expressed this sometimes in the symbol from the book of Revelation, the idea of the millennium; the demonic forces are banned for a thousand years, but they are not overcome. They will return from their prison in the underworld. This is highly mythological, but yet profound. It says that the demonic can be conquered for a time; a particular demonic structure can be overcome. But the demonic always returns, just as Jesus described in the case of the individual into whom more demons rush after the one has been cast out.

The third concept was the idea of theonomy. We said that the aim of the religious socialist movement was a theonomous state of society. Theonomy goes beyond autonomy, which is empty critical thought. It goes beyond heteronomy, which means authoritarianism and enslavement. Theonomy is the union of what is true in autonomy and in heteronomy, the fulfillment of a whole society with the spiritual substance, in spite of the freedom of the autonomous development, and in spite of living in the great traditions in which the Spirit has embodied himself. This was our answer. And we found that in the twelfth century of Europe there was something very close to theonomy, represented especially by the Franciscan-Augustinian school in theology.

Do not misunderstand me! We never said like the romantics that the Middle Ages was such a great period. People were evil then as always. But the structure of society had elements of theonomy in it. The entire life was concentrated in the great cathedrals; the whole of daily life was consecrated in the cathedral. This is what I mean by theonomy. If you go to Europe and see the genuinely creative products of this theonomy —not the pseudo-Gothic imitations that we have elsewhere in the world—then you can see how the whole life in these little towns—like Chartres near Paris—was arranged under the vertical line which drives up to the ultimate.

The religious socialist movement never was a movement for higher wages, etc., although there was much to be done in this respect. This was an incredibly exploitative situation. But it tried to re-establish the vertical line in new forms. In this respect I would say that the situation has not changed since 1920. The same problem exists in this country, not in the same social structure, but in the same spiritual structure. There is still a lack of the vertical line, the lack of a theonomous culture.

When religious nationalism arose in the context of the Nazi movement, it used at the beginning some of the ideas of religious socialism in order to make the demonic elevation of a finite reality to ultimacy religiously acceptable in Germany. In the first years of Hitler—when it was still possible to fight intellectually—I had to resist this misappropriation of concepts that we had used for a different purpose. If we had time we would also like to deal with religious pacifism and the social gospel movement in this country. Largely, the form of pacifism which I found when I came to this country in 1933 has been overcome because of the second World War in which only power could resist the demonic elevation of Nazism, and because of the type of theological interpretation given by Reinhold Niebuhr of the complex human situation.

8. Karl Barth

We will deal especially with the beginning of the development of Karl Barth. As I said, he came out of the religious socialist movement in Switzerland, but he did not join this movement in Germany. On the contrary, he recognized the danger, which was a real danger as the abuse of religious socialism by religious nationalism showed, that the Christian message will be identified with a particular political or social idea. Whether it be nationalism, or socialism, or democracy, or "the American way of life," which happens to be identified with the Christian message, Karl Barth would see these things as idolatrous. He saw the danger of idolatry much more clearly than the other danger of a divorce between church and society which we saw when we started the religious socialist movement. Therefore, he attacked all these movements, including religious socialism. In a sense this was itself a dangerous thing to do, because the Lutheran students in Germany were only too willing to leave the social problems alone to retreat into problems of systematic theology and biblical research. He broke the attempt to bridge the gap from the side of theology between the revolutionary labor movement and the church in Germany. This break became very clear to me when I saw, while a professor in Marburg, how the students after the first World War turned away from the great social problems created by the catastrophes of the War and settled back in their sanctuaries of theological discussions.

Nevertheless, in view of the situation which came later, what Barth did was providentially significant, for it saved Protestantism from the onslaught of the neo-collectivistic and pagan Nazism. Barth's theology is also called neo-Reformation theology, and is related to the rediscovery of Luther in the Ritschlian tradition, but it goes considerably deeper than the Ritschlians in the understanding of Luther and the doctrines of sin and grace. His theology was also called in the beginning the theology of crisis. Crisis can mean two things. In the one sense it means the historical crisis of bourgeois society in Central Europe after the first World War. Some of this was in Barth's theology, but very little. He elevated this occasional crisis, which happens at a given time in history, into a universal crisis of the relationship between the eternal and the temporal. The crisis is always the crisis of the temporal in the power of the eternal. This is the human situation in every period. But in this way too the interest in the social elements in the post-War period waned in the Barthian school in favor of the doctrinal elements.

Barth did all this in the name of his fundamental principle, the absoluteness of God. God is not an object of our knowledge or action. He expressed this in his commentary on Paul's letter to the Romans,[13] a book of great prophetic paradoxes; it was received in Germany and in all Europe as a prophetic book. It is not exegesis of Romans measured by strict historical standards, and he admitted this. But it was an attempt to restate the paradoxical character of the absolute transcendence of God which we can never reach from our side, which we can never bring down to earth by our efforts or our knowledge, which either comes to us or does not come to us. All our attempts to reach God are defined as religion, and against religion stands God's act of revelation. Here began the fight against the use of the word "religion" in theology.

When I returned to Germany in 1948 after the Hitler period, I was immediately attacked when I used the word "religion" in my writings or speeches, because religion was still felt after Barth's struggle with the Nazi Christians as an expression of human arrogance, a human attempt to reach up to the divine. In the meantime, however, it has come to be understood that revelation can reach man only in the form of receiving it, and every reception of it, whether more inwardly religious or more openly secular, is religion, and as religion is always humanly distorted. But in the earlier period Karl Barth did not acknowledge this; he identified revelation with the Christian message, and denied the revelatory character of everything except the Christian revelation. Therefore, he denied all natural theology. His famous controversy with Emil Brunner about the point of contact in man was the occasion for his most outspoken rejection of natural theology. It was not so much an attack on the whole system of Thomistic natural theology, for this was not necessary to do. But the idea which he attacked was that there is something in man as man which makes it possible for God to be recognized as God by man. What Troeltsch tried to formulate with his idea of the religious a priori was the object of his attack. Barth claimed that the image of God in man is totally destroyed. This immediately involved him in an attack on mysticism, following here the line of Ritschl and Harnack. He negated every point of identity between God and man, even in the doctrine of the Spirit who might be dwelling in man. He

13 *The Epistle to the Romans,* translated by Edwyn C. Hoskyns (New York: Oxford University Press, 1933).

said not that I believe, but that I believe that I believe; the Spirit is not in me, but is against me. But the question how can God appear to man at all remained unanswered in these ideas.

Barth's theology has also been called dialectical. But this word is very misleading. In its prophetic beginnings it was paradoxical, and later its conceptualization became supernaturalistic. But it is not dialectical. Dialectic involves an inner progress from one state to another by an inner dynamics. From this position there follow a number of other antiliberal doctrines. The Word of God is stressed in antithesis to Schleiermacher's idea of the religious consciousness, and to any form of pietistic or mystical experience. The classical christology is accepted, and the trinitarian dogma becomes his starting point. Karl Barth starts from above, from the trinity, from the revelation which is given, and then proceeds to man, and in his latest period, even very deeply into man, when he speaks of the "humanity of God."[14] Whereas, on the other hand, I start with man, not deriving the divine answer from man, but starting with the question which is present in man and to which the divine revelation comes as the answer.

A few more words about Barth's relation to historical criticism and to social political movements. He silenced the problems of historical criticism completely. The question of the historical Jesus did not touch him at all. But problems cannot be silenced. So it happened in almost a tragic way that when Bultmann wrote his article on demythologizing, a split in theology opened up, and the silenced questions broke out into the open all over the theological world. Bultmann saved the historical question from being banished from theology. This is his importance. He showed that it cannot be silenced, that our whole relationship to the Bible cannot be expressed in paradoxical and supernaturalist statements, not even if it is done with the prophetic power of Karl Barth. But we have to ask the question of the historical meaning of the biblical writings.

In regard to the political and social movements he detached himself not only from religious socialism, but also for a time from the political side of Hitler's power. He accepted it and did not speak against it in the

14 *The Humanity of God,* translated by John N. Thomas (Richmond: John Knox Press, 1960).

name of religion, although there were many occasions for doing so. For instance, on April 1, 1933, when the first great attack against the Jews was made, with the destruction of a vast amount of life and property, the churches kept quiet. They did not speak up until they themselves were attacked by Hitler. This is one of the great shortcomings of the German churches, but also of Karl Barth. But then Barth became the leader of the inner-churchly resistance against National Socialism. He finally came to a point where he recognized something which he had formerly rejected, namely, that the movement headed by Hitler is a quasi-religious movement which represents an attack on Christianity. So he wrote his famous letter to the Christians in England, asking them in the name of Christ to resist Hitler.[15] This was quite different from his earlier position.

Today Barth is more or less neutral, and in accordance with his fundamental principles does not want to identify the cause of Christ with the cause of the West. For this reason he is very seriously attacked by Western churches. He would not apply his criticism of Islam and Hitler to Communism in the same way, and thus has returned to his original position of detachment.

9. Existentialism

We have already spoken very much about existentialism in connection with Schelling, Kierkegaard, Nietzsche, and Feuerbach, whose revolts against Hegel gave rise to existentialist elements in their thought. They are the sources of present-day existentialism. But existentialism is not only a revolt; it is also a style. Existentialism has become the style of all great literature, of the arts and the other media of our self-expression. It is present in poetry, in the novel, in drama, in the visual arts, and it is my opinion that our century will in historical retrospect be characterized as the period of existentialism.

We must first try to define the term. It is a way of looking at man. But there are two possible ways of looking at man. The one way is essentialist which develops the doctrine of man in terms of his essential

[15] *This Christian Cause, A Letter to Great Britain from Switzerland* (New York: The Macmillan Company, 1941).

nature within the whole of the universe. The other way is existentialist which looks at man in his predicament in time and space, and sees the conflict between what exists in time and space and what is essentially given. Religiously expressed, this is the conflict between the essential goodness of man, the highest point of which is his freedom to contradict his essential goodness, and man's fall into the conditions of existential estrangement. This is a universal situation, and at the same time man is responsible for it.

Existentialist philosophy is a revolt against the predominance of the essentialist element in most of the history of Western philosophy. It represents a revival of the existentialist elements of earlier thought in Plato, in the Bible, in Augustine, Duns Scotus, Jacob Boehme, etc. In the great philosophers of the past we usually find a preponderance of the essentialist approach, but always with existentialist elements within them. Plato in this regard is a classical figure. His realm of ideas or essences is a realm of essentialism, of essentialist description and analysis. But Plato's existentialism appears in his myth of the human soul in prison, of coming down from the world of essences into the body which is its prison, and then being liberated from the cave. The essentialist element became most powerfully expressed in Hegel and in the great synthesis. But there were also hidden existentialist elements in Hegel which his pupils brought out finally against him and thus inaugurated the generations of existentialism in revolt. And finally, in our century existentialism has become a style. Therefore, to repeat, first existentialism appears as an element, then as a revolt, and finally as a style. That is where we are today.

This rediscovery of existentialism has a great significance for theology. It has seen the dark elements in man as over against a philosophy of consciousness which lays all the stress on man's conscious decisions and his good will. The existentialists allied themselves with Freud's analysis of the unconscious in protest against a psychology of consciousness which had previously existed. Existentialism and psychotherapeutic psychology are natural allies and have always worked together. This rediscovery of the unconscious in man is of the highest importance for theology. It has changed the moralistic and idealistic types which we have discussed; it has placed the question of the human condition at the center of all theological thinking, and for this reason it has made the answers meaningful again. In this light we can say that existentialism and Freud, together with his followers and friends, have become the providential allies of Christian theology in the twentieth century. This is similar to the way in which the Marxist analysis of the structure of society became a tremendous factor in arousing the churches to a sense of responsibility for the social conditions in which men live.

Often I have been asked if I am an existentialist theologian, and my answer is always short. I say, fifty-fifty. This means that for me essentialism and existentialism belong together. It is impossible to be a pure essentialist if one is personally in the human situation and not sitting on the throne of God as Hegel implied he was doing when he construed world history as coming to an end in principle in his philosophy. This is the metaphysical arrogance of pure essentialism. For the world is still open to the future, and we are not on the throne of God, as Karl Barth has said in his famous statement: God is in heaven and man is on earth.

On the other hand, a pure existentialism is impossible because to describe existence one must use language. Now language deals with universals. In using universals, language is by its very nature essentialist, and cannot escape it. All attempts to reduce language to mere noises or utterances would bring man back to the animal level on which universals do not exist. Animals cannot express universals. But man can and must express his encounter with the world in terms of universals. Therefore, there is an essentialist framework in his mind. Existentialism is possible only as an element in a larger whole, as an element in a vision of the structure of being in its created goodness, and then as a description of man's existence within that framework. The conflicts between his essential goodness and his existential estrangement cannot be seen at all without keeping essentialism and existentialism together. Theology must see both sides, man's essential nature, wonderfully and symbolically expressed in the paradise story, and man's existential condition, under sin, guilt, and death.

Index of Names

Abelard, xv, 194
Adams, James L., xvii
Anselm of Canterbury, xxiii, 194
Aquinas, Thomas, xxiv, 157, 162, 192, 193, 194
Aristotle, xxiv, 65, 192, 193, 221
Attila the Hun, 132
Augustine, xxi, 96, 193, 206, 244

Baader, Franz, 88
Baillie, J. B., 117
Barth, Karl, xv, xxv, xxviii, 2, 6, 7, 20, 30, 64, 76, 92, 107, 113, 173, 225, 231, 237, 240–245
Baudelaire, 208
Baur, F. C., xxxii, 138, 139, 223
Bergson, Henri, 149, 159, 193, 195
Bernard of Clairvaux, xxv
Biedermann, A., 141
Blumhardt, C., 235
Blumhardt, J. C., 235
Boehme, Jacob, xxi, xxix, 88, 146, 148, 194, 195, 235, 244
Bonaventura, xxiii, 193
Bonhoeffer, Dietrich, 63, 86, 130
Brunner, Emil, xxv, xxx, 7, 110, 111, 173, 241
Bruno, Giordano, 78, 79
Bucer, Martin, 20
Bultmann, Rudolf, xxxi, xxxii, 5, 213, 215, 225, 227–230, 242
Burkhardt, Jacob, 6

Calvin, John, xxvii, 12, 14, 20, 26, 28, 111
Cassirer, Ernst, 77
Copernicus, 159
Cremer, Herman, 224

Darwin, Charles, 159, 161, 202, 207
DeChardin, Teilhard, 125, 126
De Gaulle, Charles, 86
Descartes, René, 41, 74, 77, 120
DeWette, Wilhelm, 129
Dewey, John, 189, 210
Dionysius the Areopagite, 46
Duns Scotus, xxiv, 192, 194, 244

Earl of Shaftesbury, 79
Einstein, Albert, 33, 34
Eliade, Mircea, xxi, xxxiv
Eliot, George, 137
Eliot, T. S., 143
Engels, F., 157, 189, 190

Feuerbach, Ludwig, 139, 140, 141, 164, 182, 186, 243
Fichte, J., 81, 139, 142, 145, 146, 193, 216
Fox, George, 19
Frank, Г. II. Л., 211
Francke, August, 15, 16
Freud, Sigmund, 26, 88, 125, 146, 167, 193, 196, 199, 200, 244, 245
Fromm, Erich, 200

247

Index of Subjects

251